AMERICA'S COMING WAR WITH CHINA

A Collision Course over Taiwan

TED GALEN CARPENTER

palgrave
macmillan

First published 2005 by
PALGRAVE MACMILLAN™
175 Fifth Avenue, New York, N.Y. 10010 and
Houndmills, Basingstoke, Hampshire, England RG21 6XS.
Companies and representatives throughout the world.

PALGRAVE MACMILLAN IS THE GLOBAL ACADEMIC IMPRINT OF THE
PALGRAVE MACMILLAN division of St. Martin's Press, LLC and of Palgrave
Macmillan Ltd. Macmillan® is a registered trademark in the United States,
United Kingdom and other countries. Palgrave is a registered trademark in the
European Union and other countries.

ISBN 1-4039-6841-1 hardback

Library of Congress Cataloging-in-Publication Data
Carpenter, Ted Galen.
    America's coming war with China : A collision course over Taiwan / Ted Galen
Carpenter.
        p.   cm.
    Includes index.
    ISBN 1-4039-6841-1
    1. United States—Foreign relations—China.   2. China—Foreign relations—
United States.   3. United States—Foreign relations—2001–   I. Title.
E183.8.C5A7335   2006
327.73051'09'051—dc22
        2005049302

A catalogue record for this book is available from the British Library.

Design by compositor name here.

First edition: Pub Month Year
10 9 8 7 6 5 4
Printed in the United States of America

To Barbara,
with love and gratitude for all
of your support over the decades

CONTENTS

ACKNOWLEDGMENTS

I owe a debt of gratitude to numerous people for helping to make this book possible. My appreciation goes out to Christopher Layne, Doug Bandow, Christopher Preble, Charles V. Pena, Martin Sieff, and Ivan Eland for providing useful comments on and criticisms of the manuscript. Their insights regarding this book, as on so many other projects of mine, were extremely worthwhile. I also wish to thank Robert Guido, Peter Eyre, and Covadonga Iglesias for helping to track down sometimes elusive sources. Feliz Ventura and Charlene Chen deserve thanks for helping to prepare the initial manuscript for submission to the publisher. Diana Brady deserves great appreciation for preparing the final version.

My appreciation goes out as well to Anthony Wahl, my editor at Palgrave Macmillan, and his assistant, Heather Van Dusen, for their work on this project. Alan Bradshaw, Yasmin Mathew, and the rest of the staff at Palgrave provided significant help in keeping the production schedule on track. Martha Sencindiver did her usual fine job with the index.

I owe a very special thanks to my research assistant, Justin Logan. Justin is a promising young foreign policy scholar in his own right, and he provided invaluable help in the research and preparation of this book. Without his input, the book would have appeared far later and would have been much weaker in content. Any errors of either fact or interpretation, of course, are entirely those of the author.

Most of all, I want to thank my wife Barbara for her unflagging patience and encouragement. She has been the love of my life for nearly four decades, and this book is dedicated to her, my "number one fan."

THE DANGER OF A COLLISION COURSE

On the surface, America's relations with China seem to be rather cordial. Tensions spiked in April 2001 over the incident in which a U.S. spy plane collided with a Chinese fighter plane, but that quarrel soon receded, and ever since the September 11 terrorist attacks China and the United States have cooperated in the campaign against radical Islamic terrorism. More recently, Washington and Beijing have worked together to induce North Korea to give up its nuclear weapons program. Meanwhile, the important economic relationship has continued to grow, with bilateral trade now exceeding $160 billion a year.

Despite these components of a cooperative relationship, there are in the United States vocal advocates of a more hard-line policy toward the People's Republic of China. Indeed, in recent years critics of the current policy have redoubled their efforts on a number of issues. The hard-liners have sought to get the U.S. government to press China on its abuses of human rights, to increase arms sales to Taiwan, to restrict the export of high technology (especially dual use) products to the PRC, to sanction China for its proliferation of key weapons systems to unfriendly regimes, and to adopt a number of protectionist trade measures to reduce the bilateral trade deficit (and perhaps retard China's economic development).

Pressure from the hard-liners has had some effect on U.S. policy regarding several of those issues, but generally that impact has been only at the margins. For example, there have been more restrictions on high-tech exports to China on national security grounds than during the Clinton years. U.S. officials also have expressed public criticism of Beijing's human rights record—although that criticism has become less frequent and more muted during recent years. Perhaps most significant, the United States has imposed sanctions against Chinese companies a dozen times in the past four years for alleged proliferation activities, and Washington has exerted intense diplomatic pressure on Beijing regarding that issue.[1]

These are all measures that advocates of a hard-line policy have been pushing for years. The Cox Committee report in 1999, which charged that China was using espionage and imported strategic goods to build up the PRC's military power, especially generated pressure for restraints on technology trade among political conservatives.[2] A rather alarming July 2002 report to Congress by the U.S.-China Security Review Commission (established by the Defense Authorization Act of 2001) on the national security implications of the economic relationship between the United States and China intensified calls for action on the trade front.[3] It was significant that this congressionally established bipartisan committee of outside experts had a disproportionate number of China critics in its membership.

In evaluating the call for trade restrictions, it is difficult to separate national security motives from purely self-serving economic motives. This is particularly true with regard to the Bush administration's ongoing campaign to get China to revalue its currency. U.S. competitors have long complained that the PRC manipulates the value of the yuan, keeping it artificially low to make Chinese goods more competitive in the world market. The administration has grudgingly responded to the demand of its domestic economic constituencies that something be done about that problem. Although Beijing has been just grudgingly responsive on the currency revaluation issue, Chinese officials do seem concerned about the mounting calls in the United States for punitive measures to narrow the trade deficit. For example, in late 2003 and early 2004, China announced the purchase of billions of dollars worth of American goods, including airplanes, jet engines, and auto parts.

Some calls for commercial sanctions against China appear to involve a mixture of economic and security motives. How proponents of a hard-line policy combine those issues can be gauged by the comments of William R. Hawkins, senior fellow at the U.S. Business and Industry Council (USBIC), a prominent economic nationalist think tank in Washington. Hawkins called for countervailing duties on Chinese imports "across the board" to close the yawning trade deficit. Although one of the reasons he cited was the need to prevent the further loss of American manufacturing jobs, he also stressed that the trade deficit was not the only concern. He specifically warned Americans of an insidious Chinese ploy to narrow the deficit. "Beijing's gambit is to renew calls for a relaxation of import restrictions on sensitive technology, especially technology with military application, as the way to boost American exports. China has long chafed under security restrictions and has circumvented them whenever possible, often with the aid of the same avaricious American firms who lobby on Beijing's behalf." Americans must not succumb to that ploy, Hawkins emphasized. "All China really wants from the United States is technology, and the capital and know-how needed to replicate it. Opening the gates to Beijing in strategic trade might narrow the deficit somewhat in the short run, but in the long run the adverse impact on both U.S. competitiveness and national security would be catastrophic."[4] Hawkins also warned that Beijing's policies were "part of China's drive to become the strongest economy in Asia and to overturn the global balance of power that currently favors the United States."[5] His views represented the perfect marriage of trade protectionist motives and national security concerns. To this point, his views are shared only by a minority—but a substantial minority—in Congress, the foreign policy community, and the general public. That this minority exists is important because it shows that a significant reservoir of hostility toward the PRC already exists in the United States—a reservoir that easily could be tapped in the event of a crisis.

In the PRC, there are counterparts to the U.S. neoconservatives and economic nationalists who urge Beijing to adopt a more assertive policy toward the United States. Those hard-liners are especially numerous in the upper ranks of the People's Liberation Army. One prominent example of this assertive policy is a book, *Unrestricted Warfare*, published in 1999 by two colonels in the PLA.[6] The book's analysis and arguments are directed at one basic end: identifying weaknesses in the U.S. military and ways of exploiting them. The book goes into great detail about what the authors' perceive as America's strategic weaknesses: an undue reliance on technology, a hypersensitive aversion to casualties, and alleged weaknesses in joint war-fighting integration. In addition to the military analysis, the underlying assumption of *Unrestricted Warfare* is that the United States is an implacable enemy of China and that someday the PRC must confront its adversary militarily.

Michael Pillsbury, a leading scholar of Chinese affairs, has audited much of the available material from military strategists inside the PRC and notes that "not one of the more than 200 books" reviewed for his study "admitted that the United States could defeat China in any scenario—but many techniques can supposedly defeat U.S. forces."[7] In addition, "a common theme in PLA views of future warfare [is that] America is proclaimed to be a declining power with but two or three decades of primacy left."[8] The undertone of the Chinese analyses is a mixture of hostility and disdain toward the United States.

Wang Yiwei, assistant to the dean of China's prestigious Fudan University, penned a December 2004 article in which he noticed some disturbing trends in the attitudes of Chinese opinion leaders regarding U.S.–China relations. "In the eyes of Chinese strategists, 'the America Opportunity Theory' has been replaced by 'the America Threat Theory.' Strident voices can be heard concerning the serious situation of 'Taiwan independence,' saying that China will not scruple to have a strategic showdown with the U.S."[9]

Hard-liners are sometimes able to rouse China's population into anti-America outbursts. The most vivid example was the reaction to the U.S. bombing of the Chinese embassy in Belgrade during the Balkan war in May 1999. Although President Bill Clinton and other U.S. officials immediately sought to apologize for what Washington described as a horrible accident, the PRC was unforgiving. Chinese officials and opinion leaders openly charged that the attack was deliberate, perpetrated by anti-Chinese elements within the U.S. military and foreign policy bureaucracies. A negative reaction was probably inevitable, but what occurred during the days following the bombing incident went beyond a normal response. Mobs of Chinese young people attacked American businesses and other targets in Shanghai, Beijing, and other cities.[10] The mob violence against the U.S. embassy and the ambassador's residence was so severe—a barrage of rocks, bottles, and firebombs—that Ambassador James Sasser dared not leave the residence for three days.

Chinese authorities took steps to prevent similar violent, large-scale demonstrations during the April 2001 spy plane incident, perhaps fearing that they would again get out of control. Internet chat rooms in China teemed with anti-American sentiment, however.[11] That was significant in that internet users are likely to be more affluent, more educated, urban dwellers—in other words, the type of Chinese who would normally favor a more open political system and be friendly to America and American values. Instead, many of them expressed an extremely virulent variety of Chinese nationalism.

Those episodes suggest a sizeable undercurrent of hostility toward the United States among members of China's elite as well as the general public. In normal times, the numerous ties that link the interests of the United States and the PRC keep such sentiments in the background. In a time of crisis, though, the outcome could be very different.

The trade deficit, China's proliferation activities, and the PRC's human rights abuses pose problems in the relationship between the United States and China. So do sharp differences over China's expansive territorial claims in the South China Sea, the Bush administration's doctrine of preemptive war (which Beijing vehemently opposes), and a variety of other issues. But it is virtually impossible to imagine any of them leading to an armed conflict. The sole exception is the status of Taiwan. And, given the overall fragile nature of the

U.S.–PRC relationship, Taiwan could become the occasion for a very nasty confrontation indeed.

Beijing insists that Taiwan is merely a renegade province of the People's Republic of China, and although Chinese officials state that the PRC wants to settle the dispute by peaceful means, they also have consistently refused to renounce the use of force to achieve reunification. Renunciation is an option that they will not entertain even in private, off-the-record discussions. That is true even when the concession is presented as part of a quid pro quo for the termination of U.S. arms sales to Taiwan—something Beijing wants very much.[12] Taiwan seems to be one of those emotional "hot button" issues that galvanize mainland Chinese, including those who are less than passionate supporters of the government on other topics.

It is often difficult for Americans and other Westerners to comprehend the depth of Chinese determination to get Taiwan to "return to the motherland." But to many (and probably most) Chinese, Taiwan is the most potent remaining symbol of China's long period of weakness and dependence, which began in the early nineteenth century, and its shabby treatment at the hands of various colonial powers. For the Chinese, the inheritors of an ancient and proud culture, that treatment was profoundly humiliating and opened deep emotional wounds that have yet to heal fully. It was during the period of weakness that Britain wrested Hong Kong away from China's control; that Japan seized Taiwan (and later Manchuria); that czarist Russia amputated portions of Chinese territory along their border; and that France, Germany, and other countries established colonies or enclaves. That is why the return of Hong Kong to China in 1997 was such a crucial event—with the emotional symbolism transcending its admittedly significant economic importance. The last of the European enclaves, Macao, was restored to Beijing's jurisdiction in 1999. Taiwan is now the principal piece of traditional Chinese territory that has yet to be recovered. That fact alone makes Taiwan's status a potentially explosive issue.

There are elements within the People's Liberation Army who seem willing to threaten military force—and perhaps even use military force—to resolve the Taiwan issue. So far, the civilian leadership of the Chinese Communist Party appears to be more cautious. Beijing has not yet decided to use coercion to achieve reunification, but it is equally apparent that the PRC political elite regards the use of force as a viable option if peaceful alternatives prove ineffective. Any one of a number of developments could put a coercive strategy in motion: the emergence of a more hard-line PRC government, evidence that pro-independence sentiment on Taiwan was becoming dominant, or simply frustration on the mainland with the prospect of an indefinite stalemate. The latter danger may increase as

communism fades as a unifying force in China. The most likely substitute unifying force would be Chinese nationalism—and Taiwan is the most important,
emotionally laden, nationalist issue.

At the same time that China is becoming more confrontational about the
Taiwan issue, separatist sentiments are growing in Taiwan—especially among
younger Taiwanese. To them, China is an alien country.[13] A vibrant, distinct society has grown up on Taiwan, and many Taiwanese point out that their island has
been ruled from Beijing only 4 years out of the last 110—and the government in
question was not communist. Taiwan has developed separately from the mainland, and it is understandable if many Taiwanese want that reality ratified by having an independent state that enjoys full international recognition. True, the bulk
of the Taiwanese business community favors close ties with the mainland, and
that faction is an important force for caution and restraint, helping to counteract
the influence of the pro-independence faction.[14] But the overall trend seems
clear. Numerous public opinion surveys show that very few Taiwanese are interested in reunification with a communist China. Indeed, a growing number of Taiwanese may not be interested in reunification even if the mainland someday
becomes democratic. At the very least, there is a broad consensus in favor of the
island's current de facto independence, and most Taiwanese want some form of
political recognition from the international community.

The divergent attitudinal trends on the mainland and Taiwan leave little
room for compromise. Given the intensity of the emotions on both sides of the
Strait, it is uncertain how long the modus vivendi that has existed since Washington's rapprochement with the PRC in the 1970s can endure. Both Beijing and
Taipei seem increasingly dissatisfied with the status quo built around Taiwan's acceptance of being in political and diplomatic limbo. They also have sharply conflicting prescriptions for resolving the impasse. Beijing advocates the formula of
"one country, two systems," which would mean a status for Taiwan similar to that
granted Hong Kong, albeit with somewhat greater autonomy. Taipei categori-
cally rejects that solution. During the years of control by the Kuomintang Party
from the late 1940s until the mid-1990s, Taiwanese leaders at least implicitly accepted the concept of one China. But the formula under KMT President Lee
Teng-hui in the late 1990s shifted to "one China, two states." The model Lee and
his supporters seemed to be advocating was the two Germanys during the latter
stages of the Cold War. That option, though, was anathema to the PRC.

When the Democratic Progressive Party won Taiwan's presidency in 2000,
sentiment for an independent Taiwan intensified. Under the current president,
Chen Shui-bian, even the pro forma acceptance of one China has largely been
abandoned. According to Chen, one China is merely one possible outcome of ne-

gotiations between two sovereign and equal states: the Republic of China (Taiwan's official name) and the PRC. Moreover, a sizable portion of the Democratic Progressive Party's membership is even more radical than Chen. And the DPP's junior partner in the "Pan Green" electoral alliance—the Taiwan Solidarity Union—makes the DPP look anemic on the independence issue. To staunchly pro-independence elements in both the DPP and the TSU, the ultimate goal of negotiations with Beijing is not reunification but formal separation.

The United States has pursued a policy that seeks both to preserve friendly ties with Beijing and protect Taiwan's de facto independence. As developed during the 1980s and 1990s, that policy incorporated the doctrine of strategic ambiguity. On the one hand, Washington officially adheres to a one-China policy and does not dispute Beijing's contention that Taiwan is part of China. On the other hand, the 1979 Taiwan Relations Act mandates that the United States sell defensive arms to Taiwan and regard any PRC effort to coerce Taiwan as a grave breach of the peace. Left ambiguous is whether the United States would intervene with its own military forces in the event of a Chinese attack on the island. The point of strategic ambiguity is to keep both sides guessing about U.S. intentions. The rationale is that Taiwan would have to wonder whether the United States would really come to its rescue if Taiwanese leaders needlessly provoked Beijing by pushing an independence agenda. Conversely, Beijing would have to suspect that the United States would defend Taiwan. Therefore, both sides have an incentive to act cautiously.

Strategic ambiguity worked reasonably well until the mid-1990s, when a newly democratic Taiwan began to push the envelope regarding independence and the PRC reacted with ever more pointed warnings. During the past decade, U.S. leaders have tinkered at the margins of strategic ambiguity even as signs continue to mount that a confrontation between Beijing and Taipei is a very real danger. As the United States has tried to preserve an increasingly fragile status quo, it has often created confusion and increased the risk of miscalculation by one or both parties to the Taiwan dispute. (See chapter 6.)

An especially troubling aspect of U.S. policy is that America has little control over events relevant to the Taiwan situation. To some extent, that is a problem inherent in any international trouble spot involving the United States. It is always possible for the opposing party to trigger a crisis. But the Taiwan problem is far more complicated and dangerous. The United States has to worry not only about whether its potential adversary (China) remains prudent, but also whether its client state (Taiwan) remains prudent. Indeed, in this case, Washington may have to worry more about Taipei provoking a crisis than Beijing doing so. It is dangerous to undertake any commitment to defend a client or ally, but it is especially risky when the United States does not, and probably cannot, exercise effective control over the actions of that ally or client. And that is precisely the situation today in the relationship between Washington and Taipei. That vulnerability, whereby the security patron can be dragged into a confrontation (perhaps even a full-blown war) by an excessively assertive client, is the problem that Nikolas K. Gvosdev and Travis Tanner, scholars at the *National Interest*, aptly refer to as the "wag the dog" phenomenon.[15] Taiwan is a textbook example of that danger.

A related problem is that Taiwan is in a position to manipulate the decision-making process in the United States. Taipei spends a great deal of time, money, and effort not only to influence the course of action that the executive branch pursues but to cultivate support in Congress and the American opinion elite needed to push for policies that advance Taiwan's agenda. That is another facet of the "wag the dog" problem, since such influence can cause U.S. officials to take measures that might not be in America's best interest.

The United States is at a precarious point with regard to its policy on the Taiwan issue. "For the decade ahead, we need to keep the lid on the pressure cooker," states one high-ranking U.S. official.[16] Washington may find that such a mission is beyond its ability. At the very least, it will be an increasingly frustrating and dangerous mission. Given the trends in both Taiwan and the mainland, there is growing danger of a military confrontation between the two parties sometime in the next decade that could entangle the United States. Indeed, unless significant policy changes take place in Taipei, Beijing, or Washington, a collision course is all too probable. The next chapter presents a scenario about how such a perilous confrontation might occur.

CHAPTER 1

2013

How the War Began

The war that erupted between the United States and China in 2013 was a classic case of miscalculation by both parties. Neither Beijing nor Washington thought that the other side would escalate the long-standing tensions over Taiwan to the point of armed conflict. Yet armed conflict was the result, and the world has been paying the price ever since. For a quarter century, the world's two leading powers have been locked in a cold war that has been at least as intense as the earlier surly confrontation between the United States and the Soviet Union. The prospects for global peace and prosperity that looked so promising in the 1990s following the end of the first cold war have turned to ashes. U.S. policymakers have undoubtedly asked themselves many times whether the brief but intense war that broke out in July 2013 could have been avoided. They probably have asked themselves at least as many times whether defending Taiwan was worth the price.

As the secretary of state prepared to enter the White House on the morning of June 2, 2013, he wondered whether Taiwan's president had finally pushed Beijing too far. The day before, the Taiwanese leader announced that he would seek an amendment to the constitution changing the island's official name from the Republic of China to the Republic of Taiwan, a move that was certain to infuriate the PRC. It may not officially have been a declaration of Taiwanese independence, but it was the functional equivalent of one. And it certainly would be the surprise of the century if Beijing did not regard it as such.

Typically, Taiwan's president had made that blockbuster of an announcement without any advance notice to the United States. That seemed to be his standard operating procedure since his re-election to the presidency in March 2012. Even more than his predecessor, Chen Shui-bian, the current leader had a habit of blindsiding Taiwan's protector, the United States, with potentially dangerous initiatives. This was just the latest and most provocative one.

Although both presidents were members of the Democratic Progressive Party, the similarities tended to end there. For all of his faults, Chen Shui-bian had displayed a shrewd sense of what was and what was not possible in Taiwan's delicate relationship with mainland China. His pro-independence rhetoric could at times be a bit much, but his actual policies tended to be relatively cautious. Chen's successor showed little of that caution. His boldness was not all that surprising since he came from the hard-line independence faction in the DPP. To many hard-liners, Chen Shui-bian had been squishy and a disappointment.

The current president believed he also had a broader mandate to push his independence agenda. Throughout his presidency, Chen had had to deal with a national legislature controlled by the more moderate Kuomintang Party (KMT) and its allies. Whatever his private inclinations might have been, that political reality restrained his actions. Chen's successor had no such political constraints. The DPP now controlled 55 percent of the Legislative Yuan, and the party's even more rabidly pro-independence ally, the Taiwan Solidarity Union, controlled another 8 percent. The president himself had been re-elected with nearly 58 percent of the vote against the increasingly moribund KMT and what was left of the relatively pro-Beijing People First Party. Chen Shui-bian had never come close to getting a popular mandate of that magnitude.

The U.S. president had assembled the members of his national security team to hear the secretary of state's report on the latest news out of Taipei and Beijing. The news was not good. Throngs of DPP and TSU supporters had gone into the streets of Taipei and other cities on the island to support their president's proposed change of the country's name. Most of them were waving the green flag of Taiwan's independence movement. As yet there was no official reaction from Beijing, but the latest online edition of *People's Daily* was more than a little ominous.

The patience of the People's Republic of China is not unlimited, and the latest actions by the authorities on Taiwan are testing that patience to the breaking point. The government of the PRC has made it clear on numerous occasions that moves to establish so-called Taiwan independence are unacceptable and will lead our Taiwan compatriots to the abyss of disaster. Yet the current Taiwanese authorities and the other splittist forces seem determined to wrench Taiwan away from the motherland regardless of the danger. Make no mistake. The forces of the People's Liberation Army are prepared to defend the unity of China at whatever cost. Taiwan separatism will not be allowed to succeed. It is time for sober-minded Taiwan compatriots to let the DPP, the TSU and the rest of that ilk understand that the Taiwanese people will not follow them into the abyss. It is also time for the United States to make it clear to the Taiwan authorities that any effort to establish a so-called Republic of Taiwan will gravely endanger the peace and stability of the entire region.

The U.S. president queried his advisors about how to respond to the latest moves. The director of national intelligence reported on the latest satellite data, which showed an unusual amount of activity at several Chinese military airfields in Fujian Province, directly across the Strait from Taiwan. That was a troubling indicator, but manned aircraft was only one element of the firepower the PRC could deploy against Taiwan. China also had more than twelve hundred missiles targeted against the island, and those would play a major role if Beijing ever decided to use military force. The secretary of state recommended that the president personally issue a statement reiterating the U.S. position against any unilateral changes in the status quo by either Taipei or Beijing. The secretary further recommended that the president explicitly condemn the Taiwanese leader's call to amend the constitution as precisely the kind of unilateral change that jeopardized peace in the Taiwan Strait and make it clear that the United States would oppose such a change.

The president hesitated. Taiwan had a lot of friends in Congress and the media who would react badly to any statement that seemed to be appeasement of Beijing. He recognized that a statement of criticism had to be made, but he wanted it handled at a lower level to minimize the publicity and the resulting outcry. The president instructed the secretary of state to have the deputy secretary issue the statement—and to soften the condemnation of the Taiwan president's proposal to "the United States cannot support" instead of the United States "opposes" the proposed name change to the Republic of Taiwan. The secretary protested that more subtle formulations were unlikely to dissuade DPP hard-liners, but the president would not be moved.

Before the meeting adjourned, the chairman of the joint chiefs of staff recommended that the United States begin the process of redeploying some of its aircraft carrier battle groups in order to be prepared if the crisis escalated. Two carriers were the best candidates. The USS *Stennis* was just completing a call at Pearl Harbor, and the USS *Ronald Reagan* was conducting joint training exercises with the navies of India and several Southeast Asian nations in and around the

Strait of Malacca. The JCS chairman suggested that both carrier battle groups be relocated to waters closer to Taiwan. The president expressed his view that the diplomatic crisis would probably blow over in a short time just as all previous ones had, but he agreed that the redeployment of the two carriers was probably a prudent step.

Reactions from Beijing and Taipei to the State Department's criticism of unilateral changes in the status quo were not encouraging. Speaking at a DPP conference the following day, the Taiwanese president bluntly rejected the U.S. criticism. "The Republic of China has been a sovereign state for more than a century and a full-fledged democracy for nearly two decades," he stated. "It is up to the people of Taiwan to decide if we should change the name of our country to the Republic of Taiwan. The communist authorities on the mainland have nothing to say about it, and even a friend like the United States has no right to interfere in the affairs of a sister democracy." His comments seemed to confirm the secretary of state's worst fears, that the DPP government would not be dissuaded by gentle criticisms.

If the reaction from Taipei was disappointing, the subsequent reaction from Beijing was alarming. The Taiwan Affairs Office issued a shrill statement of condemnation coupled with a threat.

> The separatist traitors do not represent the best interests of the people of Taiwan. We urge our Taiwan compatriots to repudiate this irresponsible leadership before it is too late. The People's Republic of China has said repeatedly that it wants to settle the issue of Taiwan's reunification by peaceful means. Some provocations are simply intolerable, however. If the Taiwan authorities insist on proclaiming a so-called Republic of Taiwan, it will prove impossible for the PRC to adhere to a peaceful course.

The PRC's embassy in Washington, too, was unimpressed with the statement issued by the State Department. In a meeting with the secretary of state, China's ambassador dismissed the U.S. position as "anemic and utterly inadequate." In a rare display of anger, the ambassador stated:

> We are weary of your government's supposed adherence to a one-China policy when you constantly take actions that run contrary to that policy. We have put up with your sales of advanced weaponry to Taiwan—including offensive weapons—despite your commitment in the Third Communiqué signed by Ronald Reagan to gradually eliminate all arms sales. We have tolerated your willingness to issue visas to Taiwanese officials to visit the United States despite our protests. We have even tolerated those officials meeting with prominent mem-

bers of Congress and giving public speeches in which they condemn the PRC. But we will not tolerate having your government give quiet encouragement to a so-called Taiwan leader while he creates an entity called the Republic of Taiwan. You need to bring serious pressure to bear on him NOW, if you wish to preserve friendly relations between China and the United States.

The secretary was taken aback by the intensity of the ambassador's protest. Beijing had long been unhappy about Washington's arms sales to Taiwan as well as other aspects of U.S. policy. But most PRC protests had acquired a rote aspect to them over the years. This was different. There was an uncompromising undertone of menace to Beijing's position.

Any hope that the crisis might dissipate ended on June 4, when the Taiwanese administration formally introduced its proposed constitutional changes. Once again there was an unpleasant surprise for the United States. Not only did the executive propose to change Taiwan's name from the Republic of China to the Republic of Taiwan, but there was another provision delineating the boundaries of the new republic. The territory claimed was Taiwan itself plus Kinmen (Quemoy) and other small islands just off the Chinese mainland. Gone was any claim to represent any portion of the mainland. If the name change was not the functional equivalent of a declaration of independence, the second provision certainly was.

To this day it is uncertain why the Taiwanese president decided on such a daring course of action in June 2013. His own long-time commitment to the cause of an independent Taiwan was undoubtedly a key factor, but there appeared to be some other elements. Part of the move may even have been defensive. At the time he submitted the proposed constitutional amendments, only sixteen countries had diplomatic relations with the Republic of China. That number had been shrinking for years; a decade earlier, nearly thirty countries maintained diplomatic ties with the ROC. Beijing's strategy of isolating Taipei diplomatically was clearly working. Even the sixteen countries that still recognized the ROC were all small, poor countries, mainly in Central America, the Caribbean, and Africa. They were all prime candidates to be bribed by the PRC to change their diplomatic allegiance—as so many others already had done. Taiwan's leaders may have thought that they had nothing to lose by being bold, since the alternative was slow, but inexorable, diplomatic extinction.

Another factor appears to have been pervasive Taiwanese confidence that the United States would defend the island's security if the PRC tried to resort to coercive measures. Granted, America's obligations under the 1979 Taiwan Relations Act were not the same as a clear-cut defense commitment. The TRA obligated the United States to sell Taiwan arms of a defensive nature (loosely defined) and to regard any PRC threat or use of force as a grave breach of the peace of the East Asian region. The latter provision implied that the United States would use its own military forces to defend Taiwan from attack. Although previous U.S. administrations had sometimes cautioned Taiwanese leaders that the commitment was not unconditional and that they should refrain from provoking the PRC, the current Taiwanese president and his followers were convinced that if a crisis erupted—regardless of its origins—the United States would defend a thriving democracy against aggression from a dictatorial China.

Taiwan's supporters in the U.S. Congress and much of the American media encouraged Taipei to think in those terms. The Taiwan government had added confidence about the current administration, since the sitting American president was a conservative Republican and the conservative wing of the GOP had always been the most supportive of Taiwan's ambitions. Consequently, Taipei may have concluded that the time was propitious for making a bold bid for permanent separation from China.

The changing military balance across the Taiwan Strait may have been another factor leading to the conclusion that it was "now or never." In the late 1990s and the early years of the twenty-first century, Taiwan seemed capable of matching—and perhaps more than matching—the PRC's military capabilities. Indeed, Taiwan's modern air force with its F-16s and Mirages was probably superior to anything China could put into the air. But that situation had been slowly changing. In recent years, the PRC had been spending close to $70 billion a year on its military and was purchasing cutting-edge planes, ships, and other hardware from Russia and the nations of the European Union. Meanwhile, Taiwan had steadily trimmed its defense budget, choosing instead to spend money on a variety of domestic priorities. The military balance between Taiwan and the PRC was already shifting in favor of the latter. There was no doubt that in a few years China would have a decisive military edge over Taiwan, and then the island would have to rely entirely on the United States for its security. In 2013 the nature of the balance was still uncertain, but time clearly was not on Taiwan's side.

Whatever the specific motivations, the government in Taipei decided to cross what Beijing had repeatedly indicated was a bright red line. The PRC had made it clear that crossing that line would bring extremely unpleasant consequences, and Beijing's response to the Taiwan administration's proposed constitutional amendments was not long in coming. On June 5 the PRC president ordered the mobilization of the People's Liberation Army.

Both Taiwanese and U.S. officials seemed caught off guard by Beijing's action. Taipei immediately ordered the mobilization of its forces, including calling reserves to active duty. The United States increased the alert level for its forces stationed in South Korea and Japan. That move in turn caused some agitation in both Seoul and Tokyo. The South Korean foreign ministry issued a statement emphasizing that its mutual security treaty with the United States did not cover contingencies in the Taiwan Strait. Seoul reiterated its adherence to a one-China policy and admonished Taipei to stop provoking a crisis with the PRC. Officials in the Philippines, Thailand, Singapore, and other East Asian countries issued similar statements over the subsequent week. Even America's long-standing ally, Australia, made it clear that if an armed conflict erupted in the Taiwan Strait neither Taiwan nor the United States could expect help from Canberra.

Only Japan refrained from publicly chastising the Taiwanese and stating that it would not back the United States in a conflict with the PRC. Yet even Japan's response was hedged and murky. The prime minister reaffirmed his country's commitment to the alliance with the United States and stressed how important a vigorous U.S. military presence was to the security and stability of the East Asian and western Pacific regions. However, on the burgeoning crisis in the Taiwan Strait, the Japanese leader merely urged both Taipei and Beijing to "exercise restraint and display a commitment to settle this dispute by peaceful means."

The reaction of the U.S. government was more assertive. In opening remarks at a press conference on June 7, the president reminded China that the TRA put the United States on record that any effort by Beijing to coerce Taiwan "would be threat to the peace and security of the Western Pacific area and of grave concern to the United States." Beijing's decision to mobilize the PLA was "most unhelpful" and served to "make an already tense situation worse." The president announced that the aircraft carriers *Stennis* and *Reagan* had been deployed to "waters near Taiwan" as a precaution. He went on to urge the Taipei government to put the proposed constitutional changes on "indefinite hold" as a gesture of good faith on Taiwan's part to ease the crisis.

The president's attempt to outline a balanced policy infuriated Taiwan partisans in the United States. Within hours of the president's press conference, the House majority leader announced that he would introduce a resolution expressing support for Taiwan's right to make changes in its constitution free from threats by its communist neighbor and affirming that the United States stood ready to carry out its obligations under the Taiwan Relations Act, "including the use of force to repel aggression in the Taiwan Strait, should that become necessary." By the next day, that resolution had more than forty cosponsors.

The introduction of the resolution was an implicit criticism of the administration's policy, but that reaction was mild compared to the sentiments expressed in the right-wing press excoriating the administration for its cautious response to China's military mobilization.

> If the experience of the 1930s taught us anything, it is that free nations make a colossal blunder when they attempt to appease totalitarian aggressors. Yet the administration seems to be determined to repeat the folly of British Prime Minister Neville Chamberlain. Instead of issuing a statement making it clear that the United States will defend democratic Taiwan, the president and his advisors persist in trying to placate the communist dictatorship in Beijing. The president should state unequivocally that if China attacks Taiwan, it means war with the United States. Faced with such a clear and determined policy, it is likely that Communist China will back down, especially since its military forces are no match for those of the United States. If the gang of thugs in Beijing persist in their saber rattling, the United States should escalate the stakes by threatening to abandon the one-China policy and recognize Taiwan's independence. It is a policy that should have been reconsidered long ago in any case. If Beijing insists on disrupting the peace and tranquility of East Asia, China's communist rulers need to know that they could lose far more than they anticipate.

Whether it was the mounting criticism from his political base, the troubling information from U.S. surveillance satellites about PLA troop movements across from Taiwan, or some combination of the two factors, the president ordered the *Stennis* and *Reagan* carrier battle groups to move closer to the possible theater of action—into position in waters just east of Taiwan. Following the advice of the joint chiefs of staff and the secretary of defense, he also ordered another carrier battle group, led by the USS *Lincoln*, to leave the Persian Gulf area (which for the moment was unusually quiet) and steam for the western Pacific to support the *Reagan* and *Stennis*. As yet, he refrained from ordering any ships into the Taiwan Strait itself. Even so, Beijing's reaction was harsh. China's foreign minister issued a statement again demanding that the United States cease its interference in China's internal affairs. He described the deployment of U.S. naval forces as "extremely provocative," warning that such "threatening gestures" from the United States were jeopardizing the "entire range of China–U.S. relations."

What the foreign minister meant by the "entire range" of relations became evident within days. China's Central Bank began selling massive quantities of the U.S. treasuries that it held. For nearly a decade, China had been the primary funding source for U.S. government debt—holding more than $1.2 trillion by 2013. With Washington's annual budget deficit hovering near $800 billion, China's policy on the debt issue was no small consideration. It kept interest rates in the United States several percentage points below what they might have been if China had not been willing to soak up those debt instruments. When the central bank declined to purchase any more debt and began to unload hundreds of billions of dollars in what it already held, the impact on U.S. financial markets was immediate and devastating. On what became known as Black Thursday, the yield on the ten-year U.S. treasury note spiked, the stock market plunged more than 12 percent, following smaller but still significant declines the two previous sessions, and the dollar plummeted more than 5 percent. The following day the Federal Reserve's Open Market Committee met in emergency session and raised the Federal Funds rate by 150 basis points (1.5 percentage points) in a desperate attempt to prevent a collapse of the dollar. That move soon proved insufficient to stem an even more dramatic decline.

China was clearly playing hardball, but despite the growing tensions, pro-Taiwan forces in the United States did not relax their pressure to get the administration to stand up to Beijing. The congressional resolution demanding that China end its threatening behavior toward Taiwan and pledging that the United States would defend Taiwan against aggression moved rapidly through the House of Representatives. During the floor debate in mid-June, a steady parade of House members—mainly conservative Republicans, but including more than a smattering of liberal Democrats—rose to praise Taiwan's democracy and to denounce the PRC for everything from its belligerent military posture toward the island, to Beijing's own dismal human rights record, to the flood of Chinese imports that produced America's chronic massive trade deficit with that country. Only a handful of representatives dared to urge caution, warning that precipitous action could derail a crucial U.S. economic and political relationship, and suggesting that going eyeball to eyeball with a nuclear-armed nation had the potential for catastrophe.

The congressional tsunami of hostility toward the PRC caught many observers by surprise. The conventional wisdom had been that the U.S. business community, with its nearly $250 billion-a-year relationship with the PRC at stake, would use its considerable influence to rein in all but the most rabidly anti-PRC members of Congress. During the crisis of June 2013, that assumption was proven spectacularly wrong. Those who favored a cautious policy toward the PRC were routed by allegations that they were willing to sacrifice America's honor and values to protect the interests of amoral corporations. In the end, the House passed the resolution by a vote of 359 to 67. A similar resolution was making its way through the Senate, and it was clear that the margin of victory in that chamber would be only a little less lopsided.

Beijing's next move dramatically heightened the crisis. On June 22, PRC air, naval, and ground forces attacked the offshore islands of Kinmen and Matsu.

Within a matter of hours, Taiwan's badly outnumbered and outgunned defense forces surrendered and the red flag of the People's Republic of China rose over both territories. Taiwan's president responded by going on national television and radio and vowing that Taiwanese forces were prepared to defend the country at all cost and would not rest until the conquered islands were retaken. He also explicitly called on the United States to honor the provisions of the Taiwan Relations Act. "It is clear that the goal of China's communist regime is nothing less than the subjugation of free and democratic Taiwan. In the Taiwan Relations Act, the United States said that such coercion would threaten the peace of all of East Asia. America now needs to take decisive action to repel this aggression or its word will mean nothing."

China's attack on the offshore islands did not come entirely as a surprise to Washington. The movement of PRC military forces during the previous two weeks suggested that such a move was possible. Yet most members of the president's national security team had not thought that Beijing would really go that far. The consensus had been that Chinese leaders were using the mobilization and new deployments to ratchet up the pressure on Taipei and force the Taiwanese regime to retreat on its proposed constitutional revisions. Now that China had instead resorted to military action, the United States faced a dilemma. It was a dilemma that went back as far as the Formosa Straits crises in the 1950s. At that time, the Eisenhower administration had agonized about what to do if the PRC attacked the offshore islands but did not launch an assault on Taiwan itself. Fortunately, China had never changed matters to the point where the United States had to decide whether to respond militarily. The current administration faced no such luxury.

The administration was badly divided about how to respond. The secretary of state opposed any U.S. military intervention. Those offshore islands were not essential to Taiwan's economy or security, he said, noting that even some members of the DPP had previously expressed indifference about their fate. Opposition to military intervention also came from the secretary of the treasury, who warned that the U.S. financial markets had already been badly damaged by the ongoing tensions with China and that, if the crisis escalated, the effect on America's economic health could be devastating. The chairman of the joint chiefs of staff and the director of national intelligence strongly disagreed with the dovish position. They believed that the attack on the offshore islands was merely a prelude to an attempt to conquer Taiwan or intimidate it into surrendering. U.S. credibility was at stake, they stressed, and warned that if the United States did not respond militarily, not only Washington's commitment to defend Taiwan would be in doubt, but so would the other security commitments in East Asia and beyond. This was a clear case of Chinese expansionist aggression, the JCS chairman emphasized, and the United States had to intervene.

The national security advisor proposed a compromise. Move the *Stennis* and the *Reagan* into the Taiwan Strait, she suggested, but refrain at present from taking any direct military action against PRC forces. Such a middle position between doing nothing and initiating a shooting war with China appealed to the president. Later that day, the *Stennis* and *Reagan* battle groups began to move into the Strait. Within days the *Lincoln* also would be in position just east of Taiwan.

The president also called in the PRC ambassador for a dressing down. The secretary of state, who attended the meeting, later said that he had never seen his boss quite so angry or determined. The president warned the Chinese ambassador that the seizure of the islands was "completely unacceptable," and that Beijing's "reckless actions" risked igniting a war between the United States and China. But the ambassador was in no mood to give ground. He reiterated his government's demand that the United States cease interfering in an "internal Chinese dispute." He warned further against any "unwise escalation"—especially against sending U.S. military units into the Taiwan Strait. It was, as diplomats are fond of saying, an "extremely frank exchange of views."

Beijing was not about to back down in the face of the U.S. moves. Indeed, the next day, the PRC defense ministry announced that it was imposing a blockade on "the renegade province of Taiwan" and warned all ships to refrain from approaching Taiwanese ports. The blockade announcement combined with the seizure of the offshore islands sent Taiwan's supporters in the United States into a rage. As might be expected, right-wing pundits led the anti-PRC verbal barrage.

> China's communist government has proven itself to be an aggressor and an outlaw regime. The United States has no choice but to lead the civilized world in repelling this aggression and saving democratic Taiwan. Monsters like Adolf Hitler arise in every generation, and the PRC has shown itself to be the Nazi Germany of our generation. Some say that it would be too dangerous to confront China's brutal aggression, but we must ignore such voices of timidity and appeasement. Yes, it may cost lives—including American lives—to stop China's warmongering expansionism in its tracks. But it will cost even more later on if we let China subjugate free Taiwan. The appetite of a totalitarian aggressor is never satisfied. If the Chinese dictatorship succeeds in conquering Taiwan, where will it stop? Korea will likely be next, and Japan not long after. America's entire position in East Asia and its credibility throughout the world will be destroyed if we do not act resolutely now. But if we do have the courage to lead, other nations will follow us and stand up to the communist aggressors. To the advocates of appeasement, it should be said that it is better to have a small war now than to have a

larger and much more destructive war later. Indeed, our objective now should be nothing less than the removal of the outlaw regime in Beijing. Only then will there be lasting peace in East Asia. The president needs to decide whether he wants to be remembered as the twenty-first century's Winston Churchill or Neville Chamberlain. America's honor as well as its security is at stake. We must defend free and democratic Taiwan!

Although those pundits were confident that other nations would stand shoulder to shoulder with a resolute America in stopping China's coercion of Taiwan, the administration found out differently. Even before Washington sounded out Seoul about its position, the Korean government made it clear that not only would it refuse to join any U.S. military action against the PRC, it forbade the United States from using its own military bases in the Republic of Korea for such purposes. Other governments throughout East Asia followed suit, declaring their neutrality in any armed conflict between the United States and China.

Even Japan left the United States in the lurch. After an agonizing and contentious meeting of the Japanese Cabinet, Tokyo refused to allow the United States to use its military facilities on Japanese territory for operations against PRC forces. Washington reacted with anger and dismay, pointing out that Japan's de facto declaration of neutrality violated the spirit of the security statement adopted by the two governments in February 2005 declaring that a peaceful resolution of the Taiwan dispute was a crucial security interest of both Japan and the United States. Japan's reneging on that commitment, U.S. officials warned Tokyo, endangered the future of the U.S.–Japanese alliance. Nevertheless, Tokyo did not relent. Although there was considerable sympathy for Taiwan among the Japanese public as well as the country's political elite, the fear of PRC economic and military retaliation for Japanese support of an American military defense of Taiwan was even greater. As the crisis of 2013 built to a climax, America stood alone in protecting Taiwan.

The crisis escalated another notch in the early morning hours of July 3. China finally put to use some of the twelve hundred missiles it had been amassing for two decades. Missiles began slamming into targets throughout Taiwan just before dawn. The initial barrage consisted of fewer than one hundred missiles, and Taiwan's missile defense system intercepted more than 80 percent of that number. The physical damage inflicted by the warheads that actually hit their targets was quite modest, but the psychological impact was another matter. Taiwan's stock market tried to open briefly that morning, but after share values plunged more than 20 percent in the first hour of trading, the Taiwanese president ordered all exchanges closed for the duration of the emergency. In addition to the economic impact, thousands of civilians made a panicked exodus from Taipei and other cities, clogging the highways and creating general chaos.

Taiwan's air and naval forces quickly responded to the PRC attack. Although Taipei had reacted angrily to the blockade proclamation, it had not taken action against PRC naval vessels deployed in the Strait. Following the missile barrage, that restraint ended. Taiwanese planes attacked more than a dozen PRC surface vessels, and there were aerial dogfights over the Strait throughout the day. But the most dramatic move came when Taiwanese aircraft struck four of the missile batteries on the mainland, completely destroying two and badly damaging the other two. China responded with a second missile barrage, nearly twice as large as the first.

With all of the combat in and around the Taiwan Strait on July 3, what happened next probably should not have come as a surprise. To this day, no one is certain who fired the first shot in the conflict between U.S. and Chinese forces in the Taiwan Strait in the early morning hours on July 4. Beijing later claimed that a U.S. plane from one of the aircraft carriers strafed a Chinese destroyer in the western part of the Strait, barely ten miles off of the mainland coast, setting off the cascade of violence. The United States told a very different story. According to Washington, both aircraft carrier battle groups sought to avoid conflict with Chinese units while U.S. officials frantically pressed both Beijing and Taipei for a cease fire. At that point, Washington was even willing to concede the PLA's seizure of the offshore islands and had bluntly told Taipei that the United States was unwilling to go to war to dislodge those forces. The U.S. version of events was that China began the war with a missile attack from Chinese navy destroyers and submarines against the *Reagan* battle group.

It is impossible to determine with certainty whose version is correct, but there are several reasons to question the Chinese account. The fact that the PRC began a comprehensive campaign of electronic warfare to disrupt U.S. communications and launched several anti-satellite weapons, knocking out two key U.S. spy satellites, just as the confrontation got under way lends a good deal of credence to the American version. It seems likely that China initiated the conflict, not merely reacted to an American attack. In any case, those tactics were a bold stroke, and they proved highly effective. The advantage that the United States had enjoyed in every conflict since the First Gulf War of being able to see and manage the battlefield far better than any adversary virtually disappeared. In the Taiwan Strait war, American forces had no significant informational advantage over their Chinese opponents. That was a new and very unsettling experience.

In any case, it is indisputable that the Chinese missile assault on the *Reagan* and its support ships was massive and devastating. Three of those ships were sunk and four others damaged in the first hours of the battle. But the worst was yet to come. A coordinated attack using the new generation Advanced Sunburn missiles struck home in multiple locations on the *Reagan* itself. Shortly before 6 A.M. on July 4, 2013, the USS *Ronald Reagan* went to the bottom of the Taiwan Strait. Although vigorous rescue operations were mounted in the midst of the chaos, some 1,832 personnel perished with that ship. Chinese missile, aircraft, and submarine attacks on the *Stennis* battle group caused some damage, but the *Stennis* survived to retreat out of the Strait, losing only one of its escort vessels.

It is impossible to overstate how much the loss of the *Reagan* shocked not only the U.S. Navy but the American people. Before that episode, most people simply regarded the massive carriers in the U.S. fleet as invincible. The call for revenge against China was overwhelming, and U.S. forces in the western Pacific were not long in responding. Planes from the *Stennis* and the *Lincoln* attacked PRC air forces over the Strait, and although outnumbered, prevailed in most of the skirmishes. The counterattack against Chinese naval vessels in the Taiwan Strait was even more pronounced. The most dangerous action, though, was the decision to join the Taiwanese air force in striking airfields and other military installations on the mainland coast itself. On balance, it seemed that the U.S. and Taiwanese forces inflicted more damage than they suffered, but events were threatening to spiral out of control. It was especially ominous that both the United States and the PRC put their strategic nuclear forces on maximum alert. The United States and China teetered on the brink of all-out war.

At a White House meeting following the sinking of the *Reagan*, several members of the president's national security team were in favor of escalation. The chairman of the joint chiefs of staff could barely contain his anger. He advocated not only continuing to strike airfields and missile batteries on the mainland, but attacking military and infrastructure targets throughout the PRC. Clearly, that would require far more air power than the United States had available from the two remaining carriers. Indeed, the JCS chairman and the director of national intelligence urged the president to order the fleet of B-2 bombers from the continental United States into action. Those planes would focus on the government compound in Beijing as well as selected targets in China's prize economic jewel, Shanghai. The hawks on the president's national security team also suggested that the United States launch attacks from its bases in South Korea and Japan, whether the host governments in those countries approved the attacks or not. "What good are our so-called allies," the JCS chairman fumed, "if they won't even let us use our own facilities when we're under attack?"

Predictably, the secretary of state and the national security advisor urged caution and argued forcefully against escalation. The principal surprise in the meeting was that the secretary of defense supported their position and emphatically disagreed with her hawkish colleagues. She pointed out that China had more than two hundred nuclear warheads mounted on intercontinental ballistic missiles capable of reaching any target in the United States, and that the PRC government had put those forces on the highest alert status. If the United States started bombing Beijing and Shanghai, she warned, there was no telling where the cycle of escalation would stop. An all-out war between the United States and China, possibly involving the use of nuclear weapons, would be a disaster beyond comprehension. She pleaded with the president not to take such a fateful step.

For once, the chief executive proved to be both decisive and prudent. As painful as the decision must have been, he opted against escalation. A similar process of fear-induced restraint seemed to be taking place within the PRC government, and both sides began to pull back from the abyss of nuclear confrontation. In a series of calls on July 4 and 5 over the hotline between Beijing and Washington, the two presidents negotiated a cease fire. China agreed to stop its bombardment of Taiwan and to lift the blockade, while the United States agreed not to dispute continued PRC control of the offshore islands and to withdraw its forces from the Strait. Beijing also agreed to withdraw its forces to the western half of the Strait, if Taiwan redeployed its forces to the eastern half. Although those moves formed the basis for the cease fire, China had other demands that had to be met before the crisis could come to an end. Beijing insisted on the resignation of the Taiwanese leader, the end to any effort to change the name of the Republic of China, and the opening of talks on reunification. China reluctantly agreed that Taiwan would not have to accept the one-China principle as a prerequisite for such talks, but that it would be the first topic of discussion.

Not surprisingly, when the United States informed the Taiwanese president of Beijing's demand for his resignation, he flatly refused. The U.S. administration was at the limit of its patience with the volatile Taiwanese leader, though. Washington informed him that if he insisted on staying in office, the United States would withdraw all of its forces from the area and would no longer honor its commitment under the TRA to defend Taiwan. Faced with that ultimatum, he had little choice. On July 6, he announced his resignation to the Taiwanese people. His replacement, the vice president, promptly met Beijing's other demands— withdrawing the proposed constitutional changes and agreeing to commence negotiations on reunification.

Although the new president came from the more pragmatic wing of the DPP, those concessions were an extremely bitter pill to swallow. Yet he seemed to have little choice. Taiwan had neglected its own defenses, not even purchasing all of the military hardware that the United States had offered to sell over the years.

Taipei had put all of its hopes in U.S. military protection, and that protection had not proved sufficient. Given the damage the United States had suffered in this confrontation with China, it was clear that Washington's military protection would be even less reliable in the future. Even many DPP stalwarts now concluded that Taiwan's dream of internationally recognized independence was probably not achievable. The only remaining strategy was to stall as long as possible in reunification negotiations and then strike the best deal available.

Beijing gained a good many of its objectives in the crisis of 2013, although reunification talks would drag on for more than a decade, and when reunification finally occurred it was only in the form of a very loose confederation between Taiwan and the PRC. Moreover, China paid an extraordinarily high price for those gains. Public and congressional sentiment in the United States for retribution against the PRC was irresistible. Passage of the Anti-Aggression Act of 2013 in mid-July mandated not only the severing of diplomatic ties, but also a total embargo on commerce with the PRC and a ban on U.S. investment in China. Although the president had grave misgivings about both aspects, he did not resist when the legislation passed both houses of Congress by veto-proof majorities. The embargo did serious damage to the American economy and the global economy generally, but it had an absolutely devastating effect on China's economic health. A decade-long recession settled over that country, leading to the social upheavals that for a time threatened the unity and stability of the country.

A cold war has settled over U.S.–China relations in the quarter century since the conflict of 2013. Diplomatic ties were restored in 2019, and amendments to the Anti-Aggression Act over the years have led to a limited resumption of commerce. Nevertheless, bilateral trade in 2038 is less than 20 percent of what it was in 2012, and the United States, China, and the rest of the global economy have all suffered the consequences. Equally troubling, the bitter U.S.–Chinese strategic and economic rivalry intensified throughout East Asia, with the United States gradually but inexorably losing ground to the PRC. All of those negative results occurred because of a festering dispute over the status of one small island.

CHAPTER 2

THE ORIGINS OF THE TAIWAN PROBLEM, 1895–1979

During the seventeenth and eighteenth centuries, Taiwan experienced both colonization by Western powers and occupation and governance by the Ming and Qing dynasties.[1] The Penghu Islands, a small island group off the west coast of Taiwan now considered part of Taiwan, were considered part of China as far back as the fourteenth century. The Dutch and Spanish jockeyed for imperial influence on Taiwan itself in the seventeenth century, with both states establishing a presence on the island.

The Ming dynasty, facing military pressure from Manchurian forces that would later become the Qing dynasty, fled to Taiwan in 1661 and evicted the Dutch East India Company, de facto occupier of the island since the early 1620s. The Qing forces eventually overtook the Ming on Taiwan in 1683, and ruled Taiwan until the Treaty of Shimonoseki between China and Japan in 1895.

Under Qing rule, increasing numbers of mainlanders moved to Taiwan to participate in the lucrative trade in commodities, such as tea and camphor.[2] Although there were recurring conflicts between mainlanders and indigenous Taiwanese over resource allocation and other contentious issues, by the end of Qing rule the Taiwanese had effectively been assimilated into the Chinese empire. But as the nineteenth century drew to a close, Taiwan's status was about to change dramatically. Ironically, that change would come about because of a conflict between China and Japan over Korea.

THE SINO-JAPANESE WAR OF 1894-1895[3]

During the middle and late nineteenth century, Japan's and China's political and so-cial structures could hardly have been more different. Japan was undertaking the Meiji government's reforms—reforms that included the end of feudalism, the intro-duction of compulsory education, modernization and unification of Japan's military, modernization of the Japanese banking system, and deep judicial reforms, among others.[4] China, by contrast, was languishing in the remains of its feudal system, clinging tightly to Confucian ideals, and retaining its hostility toward Western ideals and technology. The rise of Japan as an imperial power and the decline of China were both clearly demonstrated by the war that erupted between them in 1894.

In February of that year, a popular uprising brought crisis to the Korean peninsula. A group of citizens organized under the Tonghak religious/political movement rebelled against the government, complaining of unreasonably high taxes and the growing influence of Western ideas on their society. The unrest continued to grow until finally, on June 3, King Kojong appealed to China to send troops to help quell the unrest. Four days later, China informed Japan that it intended to honor that request and send troops to Korea. The notification was given to comply with the Tianjin treaty of 1885, which bound both China and Japan to inform the other if one of them intended to deploy troops to Korea. That same day, Japan informed China that it too intended to send troops—to protect its embassy, consulates, and nationals living in Korea.[5]

The Tianjin treaty had been signed after the Japanese and Chinese legations in Korea clashed over a Japanese-led coup attempt in 1884. Chinese troops squashed the coup, and the Japanese regime backed off, agreeing to the treaty rather than risking a wider conflict.[6] In the ten years since the treaty was signed, however, Japan had undergone tremendous modernization and economic and technological growth, while Chinese power had continued to atrophy. The Japanese knew this, and saw the Tonghak rebellion as their chance to parlay the tension with China into a war to challenge Chinese regional preeminence.

The Japanese troop deployment to Korea in 1894 was between two and four times that of the Chinese. The Chinese were shocked to discover the number of Japanese forces and warships deployed; by mid-June, there were ten Japanese warships patrolling the waters off the coast of Korea.[7] Nevertheless, Chinese Foreign Minister Li Hongzhang believed either that he could secure European intervention to prevent Japanese expansion or that all-out war was otherwise avoidable. He was wrong in both cases.[8]

Although it appeared increasingly evident that Japan was serious about chal-lenging China over Korea, nearly all Western commentators expected that China would deal Japan a crushing defeat. One observer stated: "[F]or a little, weak country like Japan to fight a big, strong country like China is suicidal. Japan will be obliterated like a fly in the flame."[9] This aptly summed up the opinion of nearly all Western observers regarding the prospective outcome of the war. They too would be proven dramatically wrong.

Japan made clear its intentions when on July 23 its troops stormed King Ko-jong's palace in Seoul and took him hostage. Then on July 25, the Japanese navy sank a British-owned, Chinese-leased merchant ship, the *Gaosheng*, which was ferrying Chinese soldiers to Korea. Nearly all of the eleven hundred Chinese soldiers on board perished.[10] On August 1, Japan declared war on China, stating that China sought to "weaken the position of [Korea] in the family of nations—a position obtained for Korea through Japan's efforts—but also to obscure the significance of the treaties recognizing and confirming that position. Such conduct on the part of China is not only a direct injury to the rights and interests of this Empire, but also a menace to the permanent peace and tranquility of the Orient."[11] Japan's complaints about China's military buildup and warlike posture should not obscure the fact that it was Japan that wanted this fight, not China.

Neither China's army nor its navy stood a chance of defeating the Japanese without foreign intervention, which was not forthcoming. China's navy was composed of heavily armored, slow moving ships, whereas Japan's navy consisted of sleek, swift, modern ships. Additionally, China did not possess a national army. There were regional armies, under the control of regional commanders, and as a result, the forces from Chihli province (the region directly affected by the conflict) had to do a disproportionate share of the fighting. Even though troops from other provinces had been mobilized, China was crippled by logistical problems stemming from a lack of efficient transportation systems (attempts to build an expansive modern railway had been stalled)[12] and because the army had essentially no supply lines. Much of the army had to pillage the towns it passed through to survive. Accordingly, news that the army was coming was greeted with anxiety across the affected region.

Further, there was not a sense of national urgency in China, as contrasted with the enthusiasm that was frequently described as "war mania" in Japan. There was a continued belief in China (and in the West) that, although the Japanese were scoring strategic victories early on, they could not outlast the much larger Chinese army. The Chinese army adopted a strategy of counterpunching, and sought to wear down the Japanese forces by attrition.

Recognizing their own military deficiencies and realizing that they had overplayed their hand, the Chinese decided to mass their troops in Pyongyang, hoping to stave off Japanese advances onto Chinese territory. The disorganized

Chinese forces in Pyongyang proved to be utterly inept. After suffering a devastating defeat there, Chinese forces suffered a major naval defeat in the Yellow Sea, then another land defeat on the banks of the Yalu River, a land defeat at Port Arthur, and a final devastating combined land and naval defeat at the port of Weihaiwei.[13]

After this series of disasters, China began to reach the reluctant conclusion that it had no chance of winning the war. The arrogance and condescension that had characterized the Chinese view of Japan and its military became untenable in the face of the devastation wrought on Chinese forces at the hands of the Japanese. In an attempt to retain "face" with its citizens, the Chinese government made a series of disingenuous gestures to end the war that would have allowed it to maintain that China had not been defeated. Japan knew that China was trying to save face, and continued to press the battle until China was prepared to admit defeat. After a long history of being the smaller, weaker neighbor, Japan wanted China cowed and had no intention of stopping the war until China was ready to prostrate itself before the new regional power.

THE END OF THE WAR AND THE TREATY OF SHIMONOSEKI

The early diplomatic efforts to end the war consisted of numerous unrealistic Chinese proposals and staunch Japanese refusals.[14] During the negotiations the war ground on, and the Chinese were continuing to lose large numbers of forces (indeed, Weihaiwei was taken after the Chinese had started its attempts at diplomacy). Japanese military officials had begun to think about which Chinese territories Tokyo should demand as part of peace negotiations, but the army and navy were divided on what lands should be annexed.[15] The army proposed the more unrealistic of the schemes: it wanted possession of the Liaotung peninsula, a part of the Chinese mainland that was in striking distance of both Peking and the ancestral home of the Qing dynasty, Mukden. Japanese occupation of the Liaotung peninsula would thus not only have been of critical strategic concern to the Chinese; because of the proximity of foreign occupiers to the symbolic town of Mukden, it would have been a near-total loss of legitimacy for the ruling government.

The Japanese navy, on the other hand, wanted to annex Taiwan and the Penghu Islands. In the wake of the stunning Japanese military victory, it was becoming increasingly evident in the West that a new important player was emerging in East Asia. The general wariness in the West regarding that new regional power, combined with the talk in Japan about taking mainland territory from China, caused some Japanese to fear intervention by Western powers.[16] Demanding Taiwan and the Penghus, the navy reasoned, would be less provocative yet would provide a good strategic outpost to buffer Japan from a potential Western incursion.

Japanese Premier Ito Hirobumi and Foreign Minister Mutsu Munemitsu decided to demand both the Liaotung peninsula and Taiwan (as well as a large indemnity) as conditions for peace. Although the Chinese made every attempt to retain both territories, their continued military defeats forced them to accede. The Japanese suspected (and had good reason to suspect) that the Russians would intervene to prevent Japanese occupation of the Liaotung peninsula, but Russia had told Japan officially that it would not object to Japanese occupation of Taiwan.[17] Thus there may well have been doubts in Japan from the beginning about whether it could retain possession of the Liaotung.

China and Japan signed the Treaty of Shimonoseki on April 17, 1895, with the Chinese agreeing to cede both Taiwan and the Liaotung peninsula to Japan. On April 23, however, the Germans, French, and Russians offered Japan their "advice" that Japanese possession of the Liaotung peninsula would be a "constant menace to the capital of China, and would at the same time render illusory the independence of Korea; it would henceforth be a perpetual obstacle to peace in the Far East."[18] The German foreign minister, Baron von Gutschmid, went so far as to hint that force might be used if Japan were to refuse to disgorge the Liaotung peninsula. This joint European diplomatic warning became known as the Triple Intervention.[19] The Western powers were only concerned about Japanese occupation of territory on the Chinese mainland, however. After Japan responded favorably to the Triple Intervention on May 4, the Liaotung returned to Chinese ownership, but Taiwan remained a new part of the Japanese empire.

JAPAN'S OCCUPATION OF TAIWAN, 1895–1945

Although the Chinese government had had reluctantly agreed to transfer the island to Japan, people living on Taiwan had their own agenda. On May 23, Taiwan declared itself a republic and set up an independent government. With that government came an army and a mobilization to resist occupation by the Japanese. The founders of the 1895 Taiwanese "republic" shrewdly took Western political labels and applied them to ad hoc institutions, unsuccessfully attempting to obtain French support against the Japanese occupation.[20] It took the Japanese military five months to pacify the island, and for four more years the Taiwanese mounted an insurgency campaign that wore on the Japanese.[21] As one Japanese baron put it: "Japan had made no preparations whatever for the administration of the island at the time of its acquisition."[22]

The insurgency, which in some cases employed terrorism and sabotage, precipitated a forceful Japanese crackdown and severe suspicion on the part of the

Japanese of Taiwanese natives. Over time, a large-scale police state was established on Taiwan: by 1943, police forces—only one-sixth of which were Taiwanese natives—accounted for 14 percent of the population of Taiwan.[23]

Despite the insurgent violence that cropped up periodically until the occupation ended in 1945, the Japanese pursued an extensive plan of legal, political, and economic reforms that transformed Taiwan from a provincial, subsistence economy into a modern, relatively successful society. The colonial model used by Japan was extremely centralized, with near-total control being vested in the governor-general.

Taiwan was widely regarded in Japan as a political and economic albatross. It was an almost totally undeveloped backwater, and many Japanese were skeptical of the ability of ethnic Chinese to modernize. In some ways, however, Taiwan's backwardness was conducive to the Japanese colonial agenda. There were essentially no existing institutions that had to be changed; all modern legal, political, and economic structures could simply be imposed onto a blank political slate. Additionally, the abruptness with which Japan's empire itself came together was advantageous. As Japan expert Hyman Kublin pointed out, the colonial architects "did not . . . have to contend with the inertia, dead-weight, and accumulated debris of imperial systems that had literally grown like Topsy nor was it necessary for them to cope with the manifold vested interests created in an extended process of historical change."[24]

The infrastructure and legal reforms imposed by Japan were lasting contributions that played a large role in Taiwan's precipitous progress in the first half of the twentieth century. However, Japan as a colonial power also tended to plunder its colonies and direct monies back to the imperial government. Kublin noted that the Japanese "understood to their full satisfaction their purposes in engaging in colonialism and pursued their objectives with relentless and unswerving logic."[25] Aside from its strategic importance to Japan, Taiwan was seen as a place to demonstrate the efficacy of Japanese political and social reforms, as well as to generate revenues for the betterment of the empire.

Some reforms were of particular importance, with land reform being perhaps the most revolutionary. Until the Japanese occupation, legal claims to land on Taiwan were murky at best, and there was no fair, effective means to adjudicate conflicting claims. In a way that greatly benefited the Japanese Empire, the governor-general instituted a program by which land claims were institutionalized. In so doing, much of the land was deeded to the government—which was, of course, Japanese. Though the long-term effect of the reform was remarkably positive in that it created an enduring system of property rights on Taiwan, in the short-term Japan managed to line its pockets significantly with the reform's spoils.[26] The benefits to Taiwan in the medium- and long-term, however, were striking. The reforms updated the taxable land area of Taiwan from the previously registered eight hundred-ninety thousand acres to 1.5 million acres.[27]

Agricultural reforms were also staggering. Largely out of fear of renewed insurgency, the Japanese disarmed large numbers of indigenous hunters, forcing them into a growing, modernizing agricultural industry. Here again, though, the Japanese government had figured out ways to direct much of the immediate gains from modernization to its own coffers. It diverted many of the resources traditionally dedicated to rice production (which could be exported without processing) toward sugar production, which locked Taiwanese farmers into selling their sugar cane to Japanese sugar mills, which enjoyed monopoly status and the ability to fix prices. Japanese consumers suffered alongside Taiwanese farmers, paying higher prices for the monopoly-priced sugar than they would have on the world market.[28]

As mentioned earlier, Japanese police were omnipresent on Taiwan. The scattered yet nagging insurgency caused substantial fear in the new Japanese empire, and Japan had no intention of being run out of Taiwan by an indigenous uprising. Legal reforms were crafted in a manner that would help ensure Japanese security. The system of *pao-chia*, or mutual responsibilities, locked indigenous Taiwanese into a system in which social pressure prevented criminality, because many would be punished for the crimes of a few.

The combination of land, agricultural, and legal reforms increased the amount of land area under cultivation to 2.11 million acres in 1941. The value of Taiwan's foreign trade increased more than thirtyfold between 1897 and 1939.[29] Japanese public health measures dramatically reduced the spread of infectious disease, which had been rampant before the introduction of modern vaccinations and treatments. Infrastructure improvements were similarly remarkable: advances in roads and railways, ports and shipping, telephone and telegraph all set Taiwan on a course of social revolution away from the primitive subsistence agriculture of the 1890s toward the modern society that was to emerge there in the twentieth century. Given all of those changes, Taiwan's political, social, and economic development diverged more and more from that of mainland China. The two entities were becoming very different societies.

THE DEVELOPMENT OF A MODERN STATE IN CHINA

After the staggering defeat suffered in the Sino-Japanese War, it became increasingly difficult to deny the need for modernization and political transformation in China. Between the end of the war and China's retaking of Taiwan in 1945, there

were three periods of fundamental reform in China. Although they were ideolog-
ically and functionally different, each was staggering in scope.

While increasing numbers of Chinese leaders were embracing the notion of
transformation, Confucianism presented an obstacle to dramatic reform. Historically interpreted as obstinately opposed to revolutionary change, Confucianism
remained at the heart of Chinese political thought, and Western ideas and culture
had long been eschewed as incompatible with Chinese society.

Remarkably, the works of some Western philosophers did find their way into
Chinese political thinking. Particularly reasonable to Chinese thinkers was the
British philosopher Herbert Spencer's notion that humans (and social institutions) could evolve "organically" toward higher states of being.[30] Spencer had
also been influential in Meiji Japan, in large part because his theories, unlike
those of many Western philosophers, could be worked into a loosely Confucian
framework. The influence of Spencer and others slowly led the Chinese to embrace political transformation.

The first period of reform after the Sino-Japanese War was the so-called 100
Days Reform that took place in 1898. Inspired and led by the Chinese radical
Kang Yu-wei, the reformers advocated a staggeringly ambitious agenda for China
that included the creation of a parliament, the notion of "people's rights," the
translation and acceptance of Western works of science and philosophy, compulsory education, widespread privatization, market reforms, and many other progressive proposals.[31] It would be hard to overstate just how radical—and how
threatening to some—these proposals were. Kang won remarkable support from
the Emperor Guangxu, but eventually pressed too hard, too fast. Guangxu was
deposed and Kang was run out of Beijing.

In 1911, the Qing dynasty would breathe its last breath. A group of revolu-
tionaries, led by Sun Yat-sen and rallying behind his "Three Principles" (nationalism, democracy, and people's livelihood), overthrew the Qings. On January 1,
1912, Sun was inaugurated as the president of a new Chinese republic, but Yuan
Shikai, a powerful army commander, rose to challenge Sun, and assumed the
presidency just two months later. Yuan's rule was dictatorial, and would lead to
the birth of an opposition party, the Kuomintang.

Song Jiaoren founded the KMT in opposition to Yuan's rule, and was
promptly assassinated. However, the KMT itself grew in support, and Yuan's
power shrank. The country soon descended into anarchic warlordism. Ideological fissures deepened among intellectuals, who were often as divided as the war-
lords. The KMT and the newly formed Chinese Communist Party (CCP)
emerged as the leading political forces by the end of the 1910s. Chiang Kai-shek,
a former aide to Sun and a military leader in his own right, slowly rose to promi-

nence within the Kuomintang in the 1920s and effectively consolidated his power so that, by the end of the decade, the CCP had been scattered and the KMT was relatively stable. The Kuomintang made marked advances in infrastructure, social, and legal reforms.

However, by the mid-1930s, the CCP had regrouped and was growing in both ideological appeal and numbers. Though the KMT and CCP had cooperated to fight against the Japanese invasion of Manchuria in 1931, the ideological and personal conflicts were too great to reconcile. Even during the fighting there was tension between the KMT and CCP, with intra-Chinese skirmishes becoming common by 1940. Although both sides suffered heavy losses during the anti-Japanese war, the CCP emerged relatively stronger and would rout the KMT from the mainland entirely in 1949, effectively establishing the People's Republic of China.

THE END OF WORLD WAR II AND THE RETURN OF TAIWAN TO CHINA

As the tide was turning against the Axis powers in World War II, President Franklin D. Roosevelt, British Prime Minister Winston Churchill, and Chiang Kai-shek met in Cairo to discuss the status of Japan's colonies. The Cairo Declaration of December 1943 determined that all of the territories Japan had taken from China by force were to be returned to China as a condition of Japanese surrender. This decision was further codified in the Potsdam Proclamation of July 1945, which reinforced the conditions set forth in the Cairo Declaration.

The resolve on the part of the Allied powers did not, however, clear up some of the matters pertaining to international law. At what point would the legal status of Taiwan be determined? Was a treaty officially recognizing Taiwan as part of China needed before the transition would be complete?[32] What role would American forces play in the process of Japanese withdrawal and Chinese administration? China had been devastated militarily in the war and by some accounts had neither the maritime nor other military resources needed to take back and pacify the island on its own.[33]

Though a great deal of planning had been given to the handover at the State Department and within the joint chiefs of staff, no officials had suspected the rough landing that Chiang's regime would make on Taiwan. The Taiwanese people had by and large rejected Japanese culture, but they had come to embrace Japanese political and economic institutions. They enthusiastically greeted the reunification with China because they saw the Chinese people as their cultural brethren and believed that reunification would blend the best of both worlds:

modern political and economic systems coupled with cultural identification with the parent country.[34]

Accordingly, much of the strategizing had been based on the erroneous assumption that China would retake Taiwan as a normal province of the country. That did not happen. In the words of one U.S. official: "The [Taiwanese] people anticipated sincerely and enthusiastically deliverance from the Japanese yoke. However, [administrator] Chen Yi and his henchmen ruthlessly, corruptly, and avariciously imposed their regime upon a happy and amenable population. The Army conducted themselves as conquerors."[35] Resentment toward the Chinese who retook Taiwan lasted for years. As late as 1964, many Taiwanese expressed the view that "[t]he dogs [the derogatory term used for the Japanese] treated us better than the pigs [the term for mainland Chinese]."[36]

One reason that the Chinese reacted in such a way may have been simple surprise. When Taiwan was wrested from the Chinese in 1895, it was backward and provincial even by the standards used to judge China under dynastic rule. When the Chinese landed on Taiwan in September 1945, they found a relatively educated populace that was governed by some degree of law and had grown accustomed to stability and a relatively modern way of living. From the look of things in 1945, the fifty years apart had been much kinder to Taiwan than they had been to mainland China.

Chen Yi had been chosen as administrator of Taiwan in 1945 largely because of his expertise in dealing with Japan. Though most people expected the Japanese to leave without incident, the Chinese thought it wise to have an administrator who knew how to deal with the Japanese.[37] In addition, Chen was a close acquaintance of Chiang and was vested with full authority over Taiwan.

The Chinese under Chen went forward with a program not of integration but domination. They proceeded to nationalize the great majority of assets on Taiwan, reasoning that they were Japanese property and as such the rightful spoils of a war they had won. The indigenous people were treated not as Chinese welcomed back into the fold but as the inhabitants of conquered territory. Economic output shrank dramatically, and the expectation for political representation was quickly dispelled. It was this lack of economic and political opportunity, as well as Taiwan's overall poor treatment by the Chinese government, that caused a popular uprising in 1947.

On February 27, a woman selling cigarettes was accosted by agents of the tobacco monopoly, who accused her of selling untaxed tobacco. The confrontation escalated and the woman was killed. Thousands of Taiwanese marched the next day on the tobacco monopoly headquarters to protest her death. Chen's soldiers fired on the protestors, killing several of them. But Chen did not have adequate forces to put down an all-out insurrection, so he requested reinforcements from the mainland. Chiang granted the request and sent more troops while Chen employed strong-arm diplomacy to prevent an all-out rebellion in Taipei. Once the reinforcements, numbering nearly fifty thousand, arrived, they proceeded to slaughter thousands of indigenous Taiwanese and crush the protests.[38]

In the wake of the riots on Taiwan, Chiang removed Chen from his post as governor-general on May 15, 1947. (Chen would later join with the Communists on the mainland.)[39] The attitude of Taiwanese toward reunification went from hopeful anticipation to disenchantment and despair in a remarkably short period of time, and the riots and barbarism that accompanied China's regaining sovereignty over Taiwan contributed to the birth of the Taiwan independence movement. The riots in many ways also served as a wake-up call for the KMT, and its heavy-handed management of Taiwan gave way to more local control and more power vested in the hands of the Taiwanese themselves. These two factors would set the stage for the political and economic transformation that would occur in the subsequent decades.[40] But the overall animosity of Taiwanese toward the mainland authorities did not abate.

After Chen was deposed, conditions on Taiwan improved, but only marginally. It was not until 1948, when defeat became imminent for the KMT on the mainland, that Chiang started thinking seriously about the prospect of cultivating Taiwan as a base of operations for the Nationalist regime.[41] By early 1949, Chiang had appointed a new governor of Taiwan, Chen Cheng, who started the process of seriously reforming KMT rule of Taiwan. By the time the Nationalists lost the mainland later in 1949, the situation on Taiwan had improved but the hostility to the government lingered.

THE CCP TAKES OVER MAINLAND CHINA

While conditions on Taiwan were deteriorating for the Nationalists, a dire situation was emerging on the mainland. There had been periodic skirmishes between the Nationalist government and the Chinese Communist Party for roughly twenty years, but the government was always in a position of strength. The CCP had been making large relative gains in support and strategic advantage until the Japanese mounted a large-scale invasion from Manchuria into eastern China in 1937, which led the country to rally around the government to oppose the foreign occupiers. Even during this period of détente, however, there were rather precise delineations about which faction was supposed to be where, and when CCP units moved outside their approved area of operations skirmishes would erupt with the KMT, even amid fighting against the Japanese.

The United States, while formally allied with Chiang Kai-shek's Nationalist government, had been thinking seriously about the political fissures in China throughout World War II. American strategy in China was to push for reconciliation between the KMT and the CCP, unifying China into a strong, stable actor in northeast Asia. In hindsight, it seems clear that there was little or no will on the part of either the CCP or the KMT to mend fences. Even the public statements of both parties were extremely bellicose and unequivocal. To believe that peaceful settlement was possible was the triumph of hope over experience.

American efforts were also marred by strategic uncertainty. Some of the more sober analysts saw the growing strength of Mao Zedong's CCP and recognized that Chiang's regime was in trouble. At the same time, the existence of a new global strategic environment centered around the Cold War between the United States and the Soviet Union meant that a communist China would undesirably skew the balance of power in favor of communism, and increase the chances of a Soviet-Chinese alliance. The resulting U.S. strategy was to try to keep Chiang propped up by developing a coalition government in China. Washington tried to persuade the CCP that sharing power with the Nationalists was the best result the CCP could hope for, hinting that a total communist takeover would be unacceptable to the United States. This strategy was deeply flawed, because a coalition government was unsatisfactory to both sides. The CCP sensed its growing strength and refused to accept half-measures, and the Nationalists were *de jure* in power and clung desperately to the notion that the communist storm could be weathered.

The futility of U.S. diplomacy could be characterized by the visit of General George C. Marshall to China in December of 1945. By January of 1946, Marshall had brokered a cease-fire, developed plans for power-sharing, and persuaded the KMT to accept democratic elections in the future. Marshall returned to Washington in March, and by the time he went back to China in April he found that the cease-fire had been cast off and fighting had erupted again.[42]

Although forced to accept the reality that U.S. diplomacy could not stave off civil war, the Truman administration continued to half-heartedly support Chiang. The enthusiasm for material support waned, however, as Chiang proceeded to lose both the military and political battles in China. Until the late-1940s, the military and political defeats the Nationalists suffered were alarming, but not decisive. As the CCP continued to gain political support by promising liberation to peasants in the countryside, though, the Nationalists suffered increasingly meaningful military defeats.

Autumn of 1949 would bring the final blows to Nationalist rule. In October, as the CCP took control of Manchuria and a large swath of the surrounding provinces, the Nationalists were forced to move their capital from Canton to Chungking. In November, Communist forces routed them from Chungking, and the KMT moved its operations to Chengtu. Finally, in December 1949, after roughly six million Chinese had perished in the struggle, Chiang Kai-shek and more than a million of his followers fled to Taiwan to regroup and plan their counterattack to retake the mainland. For its part, the CCP remained on the offensive, planning to finish off the KMT in Taiwan. Though Mao himself famously proclaimed in 1936 that he did not consider Taiwan to be a "lost territory" of China[43] insofar as the fight against the KMT now carried onto Taiwan, Taiwan became a strategic objective for the CCP. Additionally, once the Allies recognized Taiwan as part of China in the Cairo Declaration, the CCP adjusted its position. The CCP then held that control over all parts of China was its objective, and it accordingly included Taiwan.[44]

THE KUOMINTANG SETTLE ON TAIWAN— BUT WHO REPRESENTS CHINA?

Although the KMT's governance of Taiwan from 1945 until 1947 had been a disaster, the internal party reforms that the KMT undertook after 1949 led to positive changes in the party's overall effectiveness.[45] Chiang Kai-shek believed that the KMT had lost the civil war not only because of deficiencies in policy and military strategy but also because of structural problems within the KMT itself. He identified factionalism on two fronts: ideological divisions that split the party, and infighting between the party's center and regional branches that diluted the coordination and execution of KMT policy.[46] Chiang initiated a successful campaign of restructuring that concentrated and focused the KMT's political influence and policy agenda.

While the KMT was busy consolidating its power on Taiwan, the reality of the Cold War strategic environment was playing an increasingly large role in U.S. policy. U.S. support had previously been tempered by the sober realization that Chiang was destined to lose the fight against the communists. After his defeat, however, military and other strategists in Washington were becoming increasingly convinced of Taiwan's strategic importance as a central part of the new policy of containing global communism. A classified report issued by General Albert C. Wedemeyer in 1947 suggested a program of supporting the Nationalist government with all necessary support short of U.S. military intervention, since Wedemeyer believed that communist domination of China would create enormous problems for the United States in the coming years.[47] Wedemeyer's proposal was rejected in favor of a policy that lent moral and diplomatic support to

Chiang's regime, while recognizing the reality of CCP's growing power and influence in China. But once the KMT fled to Taiwan, U.S. policy began to resemble Wedemeyer's proposal.

The CCP, for its part, believed that U.S. support for the ROC was rooted in a desire to use Taiwan as a launching pad for an assault on the newly minted People's Republic of China. Chiang Kai-shek's visit to Manila in July 1950 was seen by the PRC as part of a U.S. effort to unite the Philippines, South Korea, and the Republic of China as an anti-PRC alliance.[48] If Chiang had had his way, a U.S.-backed invasion would no doubt have been launched. His government continually pressed the United States to back an ROC invasion of the mainland, promising that the CCP would crumble and that the Chinese people would embrace the return of the KMT.[49] Both Truman and Eisenhower, however, were skeptical and repeatedly rebuffed Chiang's proposals to help retake the mainland.

Meanwhile, the PRC was having its own disputes regarding the best way to stub out the remnants of the Nationalist government. While the view that Taiwan was a part of China had not been particularly widespread or important within the communist leadership before the Cairo Declaration, the desire to deal a death blow to Chiang certainly was. Paranoia within the PRC regarding American intentions in Taiwan was not altogether unreasonable. The U.S. position would eventually end up claiming that Taiwan's status was undetermined until there was an "international action to determine its future."[50]

There had also been talk within U.S. policy circles about getting rid of Chiang by U.S.-backed coup and placing a pro-U.S. puppet in his place.[51] At various times, Secretary of State Dean Acheson, Assistant Secretary of State for Far Eastern Affairs Dean Rusk, John Foster Dulles, who would later become secretary of state, and Paul Nitze, the director of the State Department's policy planning staff, all pushed for the coup solution. The relationship with Chiang had been tenuous, and he was widely perceived as incompetent and corrupt. For this reason, military and financial aid had been cut off in January of 1950. The goal of the coup plan was to put someone trustworthy in place that would allow the United States to cultivate a true protectorate on Taiwan. This plan was rejected, however, partly because increasing flirtations between the PRC and Soviet Union were causing nervousness in the United States about destabilizing Chiang.[52]

In addition to their diplomatic and propaganda efforts, both the PRC and the KMT started massing troops on both sides of the Taiwan Strait. By at least one account, the PRC would very likely have been able to deal a death blow to the Nationalists in the spring of 1950. The *New York Times* reported that, compared to the Nationalists' "fewer than 150,000 well-trained and equipped troops," the PRC could bring to bear "virtually unlimited manpower and weapons. They hold a large slice of the material that the United States furnished the Nationalists and have on tap many times the number of troops on Formosa."[53] Absent U.S. intervention, the PRC would almost certainly have prevailed—even given the overall weakness of its naval forces.

The crystallization of the global communist threat in U.S. eyes was accelerated by the North Korean invasion of South Korea on June 25, 1950. Worried that the Chinese might see the Korean War as an opportunity to seize Taiwan, the Truman administration deployed the Seventh Fleet on June 27 to "neutralize" the Taiwan Strait; that is, to prevent any offensive acts by either the ROC or PRC while the Korean conflict was raging. The neutralization notwithstanding, the PRC escalated its own rhetoric and actions, claiming in July that not even U.S. military intervention could prevent the "liberation" of Taiwan. The PRC staged large demonstrations, rallying public support for action against Chiang.[54]

Meanwhile, both the Chinese and American governments were considering their options regarding the Korean War. Zhou Enlai, the number two leader in the PRC government, wrote that:

> For us, the Korean question is not simply a question concerning Korea, it is related to the Taiwan issue. The U.S. imperialists have adopted a hostile attitude towards us and set up their defence line in the Taiwan Strait while paying lip service to non-aggression and non-intervention. . . . From the information we got, they wanted to calm China first and, after occupying North Korea, they will come to attack China.[55]

For the United States, the fear of a communist takeover of the Korean peninsula led to a U.S.-sponsored U.N. resolution to condemn the North Korean invasion. The United States also mobilized its forces to help South Korea repel the invaders. The prospect of Chinese intervention caused further apprehension in the United States. Mao had been in Moscow from December 1949 to February of 1950, and the United States was worried that a Sino-Russian alliance was blossoming. The Sino-Soviet Treaty of Friendship, Alliance and Mutual Assistance in 1950 confirmed American fears that the two communist giants were forming a hostile bloc in East Asia.[56]

When the PRC did intervene in the Korean conflict in late October, both the Truman administration and Congress codified their beliefs that China was an existential enemy of the United States and should be considered such, in Taiwan as well as in Korea. This gave ammunition to the "China (pro-KMT) Lobby" and its sympathizers, and any notion of backing away from Chiang was discarded.[57]

The deployment of the Seventh Fleet seemed to work, and by the close of 1950 U.S. intelligence was reporting that a PRC invasion of Taiwan (always more probable than an ROC attack on the mainland) was becoming less and less likely. The PRC had always seen Truman's claim that the Seventh Fleet was positioned to defend both parties from each other as disingenuous, as there was little likelihood that Chiang would have been able to mount a credible attack on the mainland in 1950.

Additionally, it became clearer over the months to come that the Korean War was not going to close with a decisive U.S. victory. This created an awkward diplomatic environment, because the PRC envisioned that as a precondition for the end of hostilities it could demand that the United States recognize the PRC and remove the Seventh Fleet from the Taiwan Strait. However, since the "neutralization" of the Taiwan Strait was an American enterprise but the Korean War was undertaken as a UN operation, the two matters were completely separable, and the armistice in Korea did not lead to U.S. diplomatic recognition of the PRC or the end of U.S. protection of Taiwan.[58]

The Korean War also intensified vehement anti-PRC sentiment in the United States, particularly in Congress. It emboldened the China Lobby, which was originally spawned from a split between U.S. Ambassador to China Patrick J. Hurley and junior diplomats at the U.S. embassy. A political war was fought during 1944–45 to determine U.S. China policy, with Hurley advocating all-out support for the KMT and the junior diplomats recognizing that the CCP was destined to win the civil war. Hurley would eventually resign in frustration, but upon returning to the United States he approached members of Congress to cultivate robust support for Chiang there.[59]

By the time of the Korean War, the China Lobby was represented by such people as New York businessman Alfred Kohlberg (who had commercial interests in Taiwan) and Senator William F. Knowland (R-CA)—dubbed "the Senator from Formosa" by a colleague.[60] The China Lobby assembled an effective coalition of pro-Chiang partisans who relentlessly lobbied on behalf of the ROC for measures up to and including those that would have virtually guaranteed war between the United States and the PRC, such as the deployment of U.S. ground troops to Taiwan with General Douglas MacArthur coordinating Far East policy.[61]

The role of the China Lobby, combined with widespread public anger at the PRC for its intervention in Korea, meant that under U.S. protection Taiwan would remain separate from the mainland. Washington continued to recognize the ROC as the legitimate government of China, and the Seventh Fleet stayed on to maintain the neutrality of the Strait. Taiwan's status was rapidly becoming a dangerous flashpoint between the United States and China.

THE FIRST TAIWAN STRAIT CRISIS

In early September of 1954, the PRC started shelling Quemoy, a tiny cluster of islands occupied by tens of thousands of Nationalist troops, as well as Matsu, another tiny island northwest of Taiwan.[62] The Quemoys were practically "wading distance" off the coast of mainland China, near the port of Xiamen. The inconclusive nature of the Chinese civil war led to a situation in which Nationalist forces continued to occupy a series of small islands just off the Chinese coast. The status of those islands and what strategic importance they held would precipitate a crisis that would bring the United States extremely close to war with the PRC in 1955.

In the Eisenhower administration, two camps had emerged. One camp, epitomized by Admiral Arthur Radford, chairman of the joint chiefs of staff, and, to lesser degrees, by Secretary of State John Foster Dulles and President Eisenhower himself, believed that the United States should extend a security guarantee to the offshore islands as well as Taiwan and the Penghu (Pescadores) Islands.[63] The other camp was much more cautious, and this group included National Security Advisor Robert Cutler, Defense Secretary Charles Wilson, Army Chief of Staff General Matthew Ridgway, and Treasury Secretary George Humphrey.

The differing approaches regarding the Taiwan Strait reflected the larger disagreement between the "containment" strategy advocated by George Kennan and the "rollback" strategy advocated by Dulles in dealing with the global threat of communism. Dulles and other advocates of rollback were dispositionally inclined to advocate the prevention of communist advances of any size or strategic significance. Ideology aside, however, there was serious debate among members of the NSC as to whether the loss of the offshore islands would precipitate an all-out assault on the ROC. Everyone on the NSC was united in supporting Chiang in defense of Taiwan and the Penghus even if that meant war between the United States and the PRC. Eisenhower recognized the implications of escalation as taking the United States "to the threshold of World War III."[64]

The U.S. policy immediately following the PRC shelling of Quemoy was to publicly reiterate Washington's support for the Nationalists on Taiwan and the Penghus, while avoiding clarifying whether the United States would come to the defense of the offshore islands.[65] To codify its commitment to the defense of the ROC, in December the United States signed the Mutual Defense Treaty[66] with Taiwan, which was a boon to Chiang. The critical section of the MDT made official the notion that "[e]ach Party recognizes that an armed attack in the West Pacific Area directed against the territories of either of the Parties would be dangerous to its own peace and safety and declares that it would act to meet the common danger in accordance with its constitutional processes." Congress passed the so-called Formosa Resolution in January of 1955, giving the president authorization to "employ the Armed Forces of the United States as he deems necessary for the specific purpose of securing and protecting Formosa and the Pescadores against armed attack, this authority to include the securing and protection of such related positions and territories of that area now in friendly hands and the taking of such other measures as he judges to be required or appropriate in assuring the defense of Formosa and the Pescadores."[67]

The reason for the ambiguity in U.S. policy regarding Quemoy and Matsu was at least in part pragmatic: The United States would rather the Nationalists continue to hold the offshore islands if PRC uncertainty about American intentions could deter communist military advances. However, the growing consensus within the Eisenhower administration was that the United States should not defend the offshore islands unless an attack on them was only a stepping stone to a full-on communist advance to Taiwan. By February, Eisenhower was taking a more temperate tack on the offshore islands, reasoning that "we must make a distinction—(this is a difficult one)—between an attack that has *only* as its objective the capture of an offshore island and one that is *primarily a preliminary movement to an all-out attack on Formosa.*"[68] Therefore, some of the divisions in the administration could be attributed to uncertainty regarding the PRC's intentions.

The existence of the MDT, combined with Chiang's chicanery, brought the United States remarkably close to war with China. In January 1955 Nationalist planes responded to the PRC's advances on Ichiang, a small island just north of the Tachen Islands, by bombing positions on the Chinese mainland. As the Eisenhower administration saw its policy heading off the rails, a decision was made shortly thereafter to cede the Tachens, which would have been even harder to defend than Quemoy. By the beginning of February, Chiang's forces had evacuated the Tachens.[69]

Distinguishing between PRC invasion of the offshore islands as an end in itself or as a means to attacking the Penghus and Taiwan became *de facto* U.S. policy toward Taiwan, despite the misgivings of Dulles and the more hawkish members of the cabinet.[70] However, when Dulles returned from a visit to the region in the end of February 1955, he reported that the cession of the Tachens had not deterred the PRC and that it intended to move forward to Taiwan. Dulles recommended that the United States deploy tactical nuclear weapons to deter the Chinese Communists.[71]

Public comments in March by President Eisenhower and Chief of Naval Operations Robert Carney caused profound uproar in the United States, China, and the international arena generally. On March 16, Eisenhower remarked that he failed to see "why [nuclear weapons] shouldn't be used just exactly as you would use a bullet or anything else."[72] Then on March 25, Carney admitted that the United States intended to execute an attack plan on mainland China, and that he expected war to break out by April 15. On April 1, eighteen U.S. warplanes penetrated PRC airspace, and a week later a Chinese plane crashed, the Chinese blaming both the ROC and the United States for sabotage.[73]

Alongside Dulles's nuclear proposal, a broad array of policy proposals emerged in April, including a plan for pulling Nationalist troops back from all of the offshore islands while simultaneously putting in their place a U.S. naval blockade of the mainland. Dulles combined the two policies, advocating replacing Nationalist forces with a U.S. naval blockade in the Taiwan Strait and stationing nuclear weapons on Taiwan. This policy held severe implications and met opposition within the administration and from Chiang Kai-shek. (Chiang evidently feared that the United States might betray the rest of its promise once he had pulled his troops back from the offshore islands.) Ironically, Chiang's refusal to accept Dulles's proposal may have prevented war between the PRC and the United States.[74]

Abruptly, on April 23, 1955, Chinese Premier Zhou Enlai unilaterally de-escalated the cross-Strait rhetoric, stating that the PRC was open to negotiations with the United States in order to avoid war, and in May he announced that the "Chinese people are willing to strive for the liberation of Formosa by peaceful means as far as this is possible."[75] The U.S. leadership, while skeptical of the overture, supported an unofficial cease-fire at the end of May.[76] Thus ended the first Taiwan Strait crisis.

THE SECOND TAIWAN STRAIT CRISIS

While PRC and U.S. actions and statements regarding Taiwan cooled during the summer of 1955, Chiang's views were unchanged. In August, his administration publicly stated that it was preparing a plan to retake the mainland.[77] One of the reasons for the divergent ROC and U.S. policies was the continued disagreement regarding the nature of the Mutual Defense Treaty (MDT). Chiang saw the document (purposively, perhaps) primarily as an American agreement to back the Nationalist government. Since Chiang was the leader of the Nationalist government and advocated an ROC counterattack against the mainland, he assumed that the United States supported this policy by means of the MDT. The United States, however, saw the MDT as an American commitment to defend Taiwan and the Penghus from PRC invasion—nothing more. Chiang was cognizant of this difference, but continued to try to draw the United States into war with Communist China by means of the MDT.

In addition to Chiang's announcement of a plan to attack the PRC, he started rapidly building up forces on Quemoy, by one account having tripled them from thirty thousand in September of 1954 to ninety thousand in August of 1955.[78] In so doing, Chiang was able to make the case that the offshore islands had become much more important to the defense of Taiwan, insofar as they now hosted a large percentage of Nationalist troops, the loss of which would be devastating to the ROC. Chiang argued further that the morale of Nationalist troops would be crushed if they were forced to retreat. With large garrisons on the offshore islands, the Nationalists could fight forward from them, as opposed to the communists being able to do the same.[79]

Though the United States still recognized Chiang's ROC as the legitimate government of China, there were direct, ambassador-level negotiations with the PRC that had started in Geneva in 1954 and persisted off and on throughout 1955 to 1957. It was during these negotiations that the mantra of both the PRC and United States would emerge. As the American negotiators pressed for a nonaggression pledge with regard to Taiwan, the PRC maintained that Taiwan was an internal matter of Chinese politics, and that American intervention was not welcome.[80] The talks ended in December 1957, shortly before the second Taiwan Strait crisis.

In July of 1958, the PRC took decisive action against the ROC, shooting down several Nationalist aircraft, consolidating its deployment of military personnel and materiel across from the Taiwan Strait, and publicly stating that it was embarking on a policy of "liberating" Taiwan. The PRC then blockaded and bombarded Quemoy and Matsu, cutting them off from Taiwan. On August 23, the PRC began another enormous artillery bombardment of Quemoy. Within days, both U.S. Army and Navy forces were put in place to aid the Nationalists, with the Army troops ready to assist the Nationalists in assaulting the mainland, and the Naval vessels "escorting" and "protecting" ROC supply ships. It was in this environment that Eisenhower authorized allowing Chiang to attack the mainland, with the rather absurd caveat that this should be done only if doing so would not "drag us into attacking [Beijing] and the whole of China."[81] The reality was that supporting an ROC attack on the mainland would almost certainly have brought the United States to war with China.

By September Eisenhower was adopting a bellicose public tone, claiming that he was "certain" that the PRC intended to move on to invade Taiwan, and likening the PRC to Nazi Germany.[82] Chiang, however, was nonplussed, fearing that Eisenhower would fail to follow the path to war. Nationalist Ambassador to the United States George K. C. Yeh proclaimed on September 19 that air raids on the mainland were warranted by the Nationalists' "inherent right of self-de-

The Origins of the Taiwan Problem, 1895–1979 ⊧ 45

fense" and that therefore the provision of the MDT that required consultation with the United States before attacking the mainland did not apply.[83] As the Nationalists scored tactical air victories over the Communists, Chiang was emboldened, publicly suggesting on September 29 that if Quemoy was seriously threatened the Nationalists fully intended to go to war with the PRC, with or without the United States.[84]

As Dulles prepared to head to Taiwan for meetings with the Nationalist leadership in mid-October, the United States had changed strategy again, and intended once more to use both carrot and stick on Chiang. They would press him to renounce offensive attacks on the mainland and draw down his forces on Quemoy and Matsu, while simultaneously promising him increased financial and military aid. Chiang agreed to this formula during the October 21 to 23 meetings with Dulles, but quickly reinterpreted the document not as foreswearing an attack on the mainland, but as clarifying that it was not to be a "principal means" of retaking the mainland.[85]

On October 6, the PRC announced that it would lift the blockade of Quemoy and Matsu out of "humanitarian considerations" and unilaterally cease fire for one week.[86] On October 25 the PRC instigated a longer-term cease-fire, although this one had a bizarre feature. (The PRC announced that it would not shell Quemoy on even days of the month.[87]) It appears that this overture on the part of the PRC may have been for reasons other than simply fear of war with the United States. Some analysts have concluded that the PRC actually developed a fear of taking over only the offshore islands because of the possibility it would draw a clearer geographic line between Taiwan and the mainland, thus inadvertently supporting the notion of "two Chinas."[88] If the PRC developed a fear of taking only the offshore islands, it raises serious questions about what its intentions were at various points during the conflict. If this fear was held throughout the crisis, it lends credence to the argument that the PRC fully intended to move on to Taiwan.

———— •◦• ————

In both the first and second crises in the Taiwan Strait, the United States refused to support ROC offensive action, yet did not want the ROC to provide for its own defense for fear that it would be defeated and the PRC would take Taiwan. The United States saw Chiang as a welcome distraction for the PRC, and, as a bonus, the Taiwan matter caused a rift between the Soviet Union and PRC that certainly was welcomed in Washington. (The PRC, for example, was outraged that their comrades in Moscow did not so much as condemn the American threats of attacking the Chinese mainland until after the PRC had agreed to negotiations.[89]) The American policy of "strategic ambiguity" coupled with less cautious PRC leadership easily could have precipitated a conflagration that spiraled to an all-out war involving the United States as well as the PRC and the ROC. It was most fortunate that both crises ultimately ended peacefully.

TAIWAN DURING THE 1960S

Compared to the decade before and the decade that would follow, the 1960s saw a period of relative quiet over the Taiwan issue. A miniature third crisis in the Taiwan Strait emerged in 1962, when Chiang massed troops as though he intended to attack the mainland and the PRC massed troops on the other side of the Strait. Chiang issued public statements calling for anti-PRC forces on the mainland to rebel and promising ROC support for the overthrow of the PRC. President John F. Kennedy informed the PRC privately that he would not support an attack on the mainland, and then made a public statement to the same effect, which quickly calmed both sides.[90]

Significant political developments did emerge in the 1960s, such as the growing sentiment in Taiwan that it should be an independent country. Although there had always been some sentiment for that option, the notion gained traction among growing numbers of both indigenous Taiwanese and mainlanders on Taiwan in the late 1950s and throughout the 1960s. Chiang, for his part, refused to give up on his grand idea of retaking the mainland and cracked down on political dissent by arresting and imprisoning his opponents—especially those who advocated Taiwanese independence.

The United States also experienced new political developments. The end of McCarthyism changed the tone in Congress, and an increasingly open and fair debate over U.S. policy in East Asia started to emerge. By 1965, economic aid to the Nationalists had been cut off entirely, and around Washington it became increasingly acceptable to entertain the notion of shifting diplomatic recognition from the ROC to the PRC—or at least of adopting a "two Chinas" policy.[91]

In 1966, a panel of distinguished scholars and business leaders from the United Nations Association of the United States of America issued a report stating that "the United States' position in world affairs would be strengthened" by acknowledging that the China originally contemplated in the Charter has now been succeeded by two states, and that both states should be members of the United Nations."[92] Five years later, the United States put forth a proposal in the United Nations that would have conferred recognition on both the PRC and Taiwan. That proposal never came to a hearing. Instead, a proposal from Albania passed, transferring China's seat from Taiwan to the PRC.[93]

If the United States had succeeded in securing dual recognition, the dynamics of the Taiwan issue would have changed from one of diplomatic ambiguity to a clear dispute between two internationally recognized sovereign states. Although the short-term strategic considerations of the United States might not have been much different, it is likely that the actions of the United States, the PRC, and Taiwan would have looked much different over the long term. In retrospect, the inability to implement a two-Chinas policy during the late 1960s and early 1970s may have been a fateful missed opportunity.

Throughout the 1960s, Chiang continued to relentlessly press U.S. officials to back a Nationalist invasion of the mainland, advancing a cornucopia of arguments, none to any avail. At various times, Chiang tried to use instability on the Chinese mainland, fear of the PRC's nuclear capability, and the Vietnam War to make the case for U.S. support for a Nationalist attack on the PRC. Chiang argued that the massive starvation and calamity wrought by the combination of the Great Leap Forward, the Cultural Revolution, and natural disasters had disenchanted the Chinese people with Maoist Communism, making the PRC vulnerable to a Nationalist assault. He also argued that Nationalist special forces could preemptively destroy the PRC's embryonic nuclear capability—with U.S. support.[94] During the Vietnam War, Chiang made the case that destabilizing China (by supporting a Nationalist incursion) would benefit the American war effort in Vietnam.[95] That proposal, like those before it, was rebuffed.

THE SHANGHAI COMMUNIQUÉ AND CHINA POLICY IN THE 1970S

As it took power (and, to a certain degree, before), the Nixon administration pursued a different angle on China, one which would culminate in trips to China by National Security Advisor Henry Kissinger and President Nixon.[96] China policy was still a very touchy topic in the United States at the beginning of the 1970s. The PRC had been demonized in the United States as manically ideological and inherently expansionist. However, Nixon and Kissinger believed it would be to America's benefit to exploit China's fear of the Soviet Union and the Soviet Union's fear of China to increase America's room to maneuver on the global geopolitical stage. To that end, Kissinger secretly approached—through a series of back channels—the PRC to arrange for meetings. On July 1, 1971, Kissinger flew to Pakistan, ostensibly on a tour of several Asian countries, and was smuggled into China to meet with PRC leaders and arrange a summit trip for Nixon.

At the July 1971 meetings, Taiwan was not a major subject of discussion. Indeed, specific issues that might be contentious were generally avoided, reflecting the paramount concern of both the Chinese and American governments to focus on countering the power of the Soviets. Kissinger's trip proved to be surprisingly successful, albeit short on details. In mid-July, Nixon announced that he would be visiting China the following year "to seek normalization of relations between the two countries and also to exchange views on questions of concern to the two sides."[97] Kissinger would visit China again, this time publicly, in October 1971, to set the date for Nixon's trip: February 22, 1972.

During Nixon's meetings with Mao Zedong in Beijing, it became increasingly clear that Taiwan was a problem issue. Yet, in his memoirs, Kissinger wrote that "neither then, nor in any subsequent meeting, did Mao indicate any impatience over Taiwan, set any time limits, make any threats, or treat it as the touchstone of our relationship."[98] Nixon remembered it somewhat differently: "Taiwan was the touchstone for both sides."[99] Perhaps most interestingly, William Burr, a senior analyst with the National Security Archive, notes that at the 1972 meetings, "consistent with Beijing's wishes, the Americans [agreed] that Taiwan was not an 'international dispute' between Americans and Chinese, but an 'internal matter' for the Chinese to settle."[100]

The two parties issued the Shanghai Communiqué at the end of the February talks, laying a new foundation for U.S. policy toward the PRC. In that communiqué, the United States acknowledged that:

> [A]ll Chinese on either side of the Taiwan Strait maintain there is but one China and that Taiwan is a part of China. The United States Government does not challenge that position. It reaffirms its interest in a peaceful settlement of the Taiwan question by the Chinese themselves. With this prospect in mind, it affirms the ultimate objective of the withdrawal of all U.S. forces and military installations from Taiwan. In the meantime, it will progressively reduce its forces and military installations on Taiwan as the tension in the area diminishes.[101]

Certain elements within Congress, as well as the Taiwanese, responded with dismay to the revelation. The congressional opposition to the communiqué was led by Sen. James L. Buckley (R-NY), who lamented that the communiqué had done "enormous damage to American credibility" and said that he was considering refusing to campaign for Nixon as a result.[102] Some Democrats, including Senator Henry M. "Scoop" Jackson (D-WA), opposed the shift as well. A "saddened" Jackson claimed that "we are doing the withdrawing and they are doing the staying. That does not strike me as a good horse trade."[103] Chiang, of course, was floored.

The Nationalists swiftly issued a statement asserting that the PRC was "a rebel group which has no right whatsoever to represent the Chinese people."[104]

Although the 1972 Shanghai Communiqué is generally thought of as a revolution in Washington's China policy, the Nixon administration came into office purposefully seeking a new policy.[105] From the 1969 removal of the permanent patrol of the Seventh Fleet in the Taiwan Strait, to the 1970 relaxation of trade and travel restrictions to the PRC, to openly referring to the PRC as the "People's Republic of China" as opposed to "Communist" or "Red" China, the Nixon administration from its inception cultivated a new attitude toward China.[106] Nixon's trip to Beijing and the resulting communiqué was merely the culmination of a shift in Washington's China policy.

The Shanghai Communiqué also represented a shift in U.S. policy toward the Soviet Union. Kissinger's strategy was to create and exploit fissures between the PRC and Soviet Union in order to draw the PRC into a loose anti-Soviet alliance with the United States. As one commentator noted, the United States sought to "improve its own global power position by striving for a far-reaching détente and rapprochement with the weaker of its Communist opponents."[107] Although the risk of a genuine, enduring Sino-Soviet alliance was overstated at the time, Kissinger's policy of attracting China away from the Soviets did help to ensure that an alliance between the two Communist powers would not emerge.

As several scholars have pointed out, the Shanghai Communiqué was essentially an agreement to disagree. The Chinese refused to renounce the use of force, and the United States refused to repeal the MDT or eschew the use of force in defense of Taiwan. However, the communiqué proved an important step toward the normalization of relations between the PRC and United States.

American public opinion favoring recognition of the PRC as well as that government's membership in the United Nations increased during the Nixon administration. Public opinion regarding the nature of the PRC, though, remained skeptical. As late as August 1971, 56 percent of Americans still perceived China as the world's most dangerous nation.[108] Fatigue over the Vietnam War may have contributed to public sentiment in favor of engaging the nation that Americans saw as the world's most dangerous, but a pervasive wariness about the Asian giant remained.

As stories about the Watergate scandal began to emerge in the press, and as impeachment became an increasingly plausible outcome, the Nixon administration could not afford to alienate right-wing Republicans by pressing forward with an engagement policy with China.[109] After Nixon's resignation in August 1974, the reins for China policy were handed to his successor, Gerald R. Ford. The short tenure of the Ford administration saw little change in China policy. Ford sent Kissinger to Beijing in October 1975, only for him to find acting Chinese premier Deng Xiaoping to be "inflexible and stern, thus closing the door to improved Sino-American relations under the Republicans."[110]

Taipei, however, remained concerned about the trends evident in U.S. policy. In October, Congress repealed the Formosa Resolution, which had originally been issued during the first Strait crisis to give President Eisenhower authority to wage war in defense of Taiwan. By 1976, Chiang Ching-kuo (who had succeeded his father Chiang Kai-shek on the elder Chiang's death in 1975) had been reduced to threatening that the United States would be responsible "to history and the people of the world" if it abandoned the MDT.[111] The next U.S. president would do just that.

The early months of the Carter administration were characterized by uncertainty, if not a lack of content, in terms of China policy. The domestic political problems in the United States and the unwillingness of the Chinese to negotiate with Ford had slowed the engagement policy to a standstill. Neither Carter's appointee for secretary of state (Cyrus Vance) nor national security advisor (Zbigniew Brzezinski) held well-known views on China policy.[112] One author went so far as to assert that "at no point during the year did the administration show any real leadership in the area of China policy, most likely reflecting indecision at the top."[113] 1978 also would be a quiet year in terms of China policy, at least publicly. Privately, the groundwork was being laid for the severance of diplomatic ties with the Republic of China and the recognition of the People's Republic as the legitimate government of mainland China. U.S. policy on the Taiwan issue was about to enter an important new phase.

CHAPTER 3

THE TAIWAN PROBLEM EVOLVES

1979–2000

The Nixon administration had clearly put the United States on the path to engagement with the People's Republic of China. Under Presidents Carter and Reagan, two more communiqués were issued: one in 1978, which would shift diplomatic recognition to the PRC in 1979, and another in 1982, promising not to interfere in internal Chinese affairs and to limit and ultimately reduce U.S. arms sales to the Taiwanese. As a counterweight to the shift of diplomatic recognition, Congress passed the Taiwan Relations Act in 1979, which pledged to sell defensive arms to Taiwan, as well as to maintain "unofficial" relations with the authorities on Taiwan, and to treat the island as the United States treats sovereign nations.

The two new communiqués and the TRA would institutionalize a tension—if not an outright contradiction—in U.S. policy toward Taiwan and China. The rhetoric of the two communiqués, each signed by a U.S. president and Chinese premier, appeals to both the PRC and to those Americans who believe Taiwan should take more responsibility for its own defense instead of relying on the United States. For the Taiwanese, and for those Americans who believe that the United States must intervene in any PRC–Taiwan conflict, the TRA has provided an argument for their position. During the last few decades, U.S. policy has vacillated between emphasizing the TRA (pleasing the Taiwanese) and emphasizing the communiqués (pleasing the PRC). As a result, when viewed as a whole, U.S. policy has appeared unclear and sometimes mystifying to the parties involved.

From 1979 to the present, the ambiguity of U.S. policy toward Taiwan has threatened not only to undermine relations with the PRC, but has also on several occasions threatened to bring about an armed confrontation over Taiwan. As the importance of retaking Taiwan grows within both elite and public opinion in the PRC, and as antipathy toward the PRC grows on Taiwan, the ambiguous status quo crafted by the United States is becoming less and less sustainable.

THE SECOND COMMUNIQUÉ AND THE TAIWAN RELATIONS ACT

On December 15, 1978, the Carter administration abruptly announced that on January 1, 1979, the United States would shift diplomatic recognition from the Republic of China (hereinafter "Taiwan")[1] to the PRC. In this second communiqué with the PRC, the United States also again "acknowledge[d] the Chinese position that there is but one China and Taiwan is part of China." Simultaneously, the United States provided Taiwan with one year's notice that it intended to abrogate the Mutual Defense Treaty, in accordance with the MDT's provisions.

The negotiations surrounding the second communiqué were shrouded in secrecy, so much so that Taiwanese president Chiang Ching-kuo was awakened in the middle of the night to hear the news of Carter's announcement. Panic and recriminations took root among the Taiwanese. Angry mobs in Taiwan stomped peanuts in effigy of President Carter, and the ROC embassy in Washington hastily destroyed documents and shifted assets to avoid legal troubles.[2]

The Carter administration had conducted the negotiations for the shift of recognition under a veil of secrecy to prevent Taiwan's advocates in Congress from mounting a campaign against "de-recognition" of Taiwan. Accordingly, the announcement came as a surprise to most Taiwan partisans in Congress and elsewhere. Then-former Governor of California Ronald Reagan gave a speech at Pepperdine University in which he asked rhetorically but pointedly: "Have we become unreliable and capricious? Are we so lacking in common decency and morality, so motivated by the dictates of the moment that we can—by the stroke of a pen—put 17 million people over the side and escape the consequences?"[3]

The Taiwan lobby in Congress claimed that the Carter administration had circumvented proper congressional oversight of the canceling of treaties. Senator Barry Goldwater (R-AZ) was particularly incensed and mounted a challenge on constitutional grounds, alleging that the president did not have constitutional authority to abrogate the provisions of the MDT without consulting with Congress. Goldwater, who had mounted a similar (unsuccessful) case to stop President

Nixon's bombing of Cambodia, warned that the precedent that would be set by al-lowing Carter to abrogate the MDT without congressional consent would mean "heading down the road to a dictatorship."[4] Although the federal district court originally found in Goldwater's favor, that ruling was overturned on appeal, and the Supreme Court declined to hear the case. Carter's policy would stand.[5]

At the same time the United States shifted diplomatic recognition, however, Congress passed the Taiwan Relations Act. President Carter, concluding that pro-Taiwan forces in Congress had enough votes to override a veto, reluctantly decided to sign the bill. The TRA became law in April 1979. Among other provi-sions, the TRA:

- Pledged that the United States will "maintain the capacity . . . to resist any resort to force or other forms of coercion that would jeopardize the secu-rity, or the social or economic system, of the people on Taiwan;
- Promised to "make available to Taiwan such defense articles and defense services in such quantity as may be necessary to enable Taiwan to maintain a sufficient self-defense capability";
- Stated that regardless of the withdrawal of diplomatic recognition, "the laws of the United States shall apply with respect to Taiwan in the manner that the laws of the United States applied with respect to Taiwan prior to January 1"; and
- Established the American Institute in Taiwan, which would function as a de facto embassy.[6]

As with the two communiqués and the one that would follow, the language of the TRA was tortuous and legalistic. It has confounded both American analysts and PRC officials ever since its inception. For example, some American analysts, such as Peter Brookes of the Heritage Foundation, have held that the TRA rep-resents a continuation of the security guarantee under the Mutual Defense Treaty that the Carter administration had jettisoned as part of the deal for the second communiqué.[7] In fact, this analysis is almost certainly wrong. Representative Ken Kramer (R-CO) had attempted to introduce an amendment to the TRA in the House that would have inserted the portion of the MDT that claimed that an at-tack on Taiwan was in violation of U.S. interests and that the United States would respond to threats to its interests. That amendment was voted on, and defeated.[8]

Others, such as Taiwan expert Richard Bush, have countered that the passage in the TRA relating to Taiwan's security describes "capabilities only, not inten-tions."[9] Moreover, the TRA merely asserts that "efforts to determine the future of Taiwan by other than peaceful means, including by boycotts or embargoes, would be a threat to the peace and security of the Western Pacific area and of grave concern to the United States." It further directs the chief executive to "inform the Congress promptly of any threat to the security or the social or economic system of the people of Taiwan and any danger to the interests of the United States arising therefrom. The President and the Congress shall determine, in accordance with constitutional processes, appropriate action by the United States in response to any such danger."[10]

To read such statements as a defense commitment is an ambitious stretch. The United States frequently expresses "grave concern" over international crises, such as escalations of the Arab-Israeli conflict, nuclear proliferation, and countless others. Few believe that grave concern in those cases is a U.S. commitment to intervene militarily. Moreover, the prescription for the course the president is to follow in the event of a crisis involving Taiwan resembles closely the process that U.S. presidents have followed in unforeseen crises since the Korean War. The TRA gives the president no special authority or exemption from the (admittedly already debased[11]) process of acquiring congressional approval for military operations.

Beijing, however, feared that the TRA was indeed an extension of the old Mutual Defense Treaty. If the United States saw the TRA as a pledge to defend Taiwan, then in the PRC's eyes Beijing's efforts in negotiating the second communiqué had been for naught. PRC foreign minister Huang Hua retorted on March 16, 1979, during the negotiations in Congress over the TRA, that "if the bills are passed as they are worded now, and are signed into law, great harm will be done to the new relationship that has just been established between China and the United States."[12]

The bills were signed into law, however, after passing by a 339 to 50 margin in the House and an 85 to 4 margin in the Senate. The PRC's continued fear and threats regarding the TRA were assuaged by President Carter's assurances that the United States would continue to conduct its policy in accordance with both the 1972 and 1978 communiqués. The PRC also recognized that it desperately needed to cultivate relations with the United States as a counterweight to the Soviet Union and capitalize on the economic potential inherent in closer Sino-U.S. ties.[13] Consequently, Beijing soon muted its protests.

THE PROBLEM OF ARMS SALES AND THE THIRD COMMUNIQUÉ

When President Ronald Reagan took office in 1981, he faced a PRC that had been markedly agitated and confused by his campaign rhetoric. Over the course of less than a week during his presidential campaign, Reagan had issued several murky statements regarding his views on the Taiwan issue. First, he indicated that his administration would seek to restore official relations with Taipei. Then in an official statement to clarify his position, he promised not to "pretend, as Carter does, that the relationship we have with Taiwan, enacted by our Congress, is not official." That did little to clarify the issue. He was forced eventually to claim that he had "misstated" his position, and that he had only meant that relations with Taipei were "official" in the sense that they had been sanctioned by Congress.[14] Candidate Reagan's machinations caused the PRC to proclaim that "there can be no compromise on . . . the Taiwan question. It is an important question of principle."[15]

Accordingly, the Chinese were at best nervous about dealing with President Reagan. In addition to Reagan's troubling campaign rhetoric, the problem of arms sales to Taiwan had been festering during the last months of the Carter administration. In June 1980, the administration approved $280 million in new arms sales to Taiwan, which the PRC quickly denounced as in violation of the second communiqué.[16] Thus, the next administration was going to have to resolve whether continued arms sales to Taiwan could be reconciled with the new circumstances under normalization of relations with the PRC.

As President Reagan took office, he sent a variety of signals to Beijing. His appointee as secretary of state, Alexander Haig, was seen in both the United States and China as a relatively pro-PRC advocate. Countering Haig, however, were known Taiwan partisans Richard V. Allen and Michael K. Deaver as national security advisor and deputy chief of staff, respectively. The PRC remained puzzled as to what the new administration would bring in terms of a China policy.

As the administration's China policy began to come together in June 1981, Haig attempted to resolve the arms sales problem while on a trip to China by offering to sell arms to the PRC as well as to Taiwan. The PRC responded sourly, noting that their position on the Taiwan issue could not be softened by "balanced arms sales."[17]

In October Haig's counterpart, Foreign Minister Huang Hua, had come to New York to meet with Haig and was prepared for candid discussions on the arms sales issue. The PRC had been pressing for a deadline after which U.S. arms sales to Taiwan would cease altogether. Reagan and his staff saw any deadline as a sell-out of Taiwan, and had consistently refused to entertain the notion. The negotiations that took place in New York set the stage for the third communiqué that would be signed in August of 1982.[18]

However, in the interim there was a specific arms sale issue that threatened to torpedo any advance in U.S.–PRC relations. During the final months of his administration, President Carter had relaxed his previously stringent controls on arms sales to Taiwan, allowing for the development of a scaled back fighter, the FX, which he felt could be justified as "defensive."[19] Taiwan promptly expressed its interest in purchasing the relatively advanced U.S. FX fighter planes. The PRC vigorously opposed such a sale, since the FX was a dramatic step up compared to the F5-E planes that Taiwan was using at the time. Taiwan's request had been left unanswered by the Carter administration, and had come to the Reagan administration for resolution.

In January 1982, the Reagan administration announced that it would reject Taiwan's request for the FX, but that it would continue to allow Taiwan to co-produce the F5-E. Although the administration had hoped that this decision would appease the PRC, the Chinese leadership was still skeptical of Reagan, and remained fixated on the matter of a deadline for the termination of all arms sales. Even though continued co-production of the F5-E was enough to anger the PRC, causing Chinese officials to proclaim their displeasure at the announcement, they agreed to meet with Assistant Secretary of State John Holdridge for the sessions that would generate the third communiqué.[20]

The third communiqué, like its predecessors, was remarkably ambiguous. Although it did not meet the Chinese demand for a deadline for ending arms sales to Taiwan, it did respond to the PRC's official position that it was seeking "peaceful resolution of the Taiwan problem" with a promise that the United States "has no intention of infringing on Chinese sovereignty and territorial integrity, or interfering in China's internal affairs, or pursuing a policy of 'Two Chinas' or 'one China, one Taiwan.'" Also, in the third communiqué,

> [T]he United States Government states that it does not seek to carry out a long-term policy of arms sales to Taiwan, that its arms sales to Taiwan will not exceed, either in qualitative or in quantitative terms, the level of those supplied in recent years since the establishment of diplomatic relations between the United States and China, and that it intends to reduce gradually its sales of arms to Taiwan, leading over a period of time to a final resolution.[21]

Given the painfully unclear language, the two sides' interpretations of the document diverged widely. President Reagan, speaking to a domestic audience, claimed that "the People's Republic has agreed that they are going to try and peacefully resolve the Taiwanese issue. We, in turn, linked our statement about weaponry to that and said that if they make progress and do, indeed, peacefully work out a solution agreeable to both sides, then, obviously, there would no longer be any need for arms. And all the reference to reducing arms is tied to progress in that."[22]

Obviously, Reagan's interpretation would drain any meaning from the document altogether. Such an interpretation basically amounts to remarking that if two sides in a dispute resolve their differences, there will no longer be a dispute—a tautological, empty statement. The PRC, on the other hand, interpreted the document as a genuine statement of U.S. policy: not to interfere in China's domestic affairs, and to scale back (or at least not expand) arms sales to Taiwan. The president's retrospective interpretation both confused and disturbed Chinese leaders. The administration's eventual expansive definition of "qualitative" and "quantitative" served only to worsen the PRC's fears.

By 1983, the Reagan administration had chosen 1979 as the year on which subsequent annual arms sales to Taiwan would be based. It also decided that the future sales must be adjusted for inflation. As former State Department official Nancy Bernkopf Tucker remarked, "[b]y using 1979 as the base, a year when Washington had increased sales to provide a boost before normalization, and converting that into 1982 dollars, the maximum rose from the $598 million actually sold in 1979 to a far more generous $830 million."[23] In addition, the Reagan administration reduced the scope of what it considered "arms" so dramatically that "[e]verything from computer chips to helicopters may fall under the broad rubric of 'technological assistance,' 'dual-use technology,' or 'technology transfer,'" thus not being included in "arms sales."[24]

Although the Chinese were angered by such an interpretation, they did not use the disagreement to undermine U.S.–China relations. Chinese leaders had become increasingly alarmed at what they saw as Soviet expansionism throughout Asia, and remained both worried about and outmatched by the Soviet military presence in the region. Beijing's response was to emphasize and bolster its ties to Washington in order to deter any extreme Soviet measures, and also to cultivate good will in Washington in order to obtain materiel with which they could modernize their own military forces.[25]

THE OTHER TRACK OF REAGAN'S CHINA POLICY

Although the PRC had responded harshly to the notion that their acquiescence on the Taiwan issue could be bought with arms sales to the mainland, the two sides continued to move closer on the issue of U.S.-to-PRC arms sales and on joint military cooperation. The Soviet Union was a growing threat in the eyes of both parties. The USSR's invasion of Afghanistan, its operations in Vietnam, and its increasingly aggressive posture toward Europe alarmed the United States. Moscow's first two moves had also unsettled Beijing. In addition, the Chinese had grown particularly alarmed at the fact that the USSR had deployed well over one hundred SS–20 nuclear missiles pointed at and within range of the PRC.[26] U.S. and Chinese interests were converging, at least as far as both countries needed to counter the Soviet threat.[27]

Accordingly, both military and economic linkages between China and the United States increased dramatically during the 1980s. As part of Deng Xiaoping's modernization campaign, he emphasized the need to obtain foreign technical expertise and equipment. One analyst noted that the Chinese went "[f]rom viewing imports as a necessary evil . . . to an acceptance of much greater trade flows and closer integration with world markets. Imported technology was seen to hold an extremely important position in China's modernisation strategy, as it became increasingly clear just how backward its technological base had become since the 1960s."[28]

For his part, Reagan was willing to work with Beijing to open U.S. markets to more Chinese goods (allowing the Chinese to direct the foreign exchange they acquired back at obtaining Western technology), as well as to relax U.S. export restrictions on advanced technology. By the spring of 1982, the Reagan administration had increased the amount and quality of technology exports to China, as well as relaxed import quotas on important Chinese exports such as textiles, furs, and skins.[29] By June 1983, China had been reclassified under the U.S. export rules, allowing it access to the dual-use technology it had desired to modernize its military.[30] By July Secretary of Defense Caspar Weinberger had promised military equipment and "working-level training missions" to China.[31]

Reagan's rapprochement with Beijng reached a climax in his visit to China in 1984. Though some observers cynically suggested that the trip was designed for domestic political purposes,[32] Reagan was well received in China, and discussed numerous substantive issues. One report even indicates that there were so many issues on the table for discussion that Reagan and PRC premier Zhao Ziyang "spent only five minutes discussing Taiwan in more than four hours of talks."[33] Although the *Wall Street Journal*'s editorial writers fretted that Reagan would continue what they saw as a U.S. policy of "trading substance for panda bears,"[34] the talks were hailed on all sides as a success.

The discussions yielded several policy initiatives. Perhaps most notably, the parties agreed to go forward with a plan for nuclear cooperation by which U.S. companies could assist China with its peaceful nuclear capabilities—which would prospectively give the United States some insight into and control over China's military nuclear program and its proliferation activities.[35]

In addition to the agreement on nuclear cooperation, Reagan and Deng Xiaoping sealed agreements on taxes (to prevent double taxation of American businesses operating in China) and on increased grain sales to China, and progress was made, but a deal not finalized, on investment policy.[36] Progress was also made on arms sales to China, which had become increasingly important to the Chinese as Sino-Russian relations continued to deteriorate.

CHINA-TAIWAN RELATIONS IN THE WAKE OF THE TRA AND THREE COMMUNIQUÉS

As the United States was implementing its policy of supporting de facto Taiwanese independence while simultaneously engaging diplomatically with China, the Chinese leadership attempted to reach out to Taiwan. On New Year's Day 1979, the PRC issued a message to "compatriots in Taiwan," which was a public appeal directly to the Taiwanese people. The message quickly put to work the political gains the PRC had obtained from diplomatic recognition by the United States (as well as the Treaty of Peace and Friendship brokered with Japan) to press the point that the world was turning against the idea of an independent Taiwan. It advocated serious moves to end the split, stating that separation was "artificial and against our national interests and aspirations," and promising that reunification would be managed "so as not to cause the people of Taiwan any losses." In the meantime, it called for increased contact through social and cultural exchanges.

China would continue to attempt to use soft power to bring Taiwan to the table. In September 1981 China again called for exchanges on social, sporting, and cultural fronts, as well as promising a large degree of autonomy for Taiwan should it be absorbed by China. This was the beginning of the "one China, two systems" policy that China came to publicly endorse in the 1980s.[37]

The one China, two systems model was taken even further when, in June 1983, Deng told a Chinese-American professor that he was willing to take another step toward peaceful resolution. In the course of that conversation, he offered to allow Taiwan to acquire weapons abroad, maintain total control over its domestic policy, issue its own passports, and even keep its own flag and use the name "China, Taipei" in international contexts.[38] Taiwan did not reciprocate these overtures from the mainland. In fact, Chiang Ching-kuo responded by noting tersely that "to talk peace with the Chinese Communists is to invite death."[39]

POLITICAL AND ECONOMIC REVOLUTION IN TAIWAN

After the death of Kuomintang Party leader Chiang Kai-shek in 1975, the reins of the Taiwanese government were handed over to his son, Chiang Ching-kuo. The younger Chiang had been educated in the Soviet Union, and had risen through the ranks of the KMT to become premier in 1972, eventually becoming president in 1978. Chiang Ching-kuo would preside over a revolution in Taiwanese political and economic affairs, contributing to the remarkable liberalization of both Taiwan's economy and its political environment.

Chiang had worked within the government to develop a base of support before his ascendancy to the presidency.[40] However, there were demographic shifts taking place in Taiwan that mandated dramatic changes in political representation. Chiang Kai-shek had always insisted on keeping mainland Chinese in top government positions, effectively marginalizing native Taiwanese. As many of the mainlanders who had fled to the island in 1949 died off, it became harder to keep mainlanders in control of the political system. In addition, the relatively individualistic indigenous Taiwanese had focused heavily on economic progress, and as a result had become better educated, economically more secure, and more literate. Keeping them on the margins of political life was becoming increasingly difficult.[41]

Chiang recognized this phenomenon and began to open Taiwan's government to indigenous Taiwanese. Conservative mainlanders objected to such a policy, but as the members of the old guard slowly died off, Chiang gradually increased the number of Taiwanese involved in politics, going so far as naming as his vice-president Lee Teng-hui, a Taiwanese native, in 1984.

Aside from including native Taiwanese in the administration of Taiwan, a broader political transformation took place under Chiang's leadership. During the late 1970s, opposition groups had gathered into political parties, and had begun to challenge the KMT. One author described the KMT's response, which involved "co-opting the least partisan, arresting the most committed, and learning to live with the rest," as moving from "hard authoritarianism" to "soft authoritarianism."[42]

In this formulation, the "hard" authoritarianism that Chiang had inherited from his father constituted essentially a dictatorship that used mainlander control of the KMT and elections as ways to consolidate the power of the leader. Under the new "soft" authoritarianism, indigenous Taiwanese would be co-opted into the KMT, and although the government would remain securely under KMT rule, elections would allow for incremental responses to social change and other pressures that were growing among the governed.[43]

Since well before Taiwan's political liberalization, its economy had begun to perform impressively. The efficient use of U.S. foreign aid coupled with high foreign direct investment (FDI) led to growth rates between 8 and 10 percent annually between the years 1967 and 1986.[44] By the mid-1980s, however, Taiwan's macroeconomic policy of import substitution and targeted subsidies was flagging.

Taiwan's comparative advantage (and consequent specialization) in labor-intensive goods was being challenged by new competitors; ironically, mainland China was one of those challengers.[45]

In addition, the KMT leadership had placed a great deal of emphasis on exporting to the United States. From 1980 to 1984, Taiwan's trade surplus with the United States grew from $2.087 billion to $11.085 billion.[46] As protectionist sentiment cropped up in the United States during the 1980s, accusatory fingers were frequently pointed at Taiwan. The threat of American protectionism coupled with its decreasing competitiveness abroad forced Taiwan to make hard decisions and overhaul its economic policy.

It dramatically reduced its tariffs and non-tariff barriers, as well as seeking regional trading relationships with its Asian neighbors. From 1983–84 to 1991–92 average tariffs were reduced from 31 to 9 percent, and the number of commodities subject to non-tariff barriers fell from 26,768 to 9,053. Taiwan joined Asia-Pacific Economic Cooperation in 1991, negotiated observer status with the General Agreement on Tariffs and Trade in 1992, and continued to actively pursue membership in the World Trade Organization.[47] By the beginning of the 1990s, Taiwan had become a significant global economic player and an important trading partner of the United States.

As the economy was being overhauled, political structures in Taiwan were being modernized as well. In late September 1986, the Democratic Progressive Party declared itself an opposition party. The DPP had emerged slowly over a period of several years through unofficial groups such as the Association for Public Policy, a quasi–think tank that had come together in 1984. The DPP was less strident, though, than its parent. For example, while the APP had originally supported the principle of self-determination in the context of Taiwan's international status, the DPP adopted a more moderate and nuanced position on Taiwan's foreign policy.[48] Party advocates issued statements like "what matters is not reunification or independence, but democracy. People don't want to hear about reunification because the Nationalists use it to stop democratization. Independence is not important because we are living separately already."[49]

Chiang Ching-kuo responded to the formation of the DPP by declaring it illegal in early October.[50] However, before the DPP had emerged, Chiang had appointed a commission of scholars and academics to assess the pros and cons of political reform on Taiwan. In so doing, Chiang can be seen as having taken steps toward political liberalization and away from authoritarianism even before the emergence of the DPP. By mid-October, Chiang had announced that the government had decided to go forward with political liberalization, and would end martial law and allow for the formation of new political parties.[51]

In addition to recognizing the changing political reality in Taiwan, Chiang may have seen democratization as a way to win hearts and minds in America. By recasting the Taiwan issue not as a conflict between two authoritarian regimes but as one between a capitalist democracy and a communist dictatorship, Chiang may have seen that he could bolster support for Taiwan in the United States.[52] Indeed, the rhetoric of tyranny versus freedom has been a growing theme in American discussions of Taiwan since Taiwan's reforms began. The Tiananmen Square massacre in 1989 highlighted the differences between the PRC and Taiwan. Taiwanese leaders astutely emphasized the Tiananmen massacre, and outrage over that bloody episode gained a good deal of traction in the United States, particularly with members of Congress. The human rights issue had been in the background since Nixon's initial rapprochement with the PRC, but the images that emerged from Tiananmen forced Americans to think carefully about the nature of the Chinese regime. That in turn generated more American public and congressional support for Taiwan.

Policy elites within both the United States and the PRC, though, viewed the emergence of the DPP with skepticism and apprehension. Both elites knew of the origins of the DPP and feared that, if it were to take power in Taiwan, a direct push for independence would only be a matter of time. The KMT was also fearful of the real intentions behind the DPP's creation. PRC foreign ministry spokesman Ha Yuzhen made the Chinese position clear, stating in December 1986 that it remained "firmly opposed to any theory and acts that advocate the independence of Taiwan or self-determination."[53]

However, for a time after its creation, the DPP did not dramatically affect Taiwan's foreign policy. While it made steady gains in the Legislative Yuan, Taiwan's legislative body, Chiang Ching-kuo retained the presidency, and thus cross-Strait relations continued on a steady, if ambiguous, path. On Chiang's death in January 1988, however, his native-born Taiwanese vice-president, Lee Teng-hui, rose to power, and Lee's presidency would put Taiwan on a path to a new vision of the island's place in the world.

LEE TENG-HUI'S PRESIDENCY AND THE PATH TO THE 1996 ELECTIONS

During the first year of his administration, Lee Teng-hui made several conciliatory gestures toward the PRC. He promised to reduce the size of the Taiwanese military, as well as ending the so-called Period of National Mobilization for the Suppression of the Communist Rebellion.[54] The latter action, though, antagonized as much as reassured Beijing. As mentioned before, the PRC viewed with suspicion any measures by Taiwan that sought to diminish the notion that the two sides were warring for control of China. If the authorities on Taiwan stopped claiming that they were the legitimate government of China, then logically they must be the government of some other, discrete entity. Thus, such measures, even when ostensibly conciliatory, often offended the PRC. In any case, PRC leaders remained deeply suspicious of Lee.

Lee moved to consolidate his power within the Taiwanese government, successfully pushing through a constitutional revision that concentrated power in the office of the presidency and marginalized the premier he had appointed, Lien Chan.[55] Under Lee's presidency, however, the DPP was increasing its pressure for Taiwan to declare independence and seek self-determination. As conservative mainlanders were dying off, and as the native Taiwanese voice was growing louder in politics, the DPP was able to successfully push the KMT away from its traditional "one-China" position and toward a more ambiguous position. In response to a DPP proposal for a new constitution that would declare independence in 1991, Lee waffled, noting that formal independence wasn't necessary, since Taiwan had been de facto independent since 1949. The hard-line DPP position on independence backfired and the party performed poorly in the first National Assembly elections in December 1991. The DPP then took a different tack, downplaying the independence issue. Instead, the party stressed the idea that the president should be directly elected by the people, instead of by the National Assembly.[56]

The notion of directly electing the president shook the KMT, the PRC, and the United States. The steps toward direct elections would create much more flexibility and unpredictability in terms of Taipei's policy. The KMT's policy had always been its own, and was not contingent on popular opinion. With the advent of representative democracy, the people on Taiwan had a say in what policies their government pursued—even with regard to cross-Strait relations. In March 1992, Lee asked for an open debate in the KMT on the merits of directly electing the president. By May the National Assembly had amended the constitution to limit the president to no more than two four year terms, but had punted the question of how the president would be elected to a new deadline date of May 1995.[57]

Meanwhile, U.S. policy regarding Taiwan during the early 1990s also troubled the PRC. During his failed 1992 bid for reelection, President George H. W. Bush agreed to sell one hundred-fifty F–16 fighters to Taiwan. This decision "shocked and outraged" the PRC, and was denounced by many American analysts. Winston Lord, former ambassador to China, noted that although he had been "critical of Beijing with respect to human rights and other matters . . . I also believe you should honor an agreement."[58] Longtime China analyst A. Doak Barnett agreed, but took the criticism one step further: "Political factors in the United States are a major reason [for the sale] . . . Domestic politics have overridden broader, historic strategic considerations."[59] The sale was seen by Barnett, as well as by many others, as an attempt to garner support in an election year from the nearly six thousand American workers whose jobs were in jeopardy in the absence of increased demand for F–16s.[60]

The deal certainly appeared to be a violation of the third communiqué, and was both quantitatively and qualitatively greater than any U.S.–Taiwan weapons deal in history. The United States justified the decision by noting that China had recently purchased twenty-four Su–27 Russian aircraft, and might be seeking more.[61] But the notion that the purchase of twenty-four planes by a rapidly growing China indicated a decision to move away from a policy of peaceful reunification was strained, and the Chinese called it such. They also signaled their disgust by reviving Mao's rallying cry against U.S. "hegemonism," which had been retired for years before the F–16 sales.

During the early years of Lee's leadership, Taiwan and the PRC did attempt a diplomatic rapprochement. In late October 1992, the "unofficial" Straits Exchange Foundation (SEF), a Taiwanese body dedicated to addressing cross-Strait issues, conducted a dialogue with the Association for Relations Across the Taiwan Strait in Hong Kong. Ostensibly, the meetings were to cover mundane practical matters such as handling mail from both sides of the Strait, but the Chinese pressed the SEF on the question of "one China."

A complicated diplomatic flurry ensued, with proposals on how to express each side's conception of "one China" volleyed back and forth. The meetings ended inconclusively, but the debate over the practical matters at hand as well as the one-China principle continued. In the end, the SEF offered eight proposals for a statement on the one-China policy, five written and three oral.[62] It agreed that it would make an oral statement to the effect of the resolution that Taiwan's National Unification Council had passed on August 1, 1992.

> Both sides of the Taiwan Straits adhere to the principle of "one China," but the two sides attach different meanings to this. The Chinese Communist authorities regard "one China" to be "The People's Republic of China," and after unification, Taiwan would become a "Special Administrative Region" under its jurisdiction. Our side feels that "one China" should refer to the Republic of China, which was founded in 1912 and has continued to exist to the present; its sovereignty extends to the whole of China, but at present its governing power only extends to Taiwan, the Penghu Islands, Quemoy and Matsu. Taiwan is indeed part of China, but the mainland is also part of China.[63]

The Chinese side in the SEF-ARATS negotiations pressed the Taiwanese to include an altered version of that language in written form, but the Taiwanese objected, and stuck to their position that each side should offer an oral statement on its interpretation of "one China." The resulting agreement to disagree was dubbed the 1992 consensus. Both sides made statements to the effect that there was one China, even though they disagreed about what one China meant and what policies should result. The 1992 consensus was the high point of Taiwanese-PRC comity during Lee Teng-hui's tenure as Taiwan's president and led to a cordial meeting the following year in Singapore between Koo Chen-fu, the head of the SEF, and Wang Daohan, the head of ARATS.

By late 1993 Lee had clarified his position on cross-Strait relations, moving away from his prior ambiguity on the question of independence and toward the DPP line that self-determination should be the short-term goal of Taiwan. By November of 1993, Taipei was "unofficially" proclaiming that it saw "two separate sovereign states: the ROC on Taiwan and the PRC on [the] mainland."[64] Lee articulated this position further when he announced in 1994 that "'one China' is an American policy. Before national reunification, we will never accept a 'one China' policy."[65]

At the same time, Lee was developing an international policy that would come to be known as "practical" or "pragmatic" diplomacy. The Taiwanese foreign ministry became adept at using all sorts of different measures to cultivate nonofficial–and, where they could, official–ties with countries the world over. Most effective, and most insidious in Chinese eyes, was the "dollar diplomacy" policy of approaching small states with relatively large foreign aid or "economic development" packages with the understood quid pro quo that the target states would confer diplomatic recognition on Taiwan.[66]

Lee also had mounted a vigorous campaign to secure a seat for Taiwan at the United Nations. Though the Chinese possessed a veto by way of its permanent membership on the Security Council, any movement on the Taiwan question in the United Nations would have strained cross-Strait relations to the breaking point. The Chinese watched the campaign carefully, but Taipei's initiative made little progress. Taiwan continues to press for membership in the United Nations to this day, but the original UN reluctance to take the matter up seems to be institutionalized.

The demise of the Soviet Union and the reemergence of strategic competition on the Asian continent also changed U.S.–PRC and cross-Strait relations dramatically. During the Cold War, U.S. and Chinese policy in Asia had been dominated and constrained by concerns about Soviet strategic priorities and the

USSR's massive military power. After the Soviet Union's implosion, China emerged as a relatively stronger strategic force on the Asian continent.

Fearing that after defeating the Soviet Union the United States might aim to contain China, the PRC settled on a strategy of engagement with her neighbors. Still far too weak to directly challenge the United States, China opened, re-opened, or improved its diplomatic relations with Indonesia, Singapore, Brunei, India, and other countries. Since China was no longer able to manipulate the tri-angular relationship between itself, the Soviet Union, and the United States, it sought power through regional linkages.[67]

That power, combined with the removal of its Russian adversary, resulted in a China that had become freer to assert itself more forcefully in regional affairs and act more independently on the world stage.[68] The third Taiwan Strait crisis in 1995 and Beijing's ability to adopt a coercive strategy vis-à-vis Taiwan con-firmed that point.

THE THIRD TAIWAN STRAIT CRISIS

In the course of his policy of pragmatic diplomacy, Lee would occasionally travel to small countries to court relations with them. This policy became known as "vacation diplomacy," since the authorities in Taipei would deny that Lee was on official government business. In 1994, while on a trip to South Africa (which, ironically, would end up shifting recognition to the PRC in 1996) and Central America, Lee's plane stopped in Hawaii to refuel. Lee was refused a visa and barred from leaving the military base where his plane landed. Lee's lament that this sort of treatment was humiliating drew sympathy from Taiwanese expatriates and members of Congress who saw President Bill Clinton as appeasing the PRC. Longtime China critic Rep. Dana Rohrabacher (R-CA) called the treatment of Lee "an insult."[69]

In May 1995, both houses of Congress passed, almost unanimously, "sense of Congress" resolutions that the Clinton administration should grant Lee a visa.[70] While such resolutions are not binding, the fact that they passed by such wide margins had the effect of forcing Clinton's hand, and he changed course, issuing Lee a visa to visit his alma mater, Cornell University, in June 1995. The PRC re-sponded by warning that if Lee were to make the visit, "the consequences would be grave and would seriously harm Sino-U.S. relations."[71]

Even former high-ranking U.S. officials were concerned about the decision to grant Lee the visa. Burton Levin, former ambassador to Burma and former consul-general in Hong Kong, alleged that conservative Republicans were "using Taiwan as a club to beat China with," and that if he had to ascribe blame for the conflict over Lee's visa he would "put it on the shoulders of my countrymen."[72] Charles Freeman, who had been assistant secretary of defense for both Presidents Bush and Clinton, noted: "[T]he Lee Teng-hui visit proves that if you spend enough money on Washington lobbyists you can accomplish wonders, but it does not speak well for the clarity, vision, and strategic purpose of U.S. policy."[73] Acting on the advice of Liu Tai-ying, one of the pilots of the "dollar diplomacy" policy, Lee had hired the Washington lobbying firm Cassidy and Associates for a three-year fee of $4.5 million to push for the visa to be approved.[74]

The visit would bring an abrupt end to the "smile diplomacy" that had previously characterized the PRC's approach to Taiwan. Since the PRC's 1979 "message to compatriots on Taiwan," the PRC's public statements to Taiwan were generally firm, but optimistic. Lee's visit caused a dramatic hardening in Beijing's rhetoric and actions.

The atmosphere surrounding Lee's visit especially enraged the PRC. Lee was greeted on his arrival in Los Angeles by throngs of supporters waving Taiwanese flags. Several U.S. senators made the trip to New York to greet the Taiwanese president before his speech at Cornell. The State Department had been assured that the speech would not carry a political message relating to Taiwan, but Lee hardly shied away from politics in the talk.

The speech itself was troubling to the PRC for at least three reasons. First, the concept of "vacation diplomacy" was based on the idea that Lee appearing in various countries would put a human face on the Taiwan issue. Beijing objected to such visits in Third World countries, let alone the United States. Second, the Cornell speech was perfectly tailored to an American audience, playing to the notion of a small liberal democracy facing—against all odds—a much larger, more powerful, and tyrannical adversary. Beijing feared that the Lee visit would garner more American public support for Taiwan and further demonize the PRC.

Third, Lee's speech repeatedly used the construction "Republic of China on Taiwan." In a diplomatic confrontation that had been based so heavily on subtle rhetorical tics, the PRC feared that this syntax represented a change in policy—namely, that Lee would soon start asserting that the "Republic of China on Taiwan" was in fact its own country, separate from China.[75]

The PRC immediately attacked the Lee visit as "promoting Taiwan separatism" and continued to threaten retaliation, although it refused to specify what type. To compound matters, around the same time, the Taipei government made an open offer to donate $1 billion to the United Nations in return for a seat in the world body.[76] Although the offer was rebuffed, the PRC had been pushed over the edge.

In June 1995, the PRC canceled talks between the PRC and Taiwanese officials on reunification that had been scheduled as a result of Chinese premier Jiang Zemin's so-called eight points proposal of January 30. The eight points proposal had called for three major policy initiatives: first, increased nongovernmental contacts across the Strait coupled with peaceful negotiations to end the military tensions. Second, both sides would adhere to the principle of one China. Third, the PRC would retain the use of force as a last option in the event that peaceful negotiations failed.[77]

The proposal was a continuation of the smile diplomacy policy and called for a new round of negotiations. Many analysts had seen the move as authentically conciliatory; for example, one author on Taiwan noted that the eight points proposal "represented a distinct approach contrary to the hawkish inclination prevalent among the PRC's military brass and civilian conservatives."[78]

After canceling the July 1995 talks, China began a military escalation that would last into early 1996.[79] On July 18, the PRC announced that it would be holding one week of tests of its surface-to-surface missile program, to begin just a few days later. Taiwan protested that this was a provocation on the part of the PRC, but the PRC countered that the tests had already been scheduled. In response to queries from Western media suggesting that the tests were a response to Lee's visit to the United States, the PRC noted: "[I]n China, we have a saying: 'If your conscience is clear, you needn't fear a knock on the door in the middle of the night.'"[80]

Missiles that China fired over the following week were targeted toward Taiwan, and splashed down less than one hundred miles from the island's coast. In addition to the missile tests, China had massed large numbers of troops in Fujian province, just across the Strait from Taiwan. The PRC published eight opinion pieces in the state-run *People's Daily* that attacked Lee for presiding over a "dictatorship" on Taiwan, and that alleged Lee's position on the Taiwan issue was equivalent to a "political hallucinogenic drug."[81]

Beijing's escalation of tensions had manifold effects. First, it caused significant economic and political shocks in Taiwan. The stock exchange in Taipei plummeted roughly 5 percent on the announcement of the exercises, and would see a third of its value erased before the end of the confrontation. The Taiwan dollar dropped precipitously. Although both recovered fairly quickly, the episode sent a strong signal about the PRC's ability to influence economic events on the island.

The military escalation also provoked the United States. On December 19, 1995, the U.S. nuclear-powered aircraft carrier *Nimitz* made an unannounced passage through the Taiwan Strait. Although it was announced several weeks later that the diversion through the Strait has been the result of bad weather, all sides could see that the United States was sending a message. In response to the U.S. attempt at intimidation, the PRC recalled its ambassador from Washington and suggested that further measures would ensue if the United States insisted on interfering in China's internal affairs.

The United States did not use only military power to try to convey its position on the conflict. In October, Charles Freeman, the former assistant secretary of defense, visited Beijing and met with Xiong Guangkai, the deputy chief of staff for the People's Liberation Army. Xiong made clear how seriously the Chinese saw the Taiwan issue, telling Freeman tersely that he assumed the United States would not sacrifice Los Angeles to protect Taiwan.[82] The implication of a nuclear strike was no doubt colored by the context of the meeting, but the message was clear: Although the United States had been able to manage the first two Taiwan Strait crises as it pleased (including an implicit willingness to escalate to the nuclear level), China's own nuclear capability would prevent Washington from pressing too hard this time.

In any case, the PRC was undeterred by the U.S. decision to flex its military muscles. In February 1996 Beijing began massing troops in Fujian, eventually stationing roughly one hundred fifty thousand troops just across the Strait from Taiwan.[83] It also began another round of missile tests, this time firing missiles even closer to Taiwan. China then announced that it had both a live-ammunition military exercise and an amphibious assault exercise planned as well.

The Clinton administration, still fearful of hard-line Republicans and other pro-Taiwan forces in Congress, countered the PRC's deployments by sending the USS *Independence* to the waters off Taiwan (although not into the Strait itself). Just a few days later, the administration announced that it would also be sending the *Nimitz* back to the waters off Taiwan, along with an accompaniment of support ships, more than one hundred aircraft, and several submarines.[84] With American warships at the mouth of the Taiwan Strait, Lee was emboldened. A few days before the March 23 presidential elections, he held a rally in the southern city of Kaohsiung, repeatedly referring to Taiwan as a "democratic country," which served to further antagonize the PRC.[85]

One unintended consequence of the PRC's military actions was that the Taiwanese people, who had previously been sharply divided in the advent of the first presidential elections, rallied behind Lee.[86] The opposition DPP and New Party (which had previously been the most reunification-oriented of the three) and the ruling KMT had responded to the 1995 show of force by issuing a joint statement that Taiwan is "a country with independent sovereignty. We are determined to defend ourselves against any invasion by external forces."[87] A similar sentiment surfaced after the February 1996 provocations. In Taiwan's first democratic election in March 1996, Lee was elected in a landslide and the New Party fared very badly.[88]

After Lee's election, Republicans in Congress continued to press a more Taiwan-friendly China policy. The chairman of the Senate Foreign Relations Committee, Jesse Helms (R-NC), gave a speech at the Heritage Foundation just a few days after Lee's victory, and announced that he intended to invite the Taiwanese leader for another visit to the United States and would "enjoy the squawking about it."[89] Though an ideological commitment to Taiwan was undoubtedly a part of the Republican line on China policy, 1996 was a U.S. election year, and the Republicans clearly felt that Clinton was vulnerable on issues of national security.

RAPPROCHEMENT AND DE-ESCALATION AFTER THE THIRD CRISIS

After the military flare-ups in 1995 and 1996, it seemed that both Washington and Beijing were looking to de-escalate the tensions between the two countries. Even though a new round of arms sales to Taiwan were approved in March 1996, relations between the United States and China continued to relax. A series of diplomatic visits would further bring the two countries together.

First, Clinton invited Jiang to visit the United States, which he did over an eight-day period at the end of October and beginning of November 1997. Although the trip was more symbolic than substantive, the public comments issued by both sides led many to believe that both governments wanted to improve relations on the economic and security fronts, and that both sides would relax their positions on the most contentious issues, particularly Taiwan. At a speech in Los Angeles, Jiang casually noted that the "Taiwan question will eventually be answered" but that the United States and China should make efforts to improve relations despite "differences that cannot be ironed out for the time being."[90] This serene rhetoric was a far cry from the bellicose statements and demonstrations that the PRC had mounted previously.

The Taiwanese fretted about Clinton's apparently increasing willingness to engage with China. Although they did not wish for a crisis between the United States and the PRC, since that could endanger Taiwan, neither did they want relations between Washington and Beijing to get too cozy, lest U.S. officials decide to sacrifice important Taiwanese interests. Taiwanese foreign minister Jason Hu bluntly testified before the Taiwanese parliament that improved Sino-U.S. ties "would certainly have an impact on Taiwan and hurt Taiwan's interests."[91]

Clinton was in turn invited to visit the PRC, which he did in June and July 1998. Even some of his most vehement critics, such as House Majority Whip Tom DeLay (R-TX), conceded that during the visit Clinton "looked good, sounded good, and was saying the right things."[92] At the same time, Clinton was attacked for publicly embracing the "three nos" principle regarding the Taiwan issue: that the United States would provide no support for Taiwan's independence, no support for its inclusion in world bodies for which statehood was a requirement, and no support for the notion of "one China, one Taiwan."

Conservative activist Gary Bauer accused Clinton of "publicly undercutting the security of the 21 million people of Taiwan," and House Majority Leader Rep. Dick Armey (R-TX) lamented that Clinton was "conceding the whole [Taiwan] ballgame to the Chinese."[93] Parris Chang, at the time a member of Taiwan's National Assembly and a DPP leader, complained that Clinton was effectively "selling out" Taiwan. Chang went further to use Clinton's China visit and his embrace of the three nos to make the case that Taiwan needed to bolster its indigenous defense industry, which it did.[94]

Clinton's newfound pragmatism did represent a significant change from the rhetoric on which he rode into office. During his 1992 campaign for president, Clinton had accused President Bush of "coddling tyrants" in Beijing after the Tiananmen Square massacre. Clinton's China policy had evolved after numerous setbacks, particularly his administration's failure to successfully link trade agreements to human rights standards. His embrace of an "engagement" policy for China would help pave the way to permanent normalized trade relations (PNTR) with China, and closer Sino-U.S. relations.

ALARMIST RHETORIC AND PROVOCATIVE LEGISLATION

Elements of the Republican Congress renewed their public attacks on Clinton's China policy after Jiang's visit to the United States. Several congressmen went so far as to call Clinton's position a policy of "appeasement," and the House swiftly approved a bill to commission a study of a missile defense system for Taiwan.[95] The criticism and hyperbole continued not only from Republican members of Congress, but from hawkish think tanks and analysts as well. One conservative think tank in 1997 proclaimed: "The nature of the threat posed by China is in key ways of a greater magnitude . . . than that mounted by the Soviet Union at the height of the Cold War."[96] Although less hyperbolic, the Heritage Foundation warned that Chinese military modernization represented a "looming threat . . . to peace in Asia."[97]

At the same time, a measure to renew the PRC's most favored nation (MFN) status was slowly making its way through Congress. Though the question of renewing MFN for China came up every year, the 1997 vote ended up splitting political parties, ideological groups, and creating odd coalitions on both the pro-MFN side and anti-MFN side.

Neoconservative analyst William Kristol, liberal Rep. Nancy Pelosi (D-CA), religious advocacy groups such as the Family Research Council and the Christian Coalition, and conservative Senator John Ashcroft (R-MO) all united in opposition to MFN. Meanwhile, conservative Representative Armey, President Clinton, business interests (including Dick Cheney, then CEO of Halliburton), and conservative Christian Pat Robertson all gathered in favor of MFN. The House approved MFN for China in June, after an acrimonious debate. A month later, the Senate voted overwhelmingly in favor of retaining China's MFN status.

The debate that had taken place in the House was significant, however, because it illuminated the ad hoc alliances that were forming around U.S. China policy. On one side, there were protectionists, human rights activists, and hawks who argued that China was an emerging threat to U.S. national security. On the other side were free traders, business interests, and those who believed that constructively engaging China through economic ties would yield greater political openness and better relations with the United States. These coalitions would solidify and continue to affect U.S. China policy in the years to come. Though the "engagement" side emerged from the MFN debate on top, the "isolation" side continued to attempt to make inroads by a series of small measures.

In 1999 a group of legislators led by Senator Helms and House Majority Whip Tom DeLay introduced a measure to sell a wealth of advanced military systems to Taiwan, including missile defense components, attack submarines, Aegis guided missile destroyers, and several other components.[98] The package was so large and provocative that even some Taiwanese analysts noted that "[p]eople fully understand that this will provoke Beijing. This worries everybody."[99] Congress did not pass the measure, but the rhetoric from conservative intellectuals and the debate in Congress continued to demonstrate how hostile some American opinion leaders were toward China, and how effective Taiwan's lobbying had been.

Other issues continued to rattle U.S.-PRC relations. For example, the Chinese were unsatisfied by the U.S. response to the May 1999 bombing of the Chinese embassy in Belgrade during the NATO intervention in Kosovo. Several prominent Chinese journalists were killed, and hundreds of thousands of Chinese mounted protests at the U.S. Embassy in Beijing, besieging and vandalizing the embassy, and prompting the U.S. Ambassador to remark that he felt like a "hostage."[100] The "isolation" faction in America seized on the mob scene outside the U.S. Embassy to attempt to drum up anti-China nationalist sentiment.

The embassy bombing, coupled with the increasingly anti-China rhetoric emerging from American intellectuals and legislators, caused a cynical theory to gain traction in China; namely, that the United States embraced the Taiwan issue not out of some high principle, but rather as one way to prevent China from emerging as a world power.[101] Although President Clinton apologized for the embassy bombing, the damage had been done to public opinion in China. As analyst Joseph Cirincione of the Carnegie Endowment for International Peace noted, the difference between the embassy bombing and prior diplomatic squabbles was that in the embassy bombing case, "the animosity [had] reached deep into the populations in both countries."[102]

NEW PRESIDENTS FOR TAIWAN AND THE UNITED STATES

The slow but steady gains that the DPP had made in the Legislative Yuan and in the collective mind of the Taiwanese public, combined with a split in the KMT, resulted in the March 2000 election of Chen Shui-bian, the first DPP president of Taiwan. Before he became president, Chen had openly and actively promoted Taiwanese independence. On the campaign trail, he famously led chants of "Long live Taiwan independence!" He claimed to be the only candidate who could hold to Lee's "two states" theory, the controversial principle enunciated under the Lee presidency that very nearly amounted to a declaration of independence.[103] The PRC feared that if Chen were elected he might declare independence, and Beijing accordingly had mounted a campaign against him before the elections. As with the 1996 elections, though, Chinese interference appeared to backfire, and instead rallied strong Taiwanese public support in favor of the very position China was attempting to undermine.[104]

The PRC responded cautiously at first to Chen's election. On the one hand, Beijing stated that "under no circumstances" should they be "fooled by [Chen's] sweet talk."[105] Yet immediately after Chen's election, the PRC issued a guardedly optimistic statement, declaring that although the One China principle must be the basis of any negotiations, "[u]nder this prerequisite, we can talk about anything."[106] Considering Chen's open embrace of Taiwan's independence during the campaign just months earlier, Beijing's response seemed to be an olive branch.

Chen shrewdly recognized that the PRC would be looking at him with suspicion, and, under some considerable U.S. pressure, made a relatively conciliatory inaugural speech (see chapter 4). Nevertheless, on China Central Television, the

PRC's official response to Chen's speech accused him of clinging to his prior "splittist position," and of adopting an "evasive, ambiguous attitude" on the question of One China. The television broadcast stated that Chen's professed "'goodwill and reconciliation' lack[ed] sincerity." Also, the PRC broadcast flatly stated: "The Taiwan issue cannot be stalled indefinitely." The PRC would continue to emphasize this position in the years to come.[107]

Later in the year, a new president was elected in the United States. After a contentious election, George W. Bush emerged victorious in the 2000 presidential balloting. Like Ronald Reagan before him, President Bush would send a confusing array of signals to China regarding his position on the Taiwan issue (see chapter 6). That unclear U.S. policy, coupled with troubling developments in Taiwan and the PRC, creates a rising risk that tensions could spiral out of control and lead to a military confrontation that no one desires.

CHAPTER 4

SOME OMINOUS TRENDS IN TAIWAN

Taiwan is a very different place now than it was in the 1970s, when the current paradigm of calculated ambiguity about the island's status emerged as part of the rapprochement between Washington and Beijing. At that time, an authoritarian regime in Taipei still asserted as passionately as the regime in Beijing that there was only one China and that Taiwan was part of that country. The only disagreement was whether the Republic of China or the People's Republic of China was the legitimate Chinese government.

That situation has changed radically in the intervening three decades. Carnegie Endowment for Peace senior associate Michael D. Swaine describes the shift and its significance. "The Taiwanese government concurred that it understood the island to be part of China. But Taiwan's recent emergence as a democracy has cast doubt on—if not eliminated altogether—that commitment. The political influence of the Chinese nationalist minority on the island has waned, in favor of a growing separatist-leaning Taiwanese leadership."[1] Similarly, Harvard University scholar Ross Terrill observes: "A string of elections in Taiwan has crystallized the sovereignty of the territory and solidified its identity as an island nation unto itself."[2]

But it is not just Taiwan's political leadership that has changed. There is a whole range of factors that accurately reflect the changed sentiment within the Taiwanese population.

SHIFTING PUBLIC OPINION IN TAIWAN

Public sentiment for an independent Taiwan is growing slowly but inexorably—especially among younger Taiwanese for whom the mainland is an alien and threatening place. True, most Taiwanese still favor the status quo—de facto independence; they fear (with good reason) that seeking formal independence would likely provoke a crisis, and, further, that the island might find the impressive quality of life that it has painstakingly built up over the decades destroyed in a war with the PRC. Despite the danger, though, a significant percentage of the people favor pushing for independence.[3] That sentiment becomes quite evident when Beijing rattles its sabers and seeks to bully Taiwan. For example, a poll taken by the mass circulation *United Daily News* in July 1997 (following the PRC's provocative missile tests and military exercises in 1996) revealed that 43 percent favored formal independence.[4] That figure was up from 24 percent in a survey taken in February 1996.[5]

Even more revealing, more than half of the respondents in the July poll regarded themselves as "Taiwanese," while only 30 percent viewed themselves as "Chinese." On the issue of national identity, a poll taken by Taiwan Thinktank in December 2004 revealed similar sentiment. Sixty-one percent of respondents considered themselves "Taiwanese only." Only 14 percent saw themselves as "Chinese only," while 16 percent considered themselves both Chinese and Taiwanese.[6] The "Chinese only" faction had remained relatively stable from earlier surveys, but the dual nationality faction was eroding steadily. And the vast majority of respondents who abandoned that response were going over to the "Taiwanese only" option.

A series of polls taken over the last twelve years by the Election Study Center at Taiwan's National Chengchi University showed a somewhat different pattern, but one that was unlikely to bring any reassurance to the PRC. The poll conducted in 1992 showed that only 17 percent of respondents regarded themselves solely as Taiwanese, whereas 26 percent regarded themselves as Chinese and 46 percent regarded themselves as both Chinese and Taiwanese (the remainder had no response.) By the 1996 poll, the percentage of "Taiwanese only" respondents had risen to 25 percent, while the "Chinese only" faction had declined to 21 percent and the "Chinese and Taiwanese" option was down to 45 percent. By 1999, the Taiwanese-only faction had soared to 40 percent, the dual-identity faction remained steady at 45 percent, and the Chinese only option had plunged to 10 percent. The results in 2004 were even worse from Beijing's standpoint. The "Taiwanese only" faction had nearly tied the dual-identity response at 41 percent, while the "Chinese only" response stood at an anemic 6 percent.[7]

Although poll results on the identity issue must be viewed with some caution, since much depends on just how the questions are framed, a fairly clear pattern emerges. The sense of Taiwanese identity is growing and the sense of Chinese identity is declining. Moreover, those who consider themselves purely Taiwanese are now significantly more numerous than those who consider themselves purely Chinese. The dual-identity faction still holds the balance of power, but one wonders how long it can continue to do so.

Polling results on other issues related to possible Taiwanese independence hold no better news for the PRC. A survey taken in late 1996 indicated that 47 percent of respondents favored an independent Taiwan—if it could coexist peacefully with the PRC. Only 29 percent were opposed to independence under those circumstances.[8] Moreover, the reluctance to reunify with mainland China appeared to entail more than the understandable hostility to seeing the island absorbed by a highly authoritarian state. Only 54 percent were willing to endorse reunification with a democratic and prosperous China.[9] Even at that early stage of Taiwan's democratic incarnation, the sense of cultural and economic separation was surprisingly potent. It has grown more so in the intervening years.

Emile C. J. Sheng, a professor at Soochow University, has synthesized much of the polling data regarding public opinion in Taiwan on the independence issue, examining important characteristics such as demographic shifts, why respondents feel the way they feel, and how strongly they hold their views.[10] Sheng took the polling data on the question of Taiwan's status and refined it into two main categories and five subcategories. Respondents fell into one of two categories based on their responses to test questions. Either they were "rational," in that their responses were conditioned on favorable outcomes, or they were "affective," in that their responses did not change even in light of unfavorable outcomes. Sheng then identified five groups: rational with no predisposition on the independence issue, rationally pro-unification, rationally pro-independence, affectively pro-unification, and affectively pro-independence.[11]

Sheng's analysis suggests that a conflict has developed between affectively pro-independence respondents and the rational, nonpredisposed respondents. Indeed, the size of both groups has grown: between 1992 and 2000, the number of affectively pro-independence respondents more than doubled—from 13 percent to 30 percent. The number of nonpredisposed rational respondents has also grown—from 26 percent to 41 percent. By contrast, the number of affective pro-unification respondents shrank from 45 percent to 24 percent, and the number of rational pro-unification respondents plummeted from 12 percent to 3 percent.[12]

The history of Taiwan since the Communist victory on the mainland helps to explain the dramatic changes. When Chiang Kai-shek's government fled to Taiwan, essentially all of those leaving the mainland for the island regarded themselves as Chinese, preserving the intention of someday taking the mainland back from the PRC. With the passage of nearly six decades, most members of that generation have died. Moreover, the ethnic identity of many indigenous Taiwanese was ambivalent from the beginning of Chiang's rule. The combination of those two factors has led to the emergence of a new identity among those born in relatively liberal, prosperous Taiwan. According to Sheng, "the youngest respondents are more affectively pro-independence and less affectively pro-unification, while the oldest respondents are more affectively pro-unification and less rational than the population as a whole."[13] Thus, as the reflexively pro-unification older generation dies off, it is being replaced by two groups: non-predisposed rational citizens and strongly pro-independence citizens.

The growth of and tension between those two factions will help determine the public temper regarding cross-Strait policy. If the affectively pro-independence faction continues to gain ground (and there are subtle indications that this has been the case in the four years since Sheng conducted his analysis), Taiwan's policy could become more assertive and willing to court risks. Significantly, the affectively pro-independence faction seems to be the least concerned about military confrontation with China.[14] Members of that group may believe that China is bluffing when it threatens to use force to prevent Taiwanese independence. Another key question, though, is how the non-predisposed rational group will respond to events across the Strait. That is especially pertinent if Beijing takes an extremely hard line about Taiwanese moves toward greater separatism. Under those circumstances, it is uncertain whether reason would cause the uncommitted faction to support a more cautious policy in the face of PRC confrontational tactics, or to conclude that the PRC is incorrigible and that Taiwan must be prepared to assert and defend its separate existence. How that faction breaks during a crisis could well determine what policy a government in Taipei adopts.

The increased sense of Taiwanese identity and the mounting unfavorable attitudes toward reunification are not the only trends driving Taiwan away from the PRC and undermining Beijing's goal of reunification. The PRC's rather ham-handed management of the return of Hong Kong to its jurisdiction has also caused queasiness in Taiwan about the prospect of reunification. Beijing has repeatedly sought to intimidate the authorities and citizens of Hong Kong and has re-interpreted the promises it made about Hong Kong's autonomy when it regained control of the territory from Britain in 1997. For example, in April 2004, the Standing Committee of the National People's Congress barred direct elections for Hong Kong's chief executive in 2007 and the full legislature in 2008. When large protests erupted in Hong Kong over the decision, Beijing's response was less than subtle. The PRC dispatched eight warships to make a show of force in Victoria Harbor. At about the same time, some prominent pro-democracy advocates reported mysterious threats of violence against themselves and their families. Then, in early May, Beijing escalated the pressure, warning pro-democracy legislators in Hong Kong's Legislative Council that they were violating the law merely by proposing measures to criticize the decision of the Standing Committee.

Those developments were more than a matter of academic interest to people on Taiwan. After all, Beijing had held up the "one country, two systems" example that applied to Hong Kong as the model for Taiwan's reunification with the mainland (albeit with a greater degree of autonomy for Taiwan). The overwhelming majority of Taiwanese had never been enthusiastic about the one country, two systems formula. The events in Hong Kong in the spring of 2004 made them even less enthusiastic. Indeed, they provoked Szu-yin Ho, director of overseas affairs for the Kuomintang Party, to remark that "de jure independence makes sense, especially after what's been happening in Hong Kong."[15] Such a comment coming from a staunch advocate of Taiwanese independence might not have been surprising; coming from a stalwart of the moderate KMT should have been a warning to Beijing about the state of Taiwanese opinion.

FACTORS PROMOTING CONCILIATION

While the trend in Taiwanese public opinion is toward separatism, that is not to say that there are no factors promoting caution by Taipei and even facilitating some sentiment in favor of an accommodating policy toward the mainland. The most important force in that regard is the extensive and expanding economic connection between Taiwan and the PRC.[16] As Karen M. Sutter of the U.S.-China Business Council notes, however, "the current economic relationship is extremely skewed, with the majority of goods and services flowing from Taiwan to the PRC."[17] Among other things, that disparity means that the economic relationship is likely to be more important to Taiwan than it is to the mainland.

China expert Sheng Lijun notes that Beijing "has been heavily courting" Taiwan's business community with trade opportunities and incentives since the late 1970s, and especially since the early 1990s.[18] During the early years of that process, most of the Taiwanese firms that invested in the mainland were in traditional industries such as textiles and clothing manufacturing. Since the late 1990s, though, a growing number of high-tech firms have invested in China. A poll taken in February 2001 showed that 90 percent of Taiwan-based high-tech firms had plans to invest in the mainland.[19]

Trade and investment have expanded so extensively in recent years that China is now Taiwan's largest export market. The mainland is also the arena for nearly $100 billion in Taiwanese investment capital.[20] Indeed, that investment is increasing at a rate of between $3 billion and $4 billion each year.[21] A expatriate

Taiwanese community (largely attracted by business opportunities) has grown up in and around a number of mainland cities, especially Shanghai. As many as one million Taiwanese now work and live in the PRC.

The expanding economic ties have led to pressure on Taiwan's government to reopen direct transport, trade, and postal links with the mainland—the so-called three links—that were severed in 1949. In response to that pressure, the government of Chen Shui-bian proposed a more limited measure. Taipei agreed to open the outlying Kinmen, Matsu, and Penghu islands to direct communication and transportation with the cities of Xiamen and Fuzhou on the mainland for "small-scale trade." This step became known as the "mini three links."

There was an irony in the reluctance of Chen's government to approve the establishment of the "big three direct links," as Sheng Lijun observes—an irony that underscores how Taiwan's growing economic interdependence with the PRC may foster Beijing's reunification agenda.

> In the 1980s and early 1990s, Taipei used the "three links" as bargaining chips for Beijing's political concession. Now, the table has been turned around. Economically, Taiwan now needs the "three links" more than mainland China. Beijing now does not seem to be in a hurry, and it stresses agreement on the "one-China" principle for opening the "big three links."[22]

The economic interdependence and the size of the Taiwanese expatriate presence in the PRC are undoubtedly powerful incentives for caution, especially on Taipei's side. There are indications that those members of the expatriate community that returned to Taiwan to vote in the March 2004 presidential election voted overwhelmingly against the reelection of President Chen Shui-bian. Karen Sutter notes that "there is a concern in some quarters in Taiwan and the U.S. that from a national security perspective Taiwan is becoming overly dependent on the PRC." The key issue "is the question of leverage and the extent to which Beijing gains an advantage over Taiwan as Taiwanese firms enmesh Taiwan's economic future with that of the mainland." There is growing concern, especially within the Democratic Progressive Party but also within certain quarters of the KMT, "about how further economic integration may shift the debate about political identity. Specifically, they fear that Taiwan will be less inclined to consider the option of political independence as its economic survival and future are increasingly linked to those of the PRC."[23] In addition, Taiwan security planners are concerned that Taiwan's businesses—particularly its high-tech firms—may be indirectly helping to strengthen the PRC's military capabilities.[24]

As important as the economic linkages between Taiwan and mainland are (and they are quite significant), they are likely to be overwhelmed by the larger cultural and political changes in Taiwan that promote an ever greater sense of independence.[25] Chao Chien-min, a scholar at National Chengchi University in Taipei, emphasizes that Taiwan and the mainland are drifting further apart culturally and politically even with the extensive economic interdependence. Even as the economic integrationists "have been celebrating their cause, the [political] gap between the two sides has widened."[26]

Princeton University professor Thomas Christensen succinctly analyzes the trend. "China has used economic integration as a tool to change the minds of the Taiwan public. But that strategy has largely failed. Politically, Taiwan is getting further away, not closer."[27] Political analyst Andrew Peterson reaches a similar conclusion.

> For anyone to dismiss the pro-independence forces in Taiwan as a passing fad . . . risks a fundamental miscalculation. The independence movement in Taiwan has grown consistently during the last fifteen years and shows no signs of stalling. Pro-independence forces have conclusively defeated pro-reunification forces; the only political battle remaining is independence versus the status quo, where Taiwan is functionally independent but politically outcast by the PRC's "one-China" policy, and independence is gaining.[28]

THE TREND IN TAIWAN'S POLITICS: CHEN SHUI-BIAN'S FIRST TERM

The pattern of an assertive Taiwanese reaction to PRC bullying tactics has occurred on several occasions. As noted in chapter 3, the PRC's hostile rhetoric and menacing missile tests and other military maneuvers in 1996 helped propel Lee Teng-hui to a landslide victory in Taiwan's first presidential election. Since the whole purpose of Beijing's harsh measures was to weaken support for Lee, the strategy clearly backfired. Yet the PRC pursued a similar menacing strategy toward the island in the months leading up to Taiwan's 2000 presidential election. Once again, the strategy proved counterproductive. In a very tight three-way race among the KMT's Lien Chan, People First Party nominee James Soong, and DPP candidate Chen Shui bian, Chinese belligerence may have made a crucial difference as Chen eked out a narrow victory with 39 percent of the vote. Again, seeing a DPP government come to power was undoubtedly the last thing leaders in China desired, but Beijing's own policies probably helped bring about that result.

Chen began his term of office with a relatively conciliatory inaugural address. Responding in part to U.S. pressure not to provoke Beijing, Chen promised to avoid measures that would radically alter the status quo. "[A]s long as the CCP regime has no intention of using military force against Taiwan, I pledge that during my term in office, I will not declare independence, I will not change the national title, I will not push forth the inclusion of the so-called 'state-to-state' description in the Constitution, and I will not promote a referendum to change the status quo in regards to the question of independence or reunification. Furthermore, the abolition of the National Reunification Council or the National Reunification Guidelines will not be an issue."[29]

That statement became known as the "five assurances," or "five do nots," and they did serve to dampen the sense of alarm in Washington and Beijing about the coming to power of a DPP president. Yet even in an ostensibly conciliatory inaugural ceremony, Chen managed to stress Taiwan's separate identity in subtle ways.[30] The ceremony also was notable for its display of native Taiwanese (rather than Chinese) music, dance, and cultural traditions. One point that especially enraged the PRC was Chen's evasiveness about whether he considered himself Chinese. He used the word *huaren* instead of *zhongguoren*. Although both words translate into English as "Chinese," they have very different connotations. *Huaren* implies that one is of Chinese descent but not a citizen of China. As China expert Sheng Lijun notes, most Singaporeans refer to themselves as *huaren* (because they are of Chinese descent) but not *zhongguoren* (because Singapore is not part of China).[31] PRC leaders believed that by using the former term rather than the latter, Chen was making a statement that Taiwan and China were two separate entities. (Vice President Annette Lu and former president Lee Teng-hui emulated Chen in describing themselves as *huaren*, intensifying Beijing's suspicions and anger.)

Once in office, Chen also began to qualify some of his assurances. For example, he put forth three principles as necessary to open cross-Strait dialogue: to negotiate on the basis of equality between Beijing and Taipei, to resolve disputes by peaceful means, and to establish no preset conditions on the future of cross-Strait relations. The first provision implied that the PRC and Taiwan were two separate and equal states. In the Chinese text, the second provision actually invoked the UN Charter (which prohibits interference in the domestic affairs of another state.) The clear implication again was that the PRC and Taiwan were both independent states and that the disputes between them were bilateral international matters, not the leftover domestic business of the Chinese civil war. Finally, the third provision made it clear that reunification was not a predetermined result but only one possible option for discussion. Not surprisingly, this was all quite unacceptable to the PRC government, and Chinese leaders came to view Chen's ostensibly conciliatory gestures as a strategy of "one step backward, two steps forward" on Taiwan's march to independence.[32]

Chen also modified his inaugural assurances about not repudiating the 1991 National Unification Guidelines. On several occasions in August and September 2000, he emphasized that the guidelines had not been adopted through a democratic process. Therefore, those guidelines were "not an unchangeable totem." Stressing that reunification was merely a choice, "and not the only choice," for the people of Taiwan, Chen promised to consult the people on how to revise those guidelines.[33] That position vitiated much of the assurance that he had given Beijing in his inaugural speech.

The content of his 2001 New Year's address likewise aroused concern in the PRC. Once again, Chen appeared to be conciliatory on the surface, arguing that "the two sides should start from economic, trade, and cultural integration, and build mutual trust on a gradual basis so as to seek lasting peace and build a new mechanism for political integration."[34] But as Sheng Lijun points out, "the word 'integration' is subject to wide interpretations. It could mean a federation, confederation, or even commonwealth."[35] Chen himself later made it apparent that integration did not mean reunification, contending that the European Union was the best model for Taiwan and China.[36] Needless to say, that is not what the leaders of the PRC had in mind.

Chen's government could cite a few conciliatory substantive measures during his first year in office. His administration approved the expansion of economic ties to the mainland, including the lifting of a cap on the monetary value of any single investment. Perhaps more significant, the DPP itself moderated its tone on independence slightly. In 1999 the party had passed a resolution affirming for the first time that the Republic of China was a legitimate, sovereign entity, and that any change in the ROC's political status should only come as the result of a referendum by all the residents of Taiwan. At a party congress in October 2001, the DPP elevated that resolution to a status equal to that of the clause affirming the goal of an independent Taiwan republic and the need for a new constitution that the party had put in its platform in 1991.

DPP chairman Frank Hsieh contended that the new approach superceded the 1991 provisions, but he also attempted to pacify angry pro-independence hard-liners. He argued that with the changing of the domestic political environment and "fresh interpretations of a sovereign state," the status quo was now independence. In other words, Hsieh was insisting that Taiwan was already independent and that there was no need to alter its name or constitution.[37] DPP lawmaker Tsai Huang-liang was a little more candid about the changes, stating

that the resolution more accurately reflected mainstream public opinion in Taiwan, allowing the DPP to take a more pragmatic view of cross-Strait relations
and giving the party greater room to maneuver. Tsai stressed that there was no
change in the DPP's pro-independence objectives, however. A legislative colleague of Tsai's, Lin Cho-shui, even argued that the requirement for a referendum meant that the party would be even more committed to an independence
agenda.[38] PRC officials apparently agreed with that interpretation. Zhang
Mingqing, a spokesman for the Taiwan Affairs Office, dismissed the adoption of
the resolution as "a change in form but not in content."[39]

Despite occasional conciliatory measures, Chen pursued a variety of initiatives to emphasize Taiwan's separateness from China during his first term in
office.[40] For example, passports used by Taiwanese travelers had always borne
the name Republic of China on the cover. Chen did not order that name removed, a step that would have infuriated Beijing. His Ministry of Foreign Affairs did, however, add the phrase "Issued in Taiwan" to the cover beginning in
January 2002. (One suspects that during Chen's second term the print size for
"Republic of China" will become substantially smaller and the print size for
"Taiwan" will grow larger.) At the end of December 2001, the Government
Information Office introduced a new logo for the agency. The map of mainland China, which had been prominent on the previous logo, was now noticeably absent.[41] Such innovations may seem minor, but they have enormous
symbolic importance—and probably significant psychological importance—on
both Taiwan and the mainland.

Other political developments in Taiwan highlighted the growing confidence
and determination of the pro-independence forces. One key episode was the
founding of the Taiwan Solidarity Union as a new political party in August 2001.
Because former president Lee Teng-hui was instrumental in the formation of the
TSU (and was generally regarded as its de facto leader), the party acquired in-
stant credibility and influence. TSU members took a position on the independence issue that was even more uncompromising and radical than that embraced
by most DPP hard-liners. In campaigning for TSU candidates in elections for
the Legislative Yuan in late 2001, Lee constantly used the term "alien regime" to
describe his old party, the KMT, because of its adherence to a one-China policy.[42]
The infant party did surprisingly well in those elections, picking up 13 seats in
the 225-seat legislature.

In the autumn of 2003, Chen proposed an initiative that had even more symbolic (and practical) significance than his earlier measures. To accompany the
March 2004 presidential election, he planned to hold referenda on various security issues. Beijing reacted with shrill opposition. Although the initial referenda

questions were relatively sedate, PRC leaders feared that Chen was trying to set a precedent, and that if those referenda passed, at some later date proposals to change the name of the ROC or perhaps even to proclaim a Taiwanese republic would be put forth.

As it turned out, Chen's referenda proposal was a bit too bold and provocative. The initiative drew a public rebuke from President Bush during a visit to Washington by PRC prime minister Wen Jiabao in December 2003 (see chapter 6). Washington also put tremendous pressure on Chen to abandon the planned referendum, and, when that effort failed, to dilute the language to make it less offensive to Beijing.

Chen ultimately agreed to make the questions more innocuous. As announced in January 2004, the two referenda questions were the following:

1. The People of Taiwan demand that the Taiwan Strait issue be resolved through peaceful means. Should mainland China (the PRC) refuse to withdraw the missiles it has targeted at Taiwan and openly renounce the use of force against us, would you agree that the government should acquire more advanced anti-missile weapons to strengthen Taiwan's self-defense capabilities?
2. Would you agree that our government should engage in negotiation with mainland China (the PRC) on the establishment of a "peace and stability" framework for cross-Strait interactions in order to build consensus and for the welfare of the peoples on both sides?[43]

Despite the milder phrasing, a great many Taiwanese voters were nervous about provoking Beijing and alienating Taiwan's protector, the United States. Both the KMT and the PFP urged voters to boycott the referendum, and even though a slim majority voted to reelect Chen to the presidency, only a minority of voters cast ballots in the referendum, rendering the initiative invalid.[44] Chen had pushed a cautious Taiwanese public a little too far.

At the same time, Chen himself fared well politically. In contrast to the 2000 election, the KMT and PFP formed a "Pan Blue" alliance behind a single candidate—the venerable Lien Chan. To the surprise of most experts, Chen Shui-bian won the election. Opponents charged that he did so only because of a sympathy vote following a strange election-eve assassination attempt that left Chen and his running mate, Vice President Annette Lu, slightly wounded. Whatever the reason, Taiwanese voters reelected Chen by an extremely narrow margin. Even those who denigrated his victory, however, could not ignore the reality that he had garnered some 1.5 million more votes in 2004 than he had in 2000.

CHEN'S AGENDA IN HIS SECOND TERM

Once reelected, the president pursued his strategy to establish a distinct identity for Taiwan, despite the failure of his proposed referenda. As in 2000, his inaugural address was more low-key and conciliatory than many in the PRC and the United States expected—and that DPP hard-liners had hoped for. How much of that was due to Chen's own prudence and how much to U.S. pressure is uncertain. It was clear that Washington had warned him not to provoke Beijing with his inaugural address, putting excruciating pressure on him to adopt conciliatory language.

One passage in particular seemed designed to reassure Beijing and mollify the Bush administration. Noting that part of his mandate from the voters was to "safeguard peace and stability in the Taiwan Strait" and to "carefully manage future relations across the Strait," Chen added: "I would like to reaffirm the promises and principles set forth in my inaugural speech in 2000. Those commitments have been honored—they have not changed in the past four years, nor will they change in the next four years."[45]

He offered other, admittedly less precise, conciliatory gestures as well. "It is my belief that both sides must demonstrate a dedicated commitment to national development, and through consultation establish a dynamic 'peace and stability framework' for interactions; that we must work together to guarantee there will be no unilateral change in the status quo in the Taiwan Strait; and, additionally, we must further promote cultural, economic and trade exchanges—including the three links—for only in doing so can we ensure the welfare of our peoples while fulfilling the expectations of the international community."[46]

Yet the pattern of four years earlier seems to be repeating. Although Chen's 2004 inaugural address appeared to offer Beijing some olive branches, he did not give ground on the central issue of Taiwan's right to exist as a separate state. Even his language was likely to annoy Beijing. For example, he rarely referred to the Republic of China, the official name of the state that he headed. Far more often he referred to the entity simply as "Taiwan." PRC officials took note of such nuances. There were also numerous formulations in his address that implicitly assumed that China and Taiwan were wholly separate nations. "If both sides are willing, on the basis of goodwill, to create an environment engendered upon 'peaceful development and freedom of choice,' then in the future the Republic of China and the People's Republic of China—or Taiwan and China—can seek to establish relations in any form whatsoever. We would not exclude any possibility, so long as there is the consent of the 23 million people of Taiwan."[47] Although that statement held out the possibility of "one China" as an outcome, it certainly did not accept that concept as the starting point. Indeed, it was clear that Chen considered "one China" only one of several possible outcomes from negotiations. Beijing could take little comfort from such phrasing.

Chen also had a rather pointed warning to the PRC if it continued its policy of isolating and threatening Taiwan.

> We can understand why the government on the other side of the Strait, in light of historical complexities and ethnic sentiments, cannot relinquish the insistence on the "One-China Principle." By the same token, the Beijing authorities must understand the deep conviction held by the people of Taiwan to strive for democracy, to love peace, to pursue their dreams free from threat, and to embrace progress. But if the other side is unable to comprehend that this honest and simple wish represents the aspirations of Taiwan's 23 million people, if it continues to threaten Taiwan with military force, if it persists in isolating Taiwan diplomatically, if it keeps up irrational efforts to blockade Taiwan's rightful participation in the international arena, this will only serve to drive the hearts of the Taiwanese people further away and widen the divide in the Strait.[48]

In light of such statements, one can understand why Beijing did not share Washington's view that Chen's inaugural address was constructive and conciliatory. From the perspective of the PRC, nothing significant had changed.

Chen's key personnel appointments regarding policy toward the mainland also pointed to a hard-line substantive policy. To head the Cabinet-level Mainland Affairs Council, Chen appointed Joseph Wu, who had been deputy director of the Institute of International Relations in Taipei before joining the presidential office in 2002. Wu had written a number of papers and articles highly critical of the PRC's position on reunification, and his appointment came on the heels of Chen's designation of long-time independence activist Mark Chen as foreign minister. "With Mark Chen in the foreign ministry and Joseph Wu in the Mainland Affairs Council, this combination sends a very powerful message to the world," said Su Chi, who was chairman of the MAC under the previous KMT administration. "Both are diehard pro-independence individuals," Su lamented.[49] Even taking into account that Su was a political opponent of the DPP, his assessment seemed accurate and was shared by most observers of Taiwan's political scene.

Indeed, Chen's choice for prime minister, Yu Shyi-kun, seemed to be a firebreather as well. In September 2004 Yu warned Beijing not to even contemplate using military force against Taiwan. His government's response, he stressed, would not be purely defensive if such an attack occurred. "You fire 100 missiles at me, I fire 50 at you. You hit Taipei and Kaohsiung, I at least hit Shanghai. This is what we call balance of terror."[50] Such remarks were clearly not calculated to soothe the tensions with Beijing.

Moreover, barely months into his new term, Chen Shui-bian proposed a number of measures that were certain to anger the PRC. One of those initiatives, writing a new constitution to replace the ROC's 1947 document and approving that step by referendum in 2006, Chen had proposed during the presidential campaign. That proposal greatly agitated the PRC—and the United States—because the implication was that the fundamental law for the Republic of China would be replaced. Chinese and U.S. officials worried that establishing a new constitution would be the first step toward transforming the ROC into the "Republic of Taiwan." In response to blunt warnings from Beijing and expressions of concern from Washington, Chen's government began to adopt a more restrained position, even referring to a "new version of our constitution" rather than to a new constitution per se. Officials stressed that a new constitution would focus on such relatively mundane issues as whether the five-branch political system should be changed to a three-branch government, whether the president should be elected by a plurality or majority vote, whether the legislature should be reduced in size, and whether provincial governments should be abolished.

But even the assurances that Chen and his aides gave seemed less than definitive. Consider the language of Minister Yeh Jiunn-rong, chairman of the administration's Research, Development, and Evaluation Commission: "As President Chen said, the national sovereignty, territory, and independence versus reunification are not going to be included *in this round of constitutional reform*." Those issues, Yeh stated, "have to be addressed in another forum."[51] PRC leaders could be excused if they didn't take much comfort from such "assurances." Moreover, Chen himself sometimes waffled on the issue of constitutional changes and a plebiscite on Taiwan's status. For example, when addressing a delegation of officials from Mongolia in September, he stated: "The Republic of Mongolia has in the past successfully confirmed through a referendum the will of the people to safeguard the independence of the country. This is something Taiwan should learn from and turn to."[52] Those remarks seemed to contradict his pledge in May that Taiwan would not touch on sovereignty or independence in the planned constitutional reforms. They also cast doubt on his assurances that Taiwan's legislation authorizing referenda was not in preparation for a plebiscite on independence but merely to deepen internal democracy. If all that were not enough, PRC leaders undoubtedly remembered that Mongolia had confirmed its desire to be independent from China in a 1945 plebiscite authorized by the Chinese Nationalist government. Chen was not exactly soothing troubled waters by bringing up that memory.

True, the Chen administration did not intend to press as far as some of the hard-line advocates of independence desired. Former president Lee Teng-hui, for example, convened a meeting of an "Action for Taiwan Constitution" conclave in early July 2004. Lee suggested that the new constitution include a provision changing the name of the country to Taiwan or to such variations as "Taiwan, Republic of China," or "Republic of China on Taiwan."[53] In a later interview, Lee was even more blunt: "We should rectify our name to Taiwan." He added that "we have to keep moving forward, a step at a time." He also urged Chen to be bold. "Chinese leaders are very tough, and they see that Chen Shui-bian is weak, they will bully him." Lee chastised Chen for not being more assertive on the independence issue. "The government has backtracked a lot. Before, they said we should write a new constitution, now they only talk about amending the constitution," Lee lamented.[54]

It is a testimony to the changing dynamics in Taiwan's political elite that Chen Shui-bian and his government can be criticized for being too soft. Yet the differences between Lee and Chen appear to be more of tactics and timing than of substance. Instead of embracing such a provocative rationale that risked creating an immediate crisis with Beijing, Chen and his advisers stressed other reasons for drafting a new constitution. Taiwan was now a democratic polity, they pointed out, while the existing ROC constitution was prepared for a one-party, authoritarian state in which there was only minimal separation between party and government. Yet even their softer, more reasonable rationales did little to allay the PRC's suspicions. For example, Taiwanese leaders argued that the 1947 constitution was drafted for a large, undeveloped country, not for an industrialized country of 23 million people.

To officials in Beijing, that rationale sounded suspiciously like an argument that Taiwan, as a separate country with unique features and needs, required a constitution to reflect those attributes. The Chen government's strategy on the constitution might be more subtle than that embraced by Lee Teng-hui and his followers, but it pointed toward the same result. Chen's own statements fed that suspicion. Even as he rejected Lee's aggressive approach, saying to "hastily" push for a change in the country's name would divide the public, he stressed that such rash action must be avoided *until a majority consensus with the public is reached and formed.*"[55] That certainly implied that once a consensus was reached, the name should be changed, even though such action would enrage Beijing.

Chen's administration pursued a number of other initiatives that aroused Beijing's ire. In the autumn of 2004, Taiwan's Education Ministry drafted new guidelines for the 2006 academic year. Among other changes, it ordered high schools to create a separate textbook for Taiwanese history. Currently, that topic is covered under the broader subject of Chinese history. In addition, a separate course on Chinese culture, mandatory in the current curriculum, would become optional.[56] Taiwanese teachers, including many at the lower grades, seem to harbor a distinct nationalist agenda. Explained one elementary school teacher: "We don't teach that Taiwan is part of China anymore. We emphasize that we're Taiwanese now, and everybody accepts that."[57]

The changes that the Education Ministry mandated were restrained compared to the attitudes of officials responsible for the civil service exams. One official charged with preparing those exams stated that people who think they are Chinese are unfit to work as Taiwanese civil servants. "China is not only a foreign country, but also an enemy country," asserted Lin Yu-tee, a member of the Examination Yuan, the government's top examination agency. That agency will strip Chinese history and geography from future civil service tests. Lin stated that civil servants need to know only about their own country. "Do civil servants in the United States need to be tested on their knowledge of the Soviet Union?" he asked.[58]

Such administrative changes are building on subtle but important cultural shifts that have been building along with Taiwan's transition to democracy and that have accelerated since Chen's emergence as president. For example, Taiwan's Minnan dialect has increasingly displaced Mandarin in the island's linguistic life. *New York Times* correspondent Joseph Kahn observes:

> The use of Minnanese has soared, most notably on television, where it had been banned by the Nationalists. Mandarin-speaking Taiwanese must read subtitles to understand the sitcoms and talk shows with the highest ratings. Bookstores are full of history titles that explore Taiwan's indigenous past. Some pop singers have begun using Minnanese, even though that limits the potential market for their music.[59]

Beijing fully understands the political significance of such cultural and administrative changes. "To destroy a country, you first destroy history," China's *Liberation Army Daily* editorialized. "Cultural independence, taking political independence as its ultimate goal, will not only seriously jeopardize cross-Strait peace, it will finally push Taiwan people into the abyss of war," the People's Liberation Army's official newspaper warned.[60]

Taipei's initiatives increasingly worried the United States, and Washington pressed Chen to make some conciliatory moves toward the PRC to reverse the rising tensions. As he had in both inaugural addresses, the Taiwanese leader responded to U.S. pressure by directing ostensibly conciliatory comments toward

Beijing. Following a high-level meeting of his national security team on November 10, 2004, Chen emphasized his desire to reduce cross-Strait tensions.

> We believe that the next two years will be a crucial and opportune time for the resumption of cross-Strait dialogue and for the pursuit of long-term stability and peaceful development. Governments and leaders on both sides of the Strait should seize this opportunity and employ wisdom—to open a favorable "window of opportunity" for long-term development, and to seek security and prosperity for both our peoples. In spite of the absence of immediate response from the other side to our goodwill and sincere gestures—due to various factors—our determination and patience will not change.[61]

Chen then stated that he would direct government agencies to "actively formulate a 'sunshine policy' for the resumption of dialogue, decreasing tension, and enhancing cooperation and development across the Strait." If both sides could be "understanding and magnanimous toward each other, differences and hostility can be resolved through peaceful dialogue and rational consultations. The meeting in Hong Kong in 1992 was conducted in such a spirit."[62]

In addition to the call for dialogue, Chen proposed substantive mechanisms to reduce tensions. He offered the assurance that Taiwan would never develop nuclear, biological, or chemical weapons and called on the PRC likewise to renounce the development or use of all weapons of mass destruction. Another proposal was to create demilitarized "buffer zones" in the Strait. Military aircraft and ships of both sides were to refrain from entering those zones "unless absolutely necessary," and then only with advance notification. He also suggested establishing a "Taiwan Strait consultation mechanism" for military security. That entity was to develop a "code of conduct" for activities in the Taiwan Strait.

Yet even in his ostensibly conciliatory statement, Chen managed to phrase things in ways that were certain to rile Beijing. The proposal for a mutual renunciation of nuclear weapons, for example, implicitly required the PRC to give up the arsenal that it had possessed since the mid-1960s. His reference to "both our peoples" implied that China and Taiwan were two separate societies and states. Likewise, his models for the consultation mechanism were arrangements between North and South Korea and India and Pakistan; in other words, relationships between two independent states. That was precisely the point that the PRC has always been unwilling to concede.

In any case, Beijing and Washington had very different reactions to Chen's remarks. The State Department praised the initiative as "positive and constructive" and stated that it laid the foundation for progress toward the resumption of dialogue between Taipei and Beijing.[63] PRC officials were decidedly unimpressed and once again accused Chen of duplicity.

On the eve of the December 2004 legislative elections, Chen Shui-bian advanced another provocative proposal. In a bid to make a sharper distinction between Taiwan and China, he proposed to "rectify" the names of all relevant government agencies and state-owned corporations within two years. Thus, China Airlines would likely become Taiwan Airlines, China Shipbuilding Corp would become Taiwan Shipbuilding Corp, and so on. Chen even proposed to change the names of Taiwan's overseas missions. Currently, most of them go under the cumbersome name of Taipei Economic and Culture Office or the slight variation with the de facto embassy in the United States, the Taipei Economic and Cultural Representative Office. Chen did not immediately indicate what the new name would be, but the goal would be to clearly indicate Taiwan's identity. His official rationale was that "internationally, we should actively make the differentiation between Taiwan and China to avoid unnecessary confusion."[64] Beijing was not fooled.

But DPP officials brushed off Beijing's anger at the proposal to remove "China" from the name of Taiwanese companies. "We do not need the approval of mainland China to change the name of a company in Taiwan," Chang Chunhsiung, the party's secretary general, brusquely told foreign journalists.[65]

Perhaps most ambitiously, Chen pledged to seek UN membership using the name Taiwan if his party and its TSU ally in the Pan Green coalition won a majority in the legislature.[66] Seeking UN membership was itself a major provocation to Beijing, but doing so under the name Taiwan was doubly so. In the past, Taiwan had used its official name, the Republic of China, in its quest to join the United Nations. Beijing would almost certainly see a bid under the name Taiwan as tantamount to a declaration of statehood. In proposing such action, Chen Shui-bian was skating on very thin ice.

Fred Lin, a Taipei businessman and DPP supporter, accurately interpreted Chen Shui-bian's strategy. He believed that the president aimed to lead Taiwan toward formal independence but had to proceed carefully given U.S. reticence and the threat from China. "Step by step," he explained.[67] That could easily be the motto of Chen Shui-bian's administration.

In addition to his incremental steps to firmly establish Taiwan's separate identity, Chen also repeatedly tried to place Taiwan's struggle with the PRC in the broader context of East Asian security and stability. Speaking at a conference on global democracy in August 2004, he warned that a bellicose China was a threat not only to Taiwan but to the entire region. "In recent years, China has been aggressively increasing its military might," Chen stated. "It has been increasing its annual military spending by double digits. It has been deploying missiles directly aimed at Taiwan. And it's planning to have the ability to stop U.S., Japanese, and other international forces from getting involved in the Taiwan Strait." Chen added: "China's plans to use its military to intimidate Taiwan is not only a challenge to Taiwan's democratic system, it's a challenge to the region's safety and security."[68]

TAIWAN'S DECEMBER 2004 LEGISLATIVE ELECTIONS

The conventional wisdom is that the Pan Green coalition's setback in the December 2004 legislative elections would produce a significant easing of cross-Strait tensions. There is no doubt that the election was an unpleasant surprise to the DPP-TSU coalition. Public opinion polls taken in the weeks before the balloting indicated that the Pan Green forces would win a majority of seats and take control of the legislature. Indeed, in the days just prior to the election there seemed to be a surge of support for the most radical pro-independence positions. There was some speculation that the TSU might win as many as twenty seats compared to thirteen in the 2001 elections.[69] Chen himself sharpened his rhetoric during the final days of the campaign. As one post-election observer noted, "Mr. Chen moved even more firmly toward the pro-independence camp in a bid to help his Democratic Progressive Party and its allies attain a legislative majority. His campaign pledges often seemed to flatly contradict his promises to reduce tensions with China."[70]

But the *Financial Times* correctly observed that one could read too much into the election outcome.

> Another danger is that Chinese leaders will draw the wrong conclusions from the election result, mistakenly believing that the Taiwanese have abandoned hopes for independence and are coming around to Beijing's point of view. That is not so. Mr. Chen's Democratic Progressive Party (DPP) actually did slightly better than before, gaining two seats. What seems to have happened is that voters sought the middle ground, rejecting radicals in both camps, reducing their support for the KMT's pro-China allies and for a pro-independence party allied with the DPP.[71]

This is an accurate observation, but the rejection of "extreme" positions was not symmetrical. The TSU lost one seat, going from thirteen to twelve. But the appeasement-oriented People First Party received an even stronger rebuke from voters, dropping to thirty-four seats from forty-six in the 2001 elections. The DPP actually gained two seats—to eighty-nine—while the KMT went from sixty-eight seats to seventy-nine.[72] In other words, the DPP gained slightly at the expense of its more radical alliance partner, while the KMT gained dramatically at the expense of its more pro-Beijing partner.

That result is all the more interesting since the KMT has been moving noticeably in the direction of a friendlier attitude toward a separate Taiwan identity, in part to increase the party's political viability in its competition with the DPP. "Particularly among the young and in the south, there has been a dramatic change" in national identity, observed Liao Dai-chi, a political expert at National Sun Yat-sen University. "Any politician has to stand with 'Taiwan identity' to win election."[73] KMT leaders—especially younger figures in the party—are reaching a similar conclusion. Even Lien Chan almost never mentioned reunification in his campaign for the presidency in 2004. Additionally, he campaigned in Minnanese and stressed his own ethnic Taiwanese upbringing.[74]

Ma Ying-Jeou, the charismatic KMT mayor of Taipei and widely regarded as the party's probable presidential candidate in 2008, concedes that expressing any support for the one-China concept would be political suicide in Taiwan.[75] Indeed, Ma's own position on the proper short- and medium-term relationship between Taiwan and the mainland is not dramatically different from the position that DPP partisans push. Ma's preferred model is the two Germanies during the latter stages of the Cold War, when both states had membership in the United Nations and were recognized by most countries in the international system. Few DPP politicians would quarrel with that proposal, but the model is anathema to PRC leaders. In short, Beijing might find a KMT administration (especially if Ma is the president) only slightly more palatable than the Chen administration.

The results of the popular vote also confirmed the weakness of the political factions that wish to accommodate Beijing. The DPP's share of the vote rose slightly, from 38.57 percent in 2001 to 39.56 percent in 2004, while the TSU's declined from 5.78 percent to 5.33 percent. The KMT's share went from 30.22 percent to 35.11 percent. But the PFP's share plunged by a quarter—from 20.44 percent to 15.11 percent. The ardently pro-reunification New Party kept its minuscule vote total (0.44 percent) steady.[76] The pathetic status of the New Party is itself testimony to the trend in Taiwanese opinion. In 1998 the New Party had polled a respectable 4.89 percent, and in 1995 it had been a significant political force with 12.8 percent. The virtual demise of the New Party and the growing weakness of the PFP suggests that there is almost no constituency for a staunchly pro-reunification position and not much support even for the more cautious, conditional variety.

The bottom line is that Taiwanese voters appeared uneasy about following Chen's increasingly assertive separatist agenda, much less the even more brazen agenda of the TSU. At the same time, they seemed even less enthusiastic about PFP's "soft on the PRC" stance. Beijing could take some relief in the election results, but only a little. "China (and the United States) will be breathing a temporary sigh of relief," said Zhu Fend, the head of the international security program at Peking University.[77]

TAIWAN'S REACTION TO CHINA'S ANTI-SECESSION LAW

Within days after Taiwan's legislative elections, Hu Jintao's government in Beijing responded by placing before the National People's Congress a proposed law that would ban any province from seceding from the PRC—a measure that was clearly directed against Taiwan. Taiwanese officials reacted angrily and made it clear that they would not be intimidated. In doing so, they accurately reflected the views of the Taiwanese people. A poll taken by Taiwan Thinktank in December 2004 revealed that 80 percent of respondents considered the law entirely illegitimate, and 64 percent believed that the enactment of anti-secession legislation would escalate cross-Strait tensions. Some 60 percent believed that it would be necessary for Taiwan to pass a "defensive resolution" if it appeared that the anti-secession law might endanger the island's sovereignty. And nearly 90 percent called on all political parties to unite to face this latest threat posed by the mainland.[78]

In a New Year's address, Chen Shui-bian was especially blunt and confrontational in responding to the anti-secession law. He charged that the law was designed to provide a legal basis for Beijing to unilaterally dictate the outcome of cross-Strait issues and perhaps even to justify an invasion of Taiwan. Chen did his utmost to portray the move as doing far more than threatening Taiwan's security. "Such actions will not only unilaterally change the status quo of peace in the Taiwan Strait, but will also pose the greatest threat to regional stability and world peace."[79]

His choice of language was not accidental. The reference to "unilaterally" changing the status quo was a direct appeal to the Bush administration and the American people. Since Bush's statement in the White House Rose Garden in December 2003, the administration had repeatedly invoked the formula of no unilateral changes. Chen was challenging Bush (and stirring up Taiwan's supporters in Bush's political base) not to apply that standard only to the Taiwanese government. His warning that Beijing's move threatened the peace of the entire region was designed to invoke the language of the Taiwan Relations Act and perhaps to appeal for political support from other nations in East Asia.

But Chen did not direct his statement only to third parties. He had a blunt warning for Beijing as well. "We once again urge the Chinese Communist Party authorities not to underestimate the will of the Taiwan people in defending the sovereignty, security and dignity" of their country.[80] If Beijing had hoped to intimidate Chen's government by introducing the anti-secession law, it had clearly failed.

Once again, though, Chen demonstrated that his policy was more nuanced than one of unrelenting confrontation toward the PRC. Two days later, the Taiwanese government mandated the Taipei Air Transportation Association to conduct talks with Beijing on authorizing charter flights between the mainland and Taiwan over the Lunar New Year in February. Although cross-Strait charter flights had been organized in 2003, Beijing had rejected all overtures from Taipei regarding the issue since that time. This time, though, China announced through the Xinhua news agency that it would "work hard to promote the launching of charter flights across the Taiwan Strait during the Lunar New Year, and welcomes Taiwan people to come for talks over the issue."[81] Although the awkward formulation of welcoming "Taiwan people" confirmed that Beijing remained as determined as ever to give no recognition to Chen's administration, the move was a welcome respite after months of major tensions.

Taiwan's Mainland Affairs Council expressed satisfaction at the response, even though it couldn't resist a jibe that Beijing had "finally reacted to our appeals."[82] To those who pay attention to diplomatic nuances, though, it was clear that Taiwan had made the primary concession. Taipei had always insisted that talks on direct flights should be conducted on a governmental level. Beijing had insisted on "civilian" talks. By authorizing the Taipei Air Transportation Association to conduct the negotiations, the Chen administration had implicitly agreed to the PRC's formulation. Nevertheless, the Mainland Affairs Council tried to put the best face on the outcome and emphasized that flights should be conducted with the participation of Taiwanese as well as mainland Chinese airlines, in both directions, and without stopovers. (For years there have been de facto air routes between Taiwan and the mainland through Hong Kong.)

Progress on the air flights issue came on the occasion of the death of 87-year-old Koo Chen-fu, who had been Taiwan's chief negotiator with the PRC during the early and mid-1990s when tensions between Beijing and Taipei were far lower. Koo, chairman of the Straits Exchange Foundation, and his PRC counterpart, Wang Daohan, conducted the highest-level cross-Straits dialogue since 1949 when they first met in Singapore in 1993. They met on several occasions in the following years, but such meetings became increasingly pointless after the imbroglio over Lee Teng-hui's visit to the United States in 1995 and the extreme tensions that accompanied Taiwan's presidential election in 1996. Beijing terminated the meetings entirely in 1999 after Lee described the relationship between

Taiwan and the PRC as "special state to state relations."[83] They had never re-sumed. Both Taipei and Beijing seemed intent on using Koo's death as an oppor-tunity for at least tentative dialogue on a limited issue. Negotiators concluded an agreement in mid-January authorizing forty-eight charter flights between Janu-ary 29 and February 20 involving six Chinese and six Taiwanese airlines.[84] Tai-wanese officials immediately called on Beijing to engage in dialogue on a wide range of economic issues.[85]

The easing of tensions was certainly welcomed in Washington and through-out East Asia, but only the most optimistic believed that the gestures significantly or permanently altered the confrontational environment between the two sides. Indeed, many influential Taiwanese thought that the agreement, while positive, would not necessarily lead to an improvement in ties between Taipei and the mainland. "It can help to reduce tension–to create a friendly atmosphere," said George Tsai, an international relations fellow at National Chengchi University, but he added that it was "premature" to assume that it would lead to a break-through in relations. In particular, he doubted whether "Taiwan will go any fur-ther at this moment unless we can get some political benefit out of it."[86] Cheng Hsiao-meng, a Taiwanese businessman, expressed similar caution. "We'll have to wait and see if this is a breakthrough that will start more improvements in cross-Strait relations, or just a short, temporary change," he concluded.[87]

In a matter of days, developments confirmed the caution that Tsai and Cheng had expressed. In an interview with Japan's *Mainichi Shimbun*, Chen Shui-bian warned that Beijing's proposed anti-secession law was alienating Taiwan's population, citing a poll by the Mainland Affairs Council that showed that 83 percent of respondents strongly opposed the legislation as a basis for reunifica-tion. Chen suggested that such overwhelmingly negative sentiment could cause the Taiwanese people to "take to the streets" and push for passage of an "anti-annexation law," or perhaps even to force the government to call a counter-referendum on the topic.[88] The latter threat was likely to confirm the worst impression Beijing had held from the beginning about the DPP's motives in inau-gurating the use of referenda. Joseph Wu, chairman of the Mainland Affairs Council, made an equally pointed warning to the PRC a few days after Chen's comments. "If China ignores Taiwan people's reaction to the anti-secession law and insists on pushing through the law, " Wu cautioned, "it will ruin the opportu-nity to improve relations brought by the Lunar New Year charters."[89]

Yet Chen again showed that there was some nuance to his policy. To the sur-prise of many observers both in Taiwan and abroad, he entered into negotiations with James Soong to resolve the gridlock in the Legislative Yuan. In late Febru-ary, they forged an understanding on the cross-Straits issue and other matters.

Although the understanding contained more than its share of ambiguity, it was apparent that Chen had softened his position on relations with China at least slightly, among other things agreeing to relax restrictions on business ties with the mainland.[90] In what was probably the most painful concession, he affirmed that any form of political ties—including eventual reunification—were possible with China.[91] Once again, it looked as though tensions between Taipei and Beijing might recede in Chen Shui-bian's second term.

Unfortunately, that optimism did not last long. The PRC leadership disregarded Taiwan's pointed warnings about the proposed anti-secession law, and on March 14, 2005, the National People's Congress passed that measure with no dissenting votes and only two abstentions. Although the law did little more than restate provisions already contained in the 2000 and 2004 defense white papers regarding the conditions under which the PRC might use force to prevent Taiwanese independence (see chapter 5), the reaction in Taiwan was immediate and vehement. The popular response culminated on March 26 with a massive demonstration in Taipei organized by the DPP against the legislation. Estimates of the turnout ranged from two-hundred-fifty thousand to one million, with most estimates around five-hundred thousand to six-hundred thousand.[92]

Although Taiwan's quarrelsome political parties had displayed uncharacteristic solidarity in opposing and denouncing the anti-secession law, that solid front did not last long. Just days after the mass demonstration in Taipei, Chiang Pin-kung, vice chairman of the KMT, arrived in China at the head of a KMT delegation for a goodwill visit. The PRC regime responded with extraordinarily conciliatory gestures, indicating that Chiang's superior, Lien Chan, would be welcome in the PRC at any time. Chiang and Chinese leaders even concluded an informal ten- point statement between the two political parties dealing mainly with economic issues, including one provision in which the PRC promised better treatment for Taiwan's agricultural exports.[93]

The reaction from Chen's government was swift and hostile. Chen scorned the labors of the KMT delegation, and described any agreements reached as meaningless. His reaction was relatively mild compared to those of some of his DPP colleagues. Chen Chin-jun, the DPP's whip in the Legislative Yuan, challenged the KMT in a classic "do you still beat your wife?" manner: "Can the KMT tell the country if they are going there to pay tribute to the communist party? Or is it a trip of surrender and betrayal?"[94] The DPP's anger extended beyond rhetorical salvos. Just days after Chiang's delegation returned, the Justice Ministry announced that it was investigating Chiang and his colleagues for violating the Mainland Relations Act. Under that act, punishment could include stiff fines and jail terms up to five years for citizens who negotiate with PRC authorities without government authorization. Justice Minister Shih Mao-lin also indicated that members of the delegation would be investigated for treason, which carries a maximum penalty of life imprisonment.[95] Although prosecution on the treason charge seemed unlikely, the reaction of Chen's government to the trip revealed the depth of anger by pro-independence forces and their determination to prevail over elements advocating a conciliatory policy toward Beijing.

On balance, the political and security environment in the Taiwan Strait is growing more tense and unpredictable. Emile C. J. Sheng argues that Chen's government will try to push symbolic measures rather than ones of great substantive importance on the independence front. But he concedes that "Taiwan might be overly optimistic in relying on U.S. support or similarly overestimate Beijing's level of tolerance, thereby leading to accidents not within the government's plan."[96] The former chairman of the DPP, Hsu Hsin-liang, is even more worried. He stated flatly in August 2004 that "under the leadership of Chen Shui-bian, cross-Strait relations will remain in deadlock and, eventually, a war will be inevitable."[97] One certainly hopes that Hsu is wrong, but there are ample signs that the danger of such an outcome is rising.

As the *Atlantic Monthly*'s Trevor Corson notes: "So far the United States has managed to prevent armed conflict by pressuring Taiwan not to declare independence. But as Taiwan's democracy matures, America's ability to influence the island is fading."[98] In reality, Taiwan is unlikely to declare independence formally. But developments in recent years make clear that the Taiwanese are taking a variety of actions that stop just short of that ultimate provocation. In doing so, Taiwan is contributing to steadily escalating tensions. At some point a Taiwanese government may miscalculate and provoke Beijing beyond endurance. To make matters worse, the PRC seems to be getting decidedly more prickly on the Taiwan issue.

CHAPTER 5

SOME OMINOUS TRENDS IN THE PRC

When National Security Advisor Condoleezza Rice stopped in Beijing on her trip to northeast Asia in July 2004, she undoubtedly hoped that the North Korea nuclear threat would be the primary issue on the agenda. Instead she got an earful from former president Jiang Zemin—at the time still the head of the People's Republic of China's powerful Central Military Commission—about China's views regarding Taiwan. Jiang stressed that China was committed to the "one country, two systems" formula for Taiwan's status and that Beijing would "never" tolerate an independent Taiwan. He went on to chastise the Bush administration for its policy of selling sophisticated arms to Taiwan—most recently submarines to patrol the Taiwan Strait and radar that can penetrate deeply into PRC territory and facilitate strikes by Taiwanese aircraft.

The substance of such comments was not new, but the tone was unusually firm and uncompromising. Moreover, Jiang's statements are only one in a series of recent developments that suggest that Beijing's patience on the Taiwan issue is running out.

A ten-member congressional delegation visiting China in early January 2005 picked up on the same troubling signals regarding Taiwan that Jiang had conveyed to Rice the previous summer. Representative Jim Cooper (D-TN) said that he returned from the trip "much more worried than I had been before." Cooper said that he was struck that "virtually every meeting [with Chinese officials] was consumed with their concern about Taiwan." Cooper and Representative Randy Forbes were especially disturbed by how often their Chinese hosts denounced U.S. arms sales to Taipei and warned that if Taiwan continued its efforts toward independence, China would have to use "nonpeaceful means" to halt that trend.[1]

Long gone is the cavalier attitude of PRC leader Deng Xiaoping, who said in the 1970s that the Taiwan issue could remain unresolved for one hundred years without unduly upsetting Beijing.[2] As Taiwan has democratized and accelerated its quest for international recognition, Beijing has become noticeably less sanguine. Indications of this change are both obvious and subtle. One example of the latter is that the tough views of "unofficial" figures such as Professor Yan Xuetong of Tsinghua University in Beijing have become increasingly prominent. Previously, Yan's hard-line views often put him at odds with the more circumspect official line. Yan has long argued that China should confront the Taiwan more urgently and directly, because the island's separatist instincts, instead of being diluted by closer economic ties with the mainland, have continued to strengthen. In recent years, official rhetoric has moved noticeably closer to his views.[3]

Indeed, as the one-hundredth anniversary of Deng's birth approached, PRC officials sought to invoke the prestige of his name behind a hard-line policy toward Taiwan. "Deng stressed in the mid-1980s that China should never abandon military means as an option in resolving the Taiwan issue, which could deter Taiwan's separatists," the Xinhua news agency quoted Chen Yunlin, director of the Taiwan Affairs Office.[4] Notably, Chen made no mention of Deng's occasional remarks that China need be in no rush to recover Taiwan.

CHINA'S HARDENING POSITION, 2000–2004

This harder-line policy has been building for some time. Indeed, it predates the election of Chen Shui-bian as Taiwan's president, a development which one would have expected to provoke Beijing. An early indicator that greater urgency was being given to Taiwan policy was a speech by PRC Vice Premier Qian Qichen on January 28, 2000, setting out China's basic principles on the Taiwan issue:

- The two sides of the Taiwan Strait must engage in political talks under the "one-China" principle;
- "Taiwan independence" can only mean war;
- The framework is "peaceful reunification" and "one country, two systems" as well as the "one-China" principle;
- Under the "one-China" principle, other issues, such as Taiwan's international participation and its political status, could be discussed by the two sides;
- China would adopt a more liberal concept of its "one country, two systems" policy with Taiwan than it had with Hong Kong and Macao;

- China was willing to discuss the issue of "international space for economic, cultural and social activities for Taiwan that suits it"; and
- Other countries should not do anything that would cause tensions or im-
  pede the reunification process. In particular, the United States should
  cease selling Taiwan advanced weaponry.[5]

Although there were some carrots in Qian's speech, there were a lot more
visible sticks. The bottom line was that China was willing to give fairly generous
surrender terms to Taiwan, but the willingness of the island to surrender and
agree to the principle of eventual reunification was an ironclad prerequisite. That
point became even clearer a few weeks later when the Chinese government issued
an eleven thousand–word white paper on the Taiwan issue. As Qian had done, the
white paper made some conciliatory gestures to Taiwan. Most notably, it did not
demand that Taipei rescind its two-states formula before negotiations could
begin. Indeed, it indicated that cross-Strait dialogue could commence on an
equal footing and with a flexible agenda. Those conciliatory gestures were over-
shadowed, though, by a section outlining the "three situations" in which China
would use force against Taiwan. The first two were familiar from previous PRC
statements: Beijing would resort to force if a turn of events led to the separation
of Taiwan from the mainland (i.e., a clear move toward formal independence),
and if foreign invasion or other measures took place that would lead to Taiwan's
separation. The third situation was unprecedented, however. The white paper
emphasized that the Taiwanese authorities could not expect to indefinitely stall
negotiations for reunification. For the first time, Beijing indicated that it might
consider such delaying tactics by themselves sufficient grounds for resorting to
military force.[6]

The election of Chen Shui-bian caught Chinese leaders a bit off guard. In
the months leading up to the March 2000 election, the PRC regime seemed to
assume that Taiwanese voters would elect Kuomintang candidate Lien Chan. It
was not until February that they began to worry seriously about a Democratic
Progressive Party victory. When Chen was proclaimed the winner on March 18,
the Communist Party's Politburo held an urgent meeting that same evening. Following that meeting the government issued a short statement on Chinese radio
and television stating that Beijing would "listen to what Chen says and watch out
for what he does." The statement also warned the DPP that election outcome
would not change the status of Taiwan as an irrevocable part of China. Later,
Chinese officials made it clear that they would watch Chen's inaugural speech to
see if he explicitly agreed with the one-China principle. They made it clear that
Chen's apparent position that one-China was simply "a topic for discussion"

rather than a guiding principle was utterly unacceptable.[7] As noted in chapter 4, Chen offered a number of conciliatory comments in his inaugural address but steadfastly refused to endorse the one-China formula. Consequently, Beijing refused to deal with him or any member of his government.

At the National Conference on the Taiwan Issue held in late March 2000, PRC officials concluded that Chen would try to perpetuate the status quo in which there were neither moves toward reunification nor a formal declaration of independence. Within that political twilight zone, Taiwan's independence movement would use the time to gradually erase the cultural and sentimental ties between Taiwan and the mainland. Beijing, the leaders concluded, would have to be prepared to wage a long-term struggle against those independence forces.[8]

At the Beidaihe meetings of the Central Committee of the Communist Party in July and August, President Jiang Zemin also counseled patience for a long-term struggle. Economic development must take priority, Jiang stressed, because as China grew more powerful economically, time would be on its side in dealing with the Taiwan issue. Only when China was "fully prepared to reclaim it by force would there be a chance for peaceful reunification."[9] Until then, the PRC had to use more moderate political forces in Taiwan to obstruct the pro- independence faction. It also would put pressure on the United States to rein-in Taiwanese leaders.

In the intervening years, the PRC has increased its confrontational posture. Throughout Chen Shui-bian's first term, Beijing tried to isolate the Taiwanese leader and his party. Beijing made it clear that DPP visitors were not welcome, and that there would be no dialogue with Taipei unless and until Chen's administration explicitly embraced the one-China formula. The PRC consistently spurned even the most conciliatory initiatives that Chen offered.

When Taipei pushed the envelope at all on the independence issue, Beijing reacted with shrill warnings. Chen's proposal to hold referenda on security issues especially infuriated the PRC. Not only did that proposal serve to highlight Taiwan's increasingly democratic political features—which an authoritarian regime trying to keep a restless population on the mainland in line and to deal with rambunctious democrats in Hong Kong regarded as inherently threatening—but Chinese leaders believed that Chen was setting a precedent for even more assertive referenda topics later on. Their warnings, both to Taipei and Washington, about probable adverse consequences, were uncompromising. The referenda, said Tang Jiaxuan, a former foreign minister and now state councilor, would not only push the Taiwanese people "further to the brink of danger," but threatened the stability of the entire region.[10] Beijing was backing up its strong rhetoric with unpleasant measures as well. The previous month, PRC authorities had detained twenty-four people, including a number of Taiwanese businessmen, on charges that they had been spying for Taipei.

CHINA CONFRONTS A SECOND TERM BY CHEN SHUI-BIAN

Just before the inauguration of Chen Shui-bian for a second term as Taiwan's president in May 2004, the PRC agency in charge of policy toward Taiwan issued a lengthy and revealing statement. On the one hand, it offered a number of prospective benefits to Taiwan if the regime there accepted the principle of one China. On the other hand, the statement made it clear that the consequences to Taiwan would be dire if the island continued its separatist ways. There was also a distinct implication that the issue must be settled in years, not decades.

Beijing maintained an uncompromising line after Chen was reelected. Responding to the October 10 National Day speech by Chen proposing dialogue with the PRC, the state-run newspaper *China Daily* ran a front-page commentary citing the conclusion of mainland scholars that the Taiwanese leader was merely "playing word games." Typical of the assessment of such experts was the comment by Niu Jun, a professor of international relations at Peking University. "It's not goodwill. The framework of his entire statement is still Taiwan independence. It's a front. It's to assure the United States that he is trying to ease cross-Strait tensions."[11] The *China Daily* commentary concluded that Chen's overture was "too insincere and too vague to be treated seriously by the mainland."[12]

The PRC government waited three days before responding officially to Chen's speech, and when it did, the tone was no friendlier than the "unofficial" assessments. "When Chen Shui-bian says he wants to ease tensions, it is false. When he says he wants independence, it is true," Taiwan Affairs Office spokesman Zhang Mingqing told a news conference succinctly. When asked if he saw anything positive or conciliatory in Chen's speech, Zhang replied: "Can you reach that conclusion from the remarks I just made? I don't think so."[13] He added a blunt warning: "If Chen Shui-bian remains bent on sticking to his splittist and Taiwan independence activities, he will never bring peace and prosperity to the Taiwan compatriots, but will only bring great catastrophe."[14] Beijing's harsh response continued a long-standing pattern of rejecting out of hand even ostensibly conciliatory gestures from the DPP government in Taipei.

A month later, Wang Zaixi, vice minister at the Taiwan Affairs Office, offered an even more pointed warning to Taiwan. "I think it is unavoidable that tension will rise in the Taiwan Straits and [that] there may even be armed conflict . . . if the island keeps bumping Beijing's 'one-China' bottom line," said Wang. "The Chen Shui-bian authorities are exploiting our restraint on the

Taiwan issue." In particular, Wang contended that Taipei was exploiting the PRC's focus on developing the mainland's economy and on hosting the 2008 Olympics. He made it clear that the Taiwanese should not assume that the PRC government would not sacrifice both of those objectives if that step became necessary to prevent the island's independence. Wang warned that Taiwan's continuing flirtation with independence was "playing with fire." He concluded that "the coming few years will be a key and highly dangerous period in the development of the Taiwan situation. Cross-Straits relations will face a severe test."[15]

Such statements would have been troubling coming from any PRC official. But Wang was not just any official. In addition to leading the agency responsible for policy toward Taiwan, he was a People's Liberation Army major general before joining the Taiwan Affairs Office. It was reasonable to conclude that the tone of his remarks at least partly reflected the thinking of his PLA colleagues. That is more than a little ominous.

In addition to sending pointed warnings to the Taiwanese, Beijing was sending signals to Washington during the last half of 2004 that they wanted and expected the United States to restrain its Taiwanese client. Following Condoleezza Rice's trip to Beijing, the PRC embassy in Washington held a rare press conference to convey its concerns about aspects of the U.S.-China relationship, especially on the issue of Taiwan. While acknowledging that the United States officially adhered to a one-China policy, embassy spokesman Sun Weide added:

> However, we are gravely concerned over the recent U.S. moves on the Taiwan question. We strongly urge the U.S. side to stop selling advanced arms to Taiwan and cut the military links between the U.S. and Taiwan, stop any official exchanges with Taiwanese authorities, stop supporting Taiwan to join the international organizations where statehood is required. Only in this way can the stable development of the China-U.S. relations as well as the peace and stability across the Taiwan Strait be guaranteed.[16]

As the embassy statement suggested, PRC leaders were especially agitated about U.S. arms sales to Taiwan and any contacts between the U.S. and Taiwanese militaries. The latter point became evident in December 2004 when Washington decided to assign military officers to the American Institute in Taiwan—its de facto embassy in Taipei. That was the first time military personnel were stationed there since the United States broke formal diplomatic relations with Taipei in 1979. China immediately denounced the move. Foreign Ministry spokesman Liu Jianchao stated: "Whatever excuse or method the U.S. side uses to develop military relations with Taiwan violates the principles of the three Sino-U.S. joint communiqués, will encourage Taiwan separatist activities and harm the peace and stability in the Taiwan region as well as China-U.S. relations."[17]

———————•◦•◦•———————

The PRC adopted a somewhat lower-key approach to Taiwan's legislative elections in December 2004 than it had with previous presidential elections. Perhaps realizing that its threatening and blustering behavior leading up to the island's presidential elections in 1996, 2000, and 2004 had been counterproductive, this time Beijing said little about the political campaign. "Beijing has been very cool this time," stated Lo Chih-cheng, executive director of the Institute for National Policy Research in Taipei. "It's not that they necessarily understand democracy better. But they realize that their activities are counterproductive."[18]

Beijing's milder strategy seemed to pay off a little better.[19] Contrary to pre-election polls that had forecast that the DPP and its even more hard-line ally, the Taiwan Solidarity Union, would win a majority and take control of the legislature, the new body would have virtually the same makeup as the old, with the combination of the KMT and the People First Party controlling a majority of the seats. One might have thought that those results would have reassured leaders on the mainland. Chen's goal of rewriting the constitution seemed problematic with the legislature still controlled by his political opponents. Yet even the results of the December elections did not really please the PRC.

Beijing reacted cautiously, and, for a surprisingly long time, for the most part unofficially. The state-run *China Daily* featured analysts who warned that the outcome was merely a setback rather than a "decisive blow" to the DPP coalition. Wu Nengyuan, a scholar at the Fujian Academy of Social Sciences, emphasized that the key issue for the PRC was "whether Chen will stop his pro-independence push or forge ahead with his separatist" agenda. Wu and other analysts concluded that it was uncertain how Chen would react. Indeed, Wu speculated that "given his obstinate insistence on a pro-independence stance, Chen may step up his push for his separatist timetable."[20] Another expert was also pessimistic. "I don't think anyone can be too optimistic about Chen," said Shi Yin-hong, a foreign policy scholar at Qinghua University in Beijing. "This election should relax the atmosphere a little bit, but really there are even fewer reasons to try to reach an agreement with Chen now."[21]

There were certainly no olive branches forthcoming from Beijing following the December elections. The official response to the election results came three days later from Li Weiyi, spokesman for the Taiwan Affairs Office. In a briefing to reporters, Li argued that "Chen's separatist activities didn't win people's hearts.

The result of the election has shown that the majority of public opinion in Taiwan is for peace and for developing relations with China." But he stressed that "all that Chen has done" has been aimed at provoking Beijing. Therefore, a reduction of cross-Strait tension could occur only "if the authorities in Taiwan recognize that there is only one China in the world and Taiwan is part of it, and if they give up their Taiwan independence stance and stop Taiwan independence activities." He added an ominous warning: "The Chinese government will not sit, watch and do nothing if Chen Shui-bian continues his pro-independence activities."[22]

Although Beijing reserved its greatest hostility for Chen's government, it did not offer any olive branches to the KMT either. Much to the surprise of outside observers, the PRC in early January 2005 pressured Hong Kong to spurn a request from Taipei mayor Ma Ying-jeou for a visa to visit the city and speak at events organized by the University of Hong Kong.[23] Ma is not only a prominent KMT politician but is considered the party's leading candidate for the presidency in 2008. One would think that Beijing would be interested in cultivating ties with a KMT moderate and showing that it reserved its policy of frosty isolation only for Chen and other staunchly independence-minded officials. By pressuring Hong Kong to exclude Ma, it sent the opposite message. Indeed, the message was made even more stark given that Ma had previously been allowed to visit Hong Kong in 2000 and 2001.

Even Hong Kong political figures normally friendly to Beijing criticized the exclusion. James Tien, chairman of the pro-business Liberal Party, said that the government had squandered an opportunity to foster Taiwan's return to the mainland. Ma's visit would have been a good showcase for the one country, two systems concept, Tien argued.[24] A Taiwanese scholar relatively friendly to Beijing reached a similar conclusion. "This move will only reinforce the belief among the Taiwanese people that there is no way they can accept this regime," said George Tsai of the Institute for International Relations at Chengchi University. "Mr. Ma is one of the politicians in Taiwan who have been more acceptable to Beijing. Rejecting him just because of a few comments demonstrates that they do not understand Taiwanese popular opinion."[25]

BEIJING ESCALATES TENSIONS:
AN ANTI-SECESSION LAW AND A DEFENSE WHITE PAPER

The Ma episode was not the only, or even the most important, indication that Beijing's attitude toward Taiwan was hardening. Just days after the legislative elections, the PRC government took a more dramatic step that demonstrated clearly that it had no interest in offering peace overtures to Taipei. Beijing announced that legislation would be introduced in the Standing Committee of the National People's Congress explicitly prohibiting secession on the part of any Chinese province.[26] Since the NPC is purely a rubber stamp body for the Communist Party leadership, there was no doubt that the law would pass the Standing Committee easily, as it did in late December. The entire National People's Congress would consider final passage of the legislation in March 2005.

Although the measure had some relevance to Tibet and to the restless Muslim population in Xinjiang, it was clearly directed primarily at Taiwan. The possibility of legislation on the issue of secession had been rumored for months. Indeed, fellow travelers of the regime had urged the government since late 2002 to pass a "unification" law that would mandate the People's Liberation Army to take military action against Taiwan if the island continued to refuse to negotiate an end to its separation from the mainland. The Taiwan Affairs Office commented officially on such proposals in May 2004. "Unification is the common wish of the Chinese people, including [the] Taiwan people," Li Weiyi, a spokesman for the TAO stated. "China will seriously consider all suggestions for unification, including by legal means." If a unification law were proposed, "we will seriously consider it and adopt it," Li confirmed.[27] The PRC leadership apparently gauged both the domestic and international reaction to those hard-line proposals before deciding on a course of action. Although the exact language of the anti-secession law was not made public when it was introduced in the NPC, Beijing fostered the impression that it was a more moderate, watered down version of the reunification trial balloons.

Although it ultimately proved to be a more moderate proposal, the timing of its introduction was troubling. Although most outside observers believed that the pro–status quo vote in Taiwan had been in response to the PRC's more quiescent strategy,[28] officials in Beijing apparently reached a different conclusion. They believed that a majority of Taiwanese voters resisted the appeal of the DPP and TSU because they feared an adverse reaction from mainland China. Therefore, according to that logic, the proper course was to stimulate Taiwanese apprehension even further.[29] The anti-secession law was designed to do just that.

In addition to being part of a campaign of psychological warfare against Taiwan, the legislation was designed to eliminate any lingering ambiguity in Beijing's position. The Taiwanese people would be put on notice that if they continued to resist reunification and persisted in the "fiction" that the island was a country separate from the PRC, they were now in direct violation of Chinese law. At the time the legislation was introduced, it was not clear whether it would contain an explicit provision authorizing the People's Liberation Army to use military force to put down a secessionist effort, but even if there was no specific provision to that effect, that was the clear implication of the law.[30] Indeed, when rumors of a reunification law surfaced several months earlier, Chen Shui-bian himself was caustic. "It's too polite to call it a reunification law. The real connotation of the law is to use military force to annex Taiwan."[31]

Taiwan's supporters in the United States reacted harshly to the proposed anti-secession law. Heritage Foundation staffer John J. Tkacik concluded: "The new legislation, as with most exercises in Chinese foreign-policy legislation, is a propaganda tool designed for two audiences. First, it readies the Chinese people for war with Taiwan, and second, it will be trotted out and exhibited as a diplomatic lever whenever Americans point to the U.S. obligation" under the Taiwan Relations Act to defend the island. As such, Tkacik warned, "this proposed Chinese legislation is highly destabilizing."[32]

Not surprisingly, Taiwan's political leadership and public regarded the latest salvo from the PRC as extremely threatening. "The law means China is looking for a legal pretext for a future attack against the island, and for a unilateral change of the present situation," said Joseph Wu, chairman of Taiwan's Mainland Affairs Council. Wu warned PRC leaders not to be excessively emboldened by the results of Taiwan's legislative elections. "We call on China's authorities to think carefully. [China] cannot repeatedly misinterpret the Taiwanese people's love of peace and determination to oppose military threats."[33] Taiwan Vice President Annette Lu was equally grim about Beijing's legal maneuver. "They are using this method to announce to the world they will do anything to swallow up Taiwan and will establish the legal basis to do so," she told reporters.[34] Lu was contemptuous of the legislation, arguing that it would have no bearing on Taiwan because the island's status did not involve a case of future secession; Taiwan was already independent. China, she stated, had no legal or historical rights to the island.[35]

If, as one American journalist speculated, the legislation was designed to get Taiwan to take Beijing's willingness to use force to prevent the island's independence more seriously, it appears to be working in one sense.[36] Taiwanese officials concede that the law is designed to create a legal basis for possible use of force. But if Beijing believes that such a measure will intimidate the Taiwanese political elite, that appears to be yet another miscalculation. The question is whether a tougher anti-secession law is in the offing. Some "unofficial" PRC opinion leaders suggested that the proposed statute contain a provision setting a deadline for Taiwan to reunify with the mainland.[37] Hu Jintao's government decided not to go that far—yet. It is a step that cannot be ruled out, however, if Taiwan continues to ignore Beijing's increasingly explicit warnings.

That point became apparent again in late December when the Chinese government issued another defense white paper. The tone of the paper regarding the

Taiwan issue underscored the PRC's growing agitation about Taipei's recent pro-independence activities and a determination to halt them.

> The situation in the relations between the two sides of the Taiwan Straits is grim. The Taiwan authorities under Chen Shui-bian have recklessly challenged the status quo that both sides of the Straits belong to one and the same China, and markedly escalated the "Taiwan independence" activities designed to split China. Incessantly trumpeting their separatist claim of "one country on each side" [of the Strait], they use referendum to engage in the separatist activities aimed at "Taiwan independence," incite hostility among the people on the island toward the mainland, and purchase large amounts of offensive weapons and equipment. They have not given up their attempt at "Taiwan independence" through the formulation of a so-called "new constitution for Taiwan." They are still waiting for the opportune moment to engineer a major "Taiwan independence" incident through the so-called "constitutional reform." The separatist activities of the "Taiwan independence" forces have increasingly become the biggest immediate threat to China's sovereignty and territorial integrity as well as peace and stability on both sides of the Taiwan Straits and the Asia-Pacific region as a whole.[38]

The white paper warned explicitly: "Should the Taiwan authorities go so far as to make a reckless attempt that constitutes a major incident of 'Taiwan independence,' the Chinese people and armed forces will resolutely and thoroughly crush it at any cost."[39] That passage was notable in that it implied that something less than a formal declaration of independence might provoke a military response. Yet it was not clear what might constitute a "major incident" of Taiwanese independence. The vague but obviously menacing tone of the document served to ratchet up tensions another notch.

Almost as important as the white paper itself were the explanatory comments made a few days later by Peng Guangqian, a major general at the PLA Academy of Military Science. Peng noted that the paper had devoted more ink than previous versions to the Taiwan question, and that it gave a "grimmer judgment" of the situation. In particular Peng argued, Chen Shui-bian's pro-independence activities were becoming "increasingly aggressive and public."[40] He warned that both the "desinification" pace of the independence movement and the drive for de jure independence needed to be watched and countered.

Peng also made explicit that China's definition of the status quo differed markedly from that held by the United States: "The Paper made it very clear that the status quo of the cross-Straits relations is that both sides of the Straits belong to one and the same China, a status quo not defined by other countries such as the United States, nor by the Taiwan leaders."[41] That was a startling definition;

Beijing's conception of the status quo does not mean the current arrangement with Taiwan's ambiguous status, it means acceptance by all parties of the one-China principle. That means that China and the United States (and Taiwan) are talking about very different things when they speak of preserving the status quo. For example, Joseph Wu argues that the actual status quo is Taiwan independence. As supporting evidence he emphasizes that, since 1996, Taiwan has held fully democratic elections "within specified boundaries by specified citizens for a government exercising exclusive control over a territory."[42] One wonders whether that huge gap in perception on an extremely important issue is fully comprehended in the three capitals.

Perhaps most troubling, Peng asserted that the white paper rejected Taiwan's proposal for confidence-building measures in the military sphere to ease tensions and reduce the danger of accidents or miscalculations in the Taiwan Strait. He noted that Taipei's proposal failed to mention the one-China principle and the prospect of reunification. "Therefore, for the mainland such kind of discussion is without foundation. There can be no peace without reunification." Terming the Taiwan suggestion "a sheer deception," Peng maintained that "the discussion of a confidence-building mechanism in the military field is possible only if it is based on the foundation of the one-China principle. Failing this, there would be no peace."[43]

A FEW ENCOURAGING SIGNS

The defense white paper and Peng's grim interpretation caused 2004 to end on an especially tense and pessimistic note. Tensions between Taiwan and the mainland did recede slightly in early 2005. To the surprise of many observers, Beijing responded favorably to Taipei's overture to authorize direct charter airline flights between the island and the mainland over the lunar New Year. After brief and productive negotiations between nongovernmental bodies (a point that Beijing insisted upon to avoid dealing directly with Chen Shui-bian's government) an agreement was reached, and the first direct flights in fifty-six years took place. At the same time, China agreed to send senior envoys to the funeral of Koo Chen-fu, Taiwan's chief negotiator on cross-Strait relations during the 1990s.[44] Beijing's offer of condolences and the dispatch of senior envoys was clearly meant to harken back to a period when there were fewer tensions across the Strait.

Perhaps more significant, Beijing seemed to backtrack a little from its previous refusal to talk to Chen or any official of his government. According to Wang Zaixi, a vice minister of the Taiwan Affairs Office: "We have no bias against talking with any particular person, nor will we be unwilling to talk just because someone is in power."[45] Summarizing a speech by Jia Qinglin, a member of the Communist Party Politburo's Standing Committee and generally considered the number four figure in the party's hierarchy, Wang stated: "We are open on who to negotiate with and what to negotiate." However, even that slightly more conciliatory approach was carefully hedged. Talks could begin with any Taiwan leaders "regardless of his past rhetoric," but only "as long as he starts now to unequivocally recognize the 1992 consensus that upholds the one-China principle." If a Taiwan leader did that, "the cross-Strait dialogue and negotiations could resume right away, and any matter could be put on the table."[46]

The PRC's willingness to talk to Chen or his representatives at all was mildly encouraging, and Beijing did retreat from the insulting language it usually used toward him. According to Wang: "Chairman Jia said we are of the view that the vast DPP membership is different from the handful of 'Taiwan independence' diehards." Therefore, "[t]he DPP members are welcome to visit the mainland in a proper capacity."[47] But China's was still insisting on Chen's acceptance of the one-China formula as a prerequisite for talks, referring to the 1992 meeting in Hong Kong when both sides verbally accepted the one-China principle but disagreed about what that principle meant.

That formulation and the tone of the comments by Wang and Jia opened the door to compromise a crack, but only a crack. It seemed unlikely that Chen's government would accept the one-China demand in any form. Sheng Lijun explains why even moderate Taiwanese have been a bit wary of the one-China principle.

> To the DPP leaders, accepting this principle constitutes a denial of their long-held party ideology and is politically disastrous. Their concern is that Beijing may not be satisfied with a nominal acceptance, without raising the ante by demanding more concrete policies. If thus "trapped," they would be led by the nose by Beijing along the no-return track of "one-China."[48]

Given the pronounced allergy of DPP types regarding the one-China principle, a truly meaningful dialogue between the two sides still seems a considerable distance away, despite Beijing's slightly softer language.

Indeed, following the passage of the anti-secession law, Beijing seemed to return to the strategy adopted by the Communist Party hierarchy in 2000 of trying to form a common front with more moderate elements in Taiwan to isolate Chen Shui-bian and the DPP. In March 2005, the PRC welcomed KMT vice chairman Chiang Pin-kung on a "party to party" visit to the mainland. Throughout Chiang's visit, his PRC hosts could not have been more hospitable, eventually negotiating a ten-point statement of common principles. Chiang's trip paved the way for a visit by KMT chairman Lien Chan at the end of April.[49] (James Soong, the leader of the People First Party, would come to the mainland in early May). Once again, the PRC political leadership was at its conciliatory best. That approach fostered the image that the KMT and the PRC were Chinese compatriots that had simply been separated by war and circumstances and should now seek reconciliation. The Chinese media began to publicize accounts of KMT achievements in the 1920s and 1930s—including the efforts of Nationalist forces to resist the Japanese invaders during the latter decade. That treatment was in marked contrast to the usual vitriolic portrayals of the KMT as a corrupt, vicious, and venal party.

The underlying message that Beijing was conveying was not especially subtle. To the Taiwanese people, the PRC was emphasizing that it was prepared to work with more moderate political forces on Taiwan. Beijing even dropped hints from time to time that it would be willing to open a dialogue with Chen and the DPP—if that faction adopted the KMT's approach. It was an effective strategy, at least in terms of dividing Taiwanese opinion.[50] From Beijing's standpoint, it was a win-win approach. Not only did it sow dissension among the Taiwanese, but the PRC appeared (to the United States and other foreign observers) to be adopting a refreshingly conciliatory policy in contrast to the tensions it had exacerbated with the passage of the anti-secession law.

BEIJING'S GROWING IMPATIENCE

None of the conciliatory atmospherics in early 2005 altered the reality that the PRC is becoming increasingly insistent about resolving the Taiwan issue. That point became even more evident with the passage of the anti-secession law by the National People's Congress on March 14, 2005. Some of the language was conciliatory. Article 1 of the statute asserted that the law was designed to promote "peaceful national reunification," and maintain "peace and stability in the Taiwan Straits" as well as "checking" Taiwanese separatism. Likewise, article 5 asserted that a strategy to "reunify the country through peaceful means best serves the fundamental interests of compatriots on both sides of the Taiwan Straits." It also offered reassurances that the PRC "shall do its utmost with maximum sincerity to achieve a peaceful reunification."[51] Other portions of the act emphasized a desire for dialogue and negotiations with the Taiwanese—and went into rather surprising specifics on those points.

Much of the language elsewhere in the statute was uncompromising and hawkish, however. Article 2 made it clear that "the state will never allow the 'Taiwan independence' secessionist forces to make Taiwan secede from China under any name or by any means." And the heart of the act, article 8, made it plain that Beijing was determined to prevail, by whatever means necessary, on the issue of reunification. "In the event that the 'Taiwan independence' secessionist forces should act under any name or by any means to cause the fact of Taiwan's secession from China, or that major incidents entailing Taiwan's secession from China should occur, or that possibilities of a peaceful reunification should be completely exhausted, the state shall employ non-peaceful means and other necessary measures to protect China's sovereignty and territorial integrity."[52]

The PRC leadership may have miscalculated the reaction to the anti-secession law, both in Taiwan and throughout the international community. The Taiwanese public responded with vehement defiance (see chapter 4), and Washington issued a statement sharply critical of the statute. Perhaps most troubling to the PRC, leaders of major powers in the European Union strongly criticized the decision to pass such legislation and indicated that the proposal to lift the EU arms embargo against China (passed after the Tiananmen Square bloodshed), which had seemed a near certainty a few weeks earlier, was now being postponed.[53] The EU's reaction may well have been a factor leading to Beijing's more conciliatory measures in April and May—including the PRC's efforts to reach out to Taiwan's opposition parties.

Beijing also is backing up the determined language of the defense white paper and the anti-secession law with substantive military measures. The PRC has expanded deployment of missiles on its side of the Taiwan Strait, and now appears to have more than six hundred missiles arrayed against Taiwan. In the summer of 2004, Chinese soldiers practiced an amphibious invasion, conducting mock air, sea, and ground operations on Dongshan, a densely populated island off the mainland coast.[54] Perhaps most ominous, there are reports that the PRC has begun a program to build a large number of amphibious landing craft. One must question whether the Beijing authorities would expend considerable financial resources on such a program unless they were at least considering the option of using force against Taiwan. In addition, the defense white paper issued in December 2004 confirmed that the air force was continuing to switch its emphasis from the defense of China to both "offensive and defensive operations."[55] Finally, as discussed in chapter 7, China is steadily modernizing its military forces, focusing especially on techniques of asymmetrical warfare that would make a U.S. attempt to shield Taiwan from coercion both dangerous and problematic.

There are indications of a growing sense of urgency on the part of the PRC elite. Robert Marquand, a correspondent with the *Christian Science Monitor*, attributes that change to an assessment of developments on Taiwan.

One reason for Beijing's sudden new threatening talk about Taiwan is an analysis at the highest echelons of government here that Taiwan is indeed rapidly consolidating a separate identity in a manner and at a speed that is impossible for Beijing to reverse. Chen's victory on March 20 was a wake up call here. That both major parties in Taiwan pushed a pro-Taiwan identity message contradicted years of party rhetoric that pro-Taiwan feelings were limited to a small group of disgruntled dissidents.[56]

There are also signs that the Chinese believe that the United States may be so tied down with other commitments that it either would not or could not defend Taiwan. Marquand detected a disturbing attitude among Chinese opinion leaders. An argument "heard in more elite circles" was that the United States would be unable to respond effectively to an attack on Taiwan because of Iraq and other missions.[57] And some members of the political elite seem rather sanguine about the probable U.S. and international reaction. Yan Xuetong, Tsinghua University professor and a strong advocate of military action, argues that a military venture designed to bring Taipei to the bargaining table instead of conquering the island would get limited international attention–"something like the Israeli-Palestinian conflict."[58] That kind of reaction Beijing could absorb. Even a more intense reaction might be manageable. One PRC expert conceded that the world would react badly to a Chinese military assault, but soon enough "everyone will get over it." Marquand notes that "pro-military thinkers bank heavily on this point."[59]

Beijing also seems to believe that it could use its growing economic leverage as well as military power to deter the United States from intervening in a conflict between the PRC and Taiwan. China's central bank is an extremely large purchaser of U.S. Treasury notes and bonds, and is now one of the principal funding sources for Washington's chronic and growing budget deficits. If China threatened to stop purchasing U.S. government debt (much less if the PRC began to dump its existing holdings), the impact on interest rates in the United States and the value of the dollar would be extremely negative. True, the financial effect on China would not be pleasant either, since the value of the dollars it already holds would decline sharply. For that reason, Beijing is unlikely ever to take such a step just for economic reasons. But using its financial position as a political club because of an emotional noneconomic issue—such as the desire to deter the United States from interfering with Beijing's efforts to recover Taiwan—is another matter entirely. Chinese leaders may be overestimating their financial leverage on the United States, but if they believe that it is a useful tool they are likely to use it— or at least threaten to do so—during a crisis over Taiwan.

It should not be surprising if Beijing's desire to regain Taiwan is growing more insistent. Taiwan's status is a hot-button issue for most mainland Chinese.

Even those Chinese who are not especially fond of the Communist regime tend to believe that the island is rightfully part of China. From their perspective, Japan stole the province from China in 1895, and, by shielding the island militarily, the United States prevented reunification following the defeat of Chiang Kai-shek's Nationalist forces in 1949.

As the PRC grows stronger economically and militarily, it is logical that the determination to regain the lost province would also grow. As mentioned, Chinese leaders suspect (with good reason) that time is not on their side. Younger Taiwanese in particular regard the mainland as a foreign country and have little enthusiasm for reunification. Beijing fears that the prospect of regaining Taiwan may be lost forever if action is not taken relatively soon. The Taiwan issue also is caught up in the larger issue of Chinese nationalism and identity. Scholar Chien-min Chao contends that with the decline of Communism as a value system, mainland China "is once again searching for an identity—a task unfulfilled since the late Qing dynasty." Chao sees that "the rise of economic power, the craving for a reincarnation of its ancient hegemonic empire, and anti-West nationalist sentiments have all converged" to create a potentially explosive mixture.[60] Regaining Taiwan is the chief goal as well as the leading symbol of that reborn nationalism and assertiveness.

Thomas Christensen, a professor of international affairs at Princeton University, makes the proper distinction about Chinese attitudes regarding Taiwan. "I don't think that China *wants* to use force," he told the *Atlantic Monthly* following a trip to the mainland in late 2004. But he had just returned from his fourth trip to China in a two-year period, and the mood he had encountered while speaking privately with assorted Chinese experts was decidedly pessimistic. "What I heard on several occasions," Christensen stated, "is that [the experts saw] a much more serious consideration of actual conflict with the United States over Taiwan."[61]

Christensen is probably right that the PRC would be most reluctant to initiate a conflict over Taiwan. China would certainly have a lot to lose by taking that step.[62] Even if Beijing managed to avoid a military clash with the United States, an attack on Taiwan would certainly disrupt the crucial and rewarding economic relationship the PRC has developed with America over the past quarter century. The upsurge of anger in the United States against China following the Tiananmen Square massacre in 1989 would be mild compared to the public and congressional reaction to a PRC military assault on democratic Taiwan. Any attempt to coerce Taiwan in that fashion would lead to public pressure and irresistible congressional momentum for comprehensive U.S. economic sanctions against the PRC. There would also be strong demands to break diplomatic relations with Beijing.

In other words, the U.S.–China relationship would be in danger of regressing at the very least to the surly hostility that existed before the rapprochement in the 1970s. Beijing is almost certainly aware of the probable economic and diplomatic consequences. And, of course, there is the danger that the United States would intervene militarily if China moved against Taiwan. That would create the prospect of a military clash that would produce substantial casualties and poison U.S.–China relations for decades, regardless of which side won. Moreover, from the PRC's perspective, there is a serious risk that it would lose such a military confrontation with the United States, with all the adverse domestic political consequences that could have for the Communist regime.

Because of those dangers, Chinese leaders would not cavalierly adopt a strategy of military coercion against Taiwan. But the prospect of permanently losing Taiwan is deemed even more unacceptable. If the Taiwanese government continues its current course, the PRC may conclude that it has no choice but to incur the risks associated with taking drastic action. The evidence may be subtle, but it is increasingly difficult to ignore that Chinese leaders are beginning to think in those terms.

Michael D. Swaine, a senior associate at the Carnegie Endowment for International Peace, aptly summarizes the PRC's attitude regarding Taiwan. Although China would prefer to avoid conflict over Taiwan, "this does not mean that it would be unprepared to go to war over the island. For China's leaders, the Taiwan issue is inextricably related to national self-respect and regime survival." Beijing's primary goal is not to assert direct territorial rule over Taiwan, "but to avoid the island's permanent loss." Losing Taiwan would deal "a severe blow to Chinese prestige and self-confidence: Chinese leaders believe that their government would likely collapse in such a scenario." Swaine notes further that PRC leaders believe that even if their government did not collapse, the loss of Taiwan would "set a dangerous precedent for other potentially secessionist-minded areas of the country, such as Tibet, Xinjiang, and Inner Mongolia."[63]

In contrast to Swaine, many other outside observers fail to understand the depth of Chinese emotions on the Taiwan issue. Ross Terrill observes: "In no way is Taiwan a threat to the Mainland. Meanwhile Taiwan and the Mainland benefit from each other economically. . . . A Taiwan that was indefinitely separate from China but not hostile to it, as Finland was to the Soviet Union, or as Panama is to the United States, could be in Beijing's interests."[64] Such a nominally independent Taiwan, Terrill speculates, could enter into a security agreement with the PRC to further reassure Beijing.

This is an eminently reasonable observation. Unfortunately, however, it is detached from the reality of the situation. PRC leaders, and from all indications, the bulk of the Chinese people as well, simply regard the existence of even a compliant independent Taiwan as illegitimate. And as long as they think in those terms, it does not matter whether they are morally right or morally wrong. What matters is that they will likely press their claim to Taiwan with increasing vigor, greatly increasing the odds of a military crisis and a collision with the United States. Minxin Pei, another scholar at the Carnegie Endowment for International Peace, correctly identifies the mood in the PRC. "Inside China, the consensus is shifting towards confrontation with Taiwan because of the growing frustration at not being able to stop the move to de jure independence. Hence a collision is looking more likely."[65]

All of this puts the United States in a delicate and dangerous position. American leaders may soon have to change Washington's policy on Taiwan or face the nightmare of having to honor its security commitment to the island, because the PRC seems increasingly inclined to push the issue of reunification.

CHAPTER 6

WASHINGTON'S MUDDLED POLICY

The administration of George W. Bush has tried to chart a balanced policy on the Taiwan issue, but it has proven increasingly difficult to stay on that diplomatic tightrope. Instead of achieving balance, the administration has increasingly sowed confusion, inviting miscalculation by Taipei or Beijing—or even worse, by both capitals. Washington is caught between its desire to maintain good relations with the People's Republic of China and its desire to shield a vibrant democracy on Taiwan. Understandably, U.S. policymakers are reluctant to concede that it might not be possible to achieve both goals.

The risks posed by Washington's "zig-zag" policy regarding Taiwan are rising, and not only because of developments on Taiwan and the mainland, as important as those are. Political dynamics in the United States itself put intense conflicting pressures on administration policymakers. As Taiwan has evolved from an authoritarian system into a full-blown democracy, its emotional and ideological support in the United States has also expanded. That is especially true among conservative Republicans, the core of President Bush's political base, but it also is present among the democracy and human-rights lobby in the Democratic Party. To pro-Taiwan elements, the tensions in the Strait involve a case of an aggressive, authoritarian regime wanting to snuff out of existence a peaceful, democratic country. Two neoconservative scholars, Dan Blumenthal of the American Enterprise Institute and Randy Scheunemann of the Project for a New American Century, express the sentiments of many opinion shapers who strongly back Taiwan. "In his historic inauguration speech last week President Bush made clear that the expansion of democracy and freedom are the central tenets of his foreign policy. On Taiwan policy, the administration should put those inspirational words into action by protecting a democracy from the aggressive designs of a dictatorship."[1]

Arrayed against the pro-Taiwan faction is a major portion of the American business community that wants nothing to jeopardize the crucial economic relationship with the PRC, a relationship that is approaching $200 billion a year in trade and investment. The economic advocates of good relations with China are allied with realist strategic analysts who regard a security commitment to Taiwan in the face of China's rising power as unsustainable over the long run. The Bush administration is finding it increasingly difficult to placate both the pro-Taiwan and more moderate domestic constituencies.

Finally, the administration's attempt at a balanced policy is put at risk because of the changing diplomatic and economic dynamics throughout East Asia. China's burgeoning economic power is causing even America's closest allies in East Asia to hedge their bets. That makes even a qualified U.S. commitment to defend Taiwan increasingly problematic, unless the United States is prepared to undertake that mission alone.

Washington badly needs to clarify its Taiwan policy, and the essential first step is for policymakers to clarify their own thinking about the issue. Unfortunately, time is running out for them to do so.

WHAT ARE AMERICA'S SECURITY OBLIGATIONS TO TAIWAN?

Part of the confusion about current U.S. policy toward Taiwan flows from the ambiguity of the Taiwan Relations Act itself. Proponents of a U.S. security shield routinely argue that the TRA (which Congress passed when the Carter administration switched U.S. diplomatic relations from Taipei to Beijing) already contains a U.S. defense commitment.[2] In testimony before the House International Relations Committee in February 2004, political science professor John F. Copper summarized that view, stating simply "the TRA commits the United States to defend Taiwan against any military threat."[3]

That is a rather strained interpretation. The TRA merely asserts that "efforts to determine the future of Taiwan by other than peaceful means, including by boycotts or embargoes, would be a threat to the peace and security of the Western Pacific area and of grave concern to the United States."[4] It further directs the chief executive to "inform the Congress promptly of any threat to the security or the social and economic system of the people of Taiwan and any danger to the interests of the United States arising therefrom. The President and the Congress shall determine, in accordance with constitutional processes, appropriate action by the United States in response to any such danger."[5]

Such vague provisions are a far cry from a defense obligation, even an implied one. Moreover, the TRA replaced the mutual defense treaty that the United States had concluded with Taipei in 1954, at a time when the United States considered the Republic of China the sole legitimate government of all China. The language of the defense treaty is strikingly different from that of the TRA. In the former document, the United States and the ROC (hereafter Taiwan) declared "publicly and formally their sense of unity and their common determination to defend themselves against external attack, so that no potential aggressor could be under the illusion that either of them stands alone in the West Pacific area."[6] To achieve the objectives of the treaty, the parties "separately and jointly by self-help and mutual aid will maintain their individual and collective capacity to resist attack and communist subversive activities directed from without against their territorial integrity and political stability."[7] Moreover, the treaty was not merely a paper promise of defense cooperation. Another provision outlined the tangible military expression of that cooperation. "The Government of the Republic of China grants, and the Government of the United States accepts, the right to dispose such United States land, air and sea forces in and about Taiwan and the Pescadores as may be required for their defense."[8]

If Congress had intended to incorporate the provisions of the mutual defense treaty into the TRA, it could have done so. But it explicitly rejected an amendment that would have incorporated the previous obligations (see chapter 3). Instead, it chose to adopt far more diluted, ambiguous, and conditional language. Nor can the provision of the TRA committing the United States to sell defensive arms to Taiwan be stretched to cover a defense commitment using U.S. military forces. Those are entirely separable issues. Washington could adopt a policy of extensive arms sales to Taiwan but not shield the island with the U.S. military. Conversely, some future American government might scale back arms sales in an effort to placate Beijing, while making it clear to the PRC that the United States would intervene militarily if Chinese forces attacked Taiwan.

The problem with the TRA is that it can be interpreted in a multitude of ways. Hawks insist that it contains at least an implied defense commitment, while doves (with a stronger case) can argue that there is no such obligation. Over the decades, a succession of U.S. administrations have pursued a de facto policy of strategic ambiguity—at times quite deliberately—to keep both Taipei and Beijing guessing about what the United States would actually do in response to a military crisis in the Taiwan Strait. The rationale is that such ambiguity will induce restraint in both capitals. The Bush administration's innovation in the first decade of the twenty-first century has been to transform strategic ambiguity, dangerous enough, into strategic confusion verging on strategic incoherence.

THE BUSH ADMINISTRATION AND THE PRC:
RELATIONS GET OFF TO A ROCKY START

Although President Bush and his foreign policy advisers now like to boast that U.S.-PRC relations are the best they have been in many years, the relationship certainly did not start out that way. Indeed, a little more than two months into the new administration a major crisis erupted in relations with China. On April 1, 2001, an American EP–3 surveillance plane was flying a mission over the South China Sea, which is generally considered international airspace but that China claims as part of its economic zone. On several previous missions U.S. surveillance planes increasingly found themselves confronted and harassed by Chinese fighter planes, although no untoward incidents had taken place. On the April 1 mission, though, the EP–3 collided with a Chinese fighter plane and was forced to make an emergency landing on China's Hainan Island.

Both sides alleged that the other was at fault and a nasty diplomatic spat ensued. The Chinese pilot had perished in the collision, and the Beijing government, almost certainly prodded by hard-liners in the defense ministry, used his death to stimulate nationalist, anti-U.S. sentiment. Chinese authorities held the crew of the EP–3 for more than a week, until the State Department issued a carefully crafted statement expressing regret that the Chinese pilot had been killed and that the U.S. plane had been forced to enter Chinese airspace for an emergency landing. Although that statement was short of the formal apology that Beijing had been demanding, it successfully resolved the incident, much to the relief of moderates in the PRC's foreign ministry and trade ministry. However, Chinese authorities did keep the plane, which was likely an intelligence bonanza for the People's Liberation Army.

Hawkish media outlets and political figures in the United States seized on the incident to demand a more confrontational U.S. policy toward the PRC regarding Taiwan, human rights, and other issues. Robert Kagan and William Kristol at the neoconservative *Weekly Standard* charged that President Bush had presided over a "national humiliation," demonstrating a policy of "weakness and fear."[9] Fred Barnes, executive editor of the *Standard*, recommended that the administration bring the U.S. ambassador home and "expel the Chinese ambassador from the United States." Barnes also asserted that "you can't have 'normal relations' with a communist dictatorship. They are not normal countries. They don't have legitimate governments like a democracy does, a democracy like Taiwan, for instance."[10]

China's diplomatic confrontation with the United States was poorly timed. A large package of arms sales to Taiwan was awaiting approval by the Bush administration, and the EP–3 incident caused both public and congressional opinion to swing sharply against the PRC. In addition, although Congress had granted China permanent normal trade relations (PNTR) the year before, the delay in Beijing's obtaining membership in the World Trade Organization meant that it would need another year's extension of normal trade relations from Congress in the interim. Pressure mounted in Congress for reconsideration of the economic engagement policy toward China.

Representative Dana Rohrabacher (R-CA), a longtime antagonist of the PRC, protested that the EP–3 crew members were "hostages held by a hostile power."[11] Even more temperate legislators like Representative Henry Hyde (R-IL), who had previously supported PNTR, stated that, given the EP–3 incident, he was less inclined to support automatic, open trade with China. Several legislators noted that the incident made them and their constituents more enthusiastic about the arms sale package to Taiwan.[12]

On April 24, 2001, the Bush administration announced approval of the largest arms sale to Taiwan since 1992.[13] Washington did deny the sale of the Arleigh-Burke class destroyers equipped with the Aegis radar system, the weapon system that most concerned Beijing. Even without the Burke destroyers, though, the Chinese were agitated. Not only did the sale signal a firm commitment from the Bush administration to continue selling arms to Taiwan, but for the first time it included submarines—something Beijing regarded almost as provocative as the Aegis system. Submarines, conceded Holmes Liao, a military analyst at the Taiwan Research Institute, were "potentially an offensive weapon."[14] Under the Taiwan Relations Act, the United States was only supposed to sell defensive weapons to Taiwan.

As the Chinese government was summoning U.S. Ambassador Joseph Prueher to protest the arms sale the next day, President Bush was being interviewed on *ABC News*. Interviewer Charles Gibson asked Bush whether the United States had an obligation to defend Taiwan from a Chinese attack. The president replied, "Yes we do, and the Chinese must understand that." Would the United States respond "with the full force of the American military?" Gibson pressed. "Whatever it took to help Taiwan defend herself," Bush replied.[15]

That was a dramatic departure from prior U.S. policy. The open endorsement of a military guarantee to Taiwan—particularly without any caveats or nuances—came as a jolt to Beijing. Previously, U.S. leaders had indicated that the United States would regard the use of force against Taiwan by the PRC as a serious breach of the peace and might, depending on the circumstances, intervene militarily. Sometimes such "strategic ambiguity" took extreme forms. During a visit to China in 1995 Assistant Secretary of Defense Joseph P. Nye was asked by his hosts what the United States would do if war broke out between the mainland and Taiwan. Nye reportedly replied: "We don't know and you don't know."[16]

The PRC issued a statement rebuking President Bush, stating that "Taiwan is a part of China, not a protectorate of any foreign nation." The statement warned that Bush's comments "undermine peace and stability across the Taiwan Strait and will create further damage to Sino-U.S. relations."[17] Chinese officials were also becoming uneasy as they examined the people supporting and advising the Bush administration. Several members of the Bush foreign policy team, including Deputy Secretary of State Richard Armitage, Richard Perle, chairman of the defense department's policy advisory board, John Bolton, who would soon become Under Secretary of State for Arms Control and International Security, Lewis Libby, Vice President Dick Cheney's chief of staff, and Deputy Secretary of Defense Paul Wolfowitz, had all signed a 1999 statement released by the Project for a New American Century that openly called for ending the one-China policy. That statement affirmed that "if the people of Taiwan do not want to be united with the mainland until China becomes a democracy, the United States has a moral obligation and a strategic imperative to honor that determination."[18] Thus the PRC had ample reason to worry about the direction of the Bush administration's Taiwan policy.

Predictably, advocates of a hard-line policy toward the PRC applauded the president's *ABC News* comments. Claremont Institute scholar and former Republican nominee for the U.S. Senate Bruce Herschensohn praised Bush's "moral instincts" and urged him to repudiate the entire one-China policy.[19] Representative Tom Lantos (D-CA) stated that the president's words marked a welcome shift in U.S. policy and that the time had come to "go beyond" a policy of strategic ambiguity.[20] The *Wall Street Journal* editors likewise praised the shift, stating that it sent a message that "the U.S. sees a strong national interest in preserving Taiwan's democracy, and that China's attempts to undermine support for the island through bluster and threats will have the opposite effect."[21]

It is likely though, that the administration also heard from an agitated business community and experts who worried that the president's impetuous statement of unconditional support for Taiwan's defense could lead to a serious rupture in relations with the PRC. Such concerns were especially pertinent coming on the heels of the dust up with Beijing over the spy plane incident. Whatever the reason, both the State Department and the White House issued statements the day after Bush's interview denying that his comments indicated any change in U.S. policy. Bush himself remarked on CNN that "nothing has really changed in policy as far as I'm concerned."[22] Former national security advisor Sandy Berger saw matters differently, alleging that Bush had gone "from a 20-year policy of strategic ambiguity to what appeared to be a firm commitment, then back to strategic confusion," all in the space of a few hours.[23]

Attempts to resuscitate strategic ambiguity did little to allay the suspicions of an angry China.[24] Beijing's leaders seemed to regard Bush's initial comments as reflecting Washington's real policy. Their suspicions were exacerbated by reports in the Taiwanese press that Admiral Dennis Blair, the commander of U.S. Pacific Command, had paid a secret visit to Taiwan to meet with military leaders there and propose more extensive cooperation between the U.S. and Taiwanese militaries.[25] To make matters still worse, stories based on high-level leaks from the Pentagon appeared in the American press, saying that the administration was considering shifting targets for some U.S. nuclear weapons from Russia to China.[26]

In June the administration proposed three suggestions for initiating a cross-Strait dialogue, and again the tilt toward Taiwan's position was evident. The three suggestions were (1) that the two sides should resume a direct dialogue without preconditions; (2) that the dialogue should begin with economic issues, and not include political issues initially; and (3) that the parties should seek to increase mutual understanding in order to enhance mutual trust. As Sheng Lijun concludes, the proposal "was a clear rejection of Beijing's request that the two sides of the Strait should, apart from economic negotiations, also have political negotiation or dialogue under the 'one-China' principle."[27] In particular, it was the first time that the United States had embraced Taiwan's position that talks should commence without preconditions. On another occasion, the Bush administration called on Beijing to acknowledge the Chen Shui-bian government, which, U.S. officials emphasized, was created through democratic elections, and suggested further that Beijing should pursue cross-Strait dialogue with a greater degree of sincerity.[28] Beijing's perception by the early summer of 2001 was that Washington's policy on the Taiwan issue was moving in a most alarming direction.

THE ADMINISTRATION SUPPORTS TAIWAN BUT COURTS BEIJING

Relations between Beijing and the new Bush administration clearly reached their nadir in the spring and early summer of 2001. Thereafter, efforts were made in both capitals to repair the relationship, and the situation gradually improved regarding most aspects of the relationship. Then came the terrorist attacks on September 11, 2001, and the administration faced a new challenge in its overall policy toward the PRC. Previously, advocates of a hard-line policy toward China both within and outside the administration seemed to act as though they could pursue such initiatives with impunity. They either did not worry about potential disruption to the important economic relationship with the PRC, or they believed that Beijing would have no choice but to accept Washington's growing support for Taiwan because ultimately China needed that economic relationship more than did America.

September 11 changed that calculation for U.S. policymakers. Now the United States needed China's assistance in the war against radical Islamic terrorism. Many of those terrorists were active in Central and Southwest Asia, and Chinese intelligence sources were much better than America's in both regions. Chinese pressure on Pakistan (a longtime PRC ally) was important to get the government of General Pervez Musharraf to cooperate with the United States against Al Qaeda and its affiliates. Without Chinese pressure, Islamabad would have been less willing to help the U.S. campaign against the Taliban regime in Afghanistan and the sanctuary that regime had given to Al Qaeda. Chinese support (or at least acquiescence) also was useful in inducing the governments of Central Asian countries to host U.S. military forces in the struggle against the terrorists.

As time went on, Washington discovered that it needed Beijing's assistance on other issues as well. The most important one involved the reemergence of the North Korean nuclear crisis in the autumn of 2002. U.S. officials quickly realized that without the PRC's help there was little prospect of resolving that crisis diplomatically. China was one of the few countries that had relatively close relations with Pyongyang, and the PRC was by far North Korea's most important trading partner. Perhaps most important, it supplied the reclusive and poverty stricken Stalinist country with some 70 percent of its energy needs. The PRC could exert significant economic and diplomatic leverage on North Korea if it chose to do so.[29]

The war on Islamic terrorism and the burgeoning North Korea crisis created important incentives for the United States to treat China with greater care than it had during the early months of the Bush administration. Nevertheless, the administration did not immediately back away from its enhanced support for Taiwan. Washington's treatment of Taiwan's political leaders was markedly different from what it had been during the Clinton administration. The Clinton foreign policy team seemed so wedded to a one-China policy that it barely tolerated "stopovers" in the United States by Taiwanese officials on their way to destinations elsewhere in the world (usually to the handful of countries that continued to have diplomatic relations with Taipei.) When Taiwan's president, Chen Shui-bian, made such a stopover in 2000, the State Department strongly discouraged him from making public appearances or even meeting privately with members of Congress. He was kept virtually incommunicado in his hotel.[30]

The Bush administration's attitude was dramatically different. Subsequent visits by Chen and other Taiwanese officials included public appearances and meetings with Washington's apparent blessing—even as Beijing seethed.[31] At one point in early 2002, Taiwan's defense minister met "informally" with Deputy Secretary of Defense Paul Wolfowitz during a security conference sponsored by a think tank in Florida.[32] That was the highest-level meeting between U.S. and Taiwanese officials since the United States switched its diplomatic recognition from the Republic of China to the People's Republic of China in 1979. The meeting also intensified PRC suspicions about the extent of U.S.-Taiwanese defense cooperation, which Beijing feared was growing rapidly.[33]

From September 2001 to late 2003, U.S. policy toward China and Taiwan seemed even more inconsistent than usual. One the one hand, Washington's support for Taiwan appeared to be stronger and firmer than it had been in decades. On the other hand, the United States was courting China and seeking Beijing's support for a variety of important U.S. policy initiatives—especially the drive to get North Korea to give up its quest for nuclear weapons.[34] Such an inconsistency could not last, especially since Chen Shui-bian's government apparently viewed Washington's exceptionally friendly attitude as a green light to push its independence agenda. Indeed, by late 2003, Taipei's policies were setting off alarm bells in Washington, especially after China issued a thinly veiled warning that it might have to go to war if Chen's government persisted in its provocations.[35] The Bush administration decided that a course correction regarding Taiwan policy was needed.

THE RHETORICAL SHIFT AT
THE END OF BUSH'S FIRST TERM

President Bush made a noticeable change in Taiwan policy during a visit by PRC Premier Wen Jiabao in December. With Wen at his side, Bush stated that the United States opposed "any unilateral action by either China or Taiwan to change the status quo." Making it clear that his warning was directed primarily to Taipei rather than Beijing, he added that "the comments and actions made by the leader of Taiwan indicate that he may be willing to make decisions unilaterally, to change the status quo, which we oppose." The president went even further, allowing Wen to characterize U.S. policy as one of "opposition to Taiwan independence."[36]

This new position was likely prompted by Chen's recent initiatives, most notably proposing to hold referenda on various security issues (including how to respond to China's massing of missiles across the Taiwan Strait) in conjunction with the presidential elections scheduled in March 2004. The PRC feared that Chen's initial foray into using referenda as a form of lawmaking could easily escalate within a few years into proposing a referendum on changing Taiwan's name from the Republic of China to the Republic of Taiwan, or perhaps even a referendum on independence itself. Beijing had made its grave concerns on this matter known to Washington, and the Bush administration had responded in a way that delighted PRC leaders.

Pro-Taiwan forces in the United States took a decidedly different attitude. Bush's public undercutting of Taiwan drew immediate and sharp rebukes from the president's political allies. Neoconservative luminaries William Kristol, Robert Kagan, and Gary Schmitt immediately issued a statement criticizing the president for rewarding "Beijing's bullying" but saying "not a word" about China's missile buildup across the Taiwan Strait and the PRC's repeated threats against Taiwan. They added that "appeasement of a dictatorship simply invites further attempts at intimidation."[37] John Tkacik, a scholar at the Heritage Foundation's Asian Studies Center, was even more caustic. Accusing the president of "losing his bearings" on the Taiwan issue, Tkacik did not attempt to conceal his dismay. "It just boggles the mind," he said. "I'm just appalled. Clinton never would have gone this far."[38]

The president's political allies were not the only people who believed that Bush went much too far in placating Beijing. The *Washington Post* weighed in with a scathing editorial criticizing Bush for essentially placing the United States "on the side of the dictators who promise war, rather than the democrats whose threat is a ballot box." Such action suggested "how malleable is his commitment to the defense of freedom as a guiding principle of U.S. policy."[39]

Although one must make allowances for hyperbole on the part of conservative hawks, there is a possibility that the Bush comments may have conveyed a message of acquiescence to Beijing beyond what the administration intended. A comment by a PRC leader reported by Willy Wo-Lap Lam, a former correspondent for the *South China Morning Post* and now a China analyst at CNN, was most disturbing. According to Lam, the senior official stated that President Bush's "unambiguous opposition" to any effort by Taipei to change the status quo meant that if "we were to respond militarily, the U.S. can't raise objections, let alone interfere."[40] That is precisely the kind of miscalculation that Washington's erratic "tightrope" policy regarding Taiwan invites and which could lead to extremely unpleasant consequences.

Lam was not the only analyst picking up on disquieting attitudes coming out of Beijing following Bush's December comments. Bonnie S. Glaser, a scholar at the Center for Strategic and International Studies, warned that the United States was sending dangerous signals to the PRC. "Some Chinese even believe," she reported, "that the U.S. may acquiesce in a limited use of force by the PLA—for example to seize an offshore island, temporarily impose a limited blockade, or fire a lone missile at a military target on Taiwan."[41] It is quite possible, of course, that such PRC calculations about U.S. intentions are wrong. But that will be little comfort to either side if Beijing's leadership has begun to think in those terms and decides to act on the underlying assumptions.

Once again, the State Department rushed to offer assurances that the president's remarks did not indicate a substantive change in U.S. policy. Indeed, a few weeks later Washington was urging the Taiwanese legislature to approve the $18 billion price tag for the weapons systems that the United States already had offered to sell to Taipei. Chen's government was running into resistance from the "Pan Blue" coalition (primarily the Kuomintang Party and the People First Party) that controlled the legislature regarding the purchase. Opposition legislators not only criticized the package as too expensive and coming at the expense of the domestic needs of the Taiwanese people, but some of them feared that it would be unduly provocative to the PRC. Needless to say, Beijing was not pleased with Washington's lobbying on behalf of the full arms package. PRC leaders were even less happy at the end of March when the Pentagon announced plans to sell long-range, early-warning radars to counter China's ongoing deployment of missiles.[42]

Yet at the same time, the Bush administration continued to urge Chen to abandon plans to hold referenda on security issues during the March presidential election. When that pressure failed to dissuade Chen, U.S. officials virtually insisted that the language of the referenda questions at least be watered down to minimize the offense that they would give to Beijing. The DPP government ultimately gave in to Washington's pressure and made the questions as innocuous as possible, a step that U.S. officials welcomed.[43] But the outcome satisfied neither Taiwan nor the PRC.[44] Chen and his supporters were irritated that the United States was interfering in Taiwan's internal political affairs, while Beijing was disappointed that the United States had not done more, preventing the balloting entirely.

In the autumn of 2004, U.S. policy again took a lurch in favor of the PRC and suggested that Washington's support for Taipei was in doubt. In an interview on CNN International during his trip to East Asia in October, then Secretary of State Colin Powell explicitly embraced the goal of eventual reunification of Taiwan with the mainland. That goal, the secretary said, was one that "all parties are seeking." His statement was astonishing, and it ignored the wishes of millions of Taiwanese who regard reunification as anathema and consider Taiwan to be a wholly separate society. Powell's comment was significant, though, because the

United States had never before taken an explicit public stand on the reunification issue.

The secretary offered even more startlingly pro-Beijing remarks in an interview with Hong Kong's Phoenix Television. Powell stressed that Washington had made it clear to all parties "that the United States does not support independence for Taiwan. It would be inconsistent with our One-China Policy." He then made that point even more explicit. "There is only one China. Taiwan is not independent. It does not enjoy sovereignty as a nation." Lest anyone still miss the thrust of his message, he added: "Independence movements or those who speak out for independence in Taiwan will find no support from the United States."[45]

The motivation for Powell's strong remarks was unclear. But they immediately produced a firestorm of criticism in Taipei and expressions of appreciation from Beijing. Chen directly contradicted Powell, saying that "Taiwan is absolutely a sovereign and independent country." Conversely, a Chinese Foreign Ministry spokesman called Powell's comments "helpful and constructive."[46] Zhang Mingqing, a spokesman for the PRC's Taiwan Affairs Office, likewise praised the comments and said that they had addressed a long-standing PRC complaint about the lack of clarity in U.S. policy.

Beijing's satisfaction was short-lived. The Bush administration's conservative supporters reacted with at least as much fury as they had to the president's December 2003 statement. John Tkacik exemplified the criticism. "It is unsettling for the United States to be seen siding with an arrogant, belligerent, and aggressive Communist dictatorship against any democracy. But Taiwan isn't just any democracy: It has been one of America's staunchest allies—despite the 1979 break in formal diplomatic relations." Yet, Tkacik charged, Secretary Powell had been persuaded "that democratic Taiwan's interests can be sacrificed to the warlike threats of Communist China."[47]

Whether in response to the discontent that conservatives expressed or in response to some other factor, State Department officials scurried to clarify that Powell's comments did not constitute a shift in U.S. policy. They even insisted that the Secretary has misspoken—that he had intended to say "peaceful resolution" not peaceful reunification. Those, of course, were very different concepts. The incident created yet more confusion in Taipei and Beijing, and it raises some intriguing questions about decision-making in Washington. Did Powell intend to articulate a significant shift in U.S. policy but saw his initiative torpedoed by hardliners on President Bush's national security team? Did he truly experience a slip of the tongue? The latter explanation seems unlikely. Secretary Powell was an experienced, intelligent diplomat who had to be aware of the extremely sensitive nature of the Taiwan issue and how every nuanced phrase expressed by any U.S. policy-maker, much less the secretary of state, would be scrutinized in Taipei and Beijing. Surely he knew the crucial difference between "resolution" and "reunification." If he had made such a gaffe, would he not have taken steps to correct it immediately? Instead, he waited more than 48 hours and then had subordinates in the State Department issue a clarification. Moreover, the comment about reunification was merely one aspect of an overall tone in the two interviews that conveyed explicit U.S. hostility to any manifestation of Taiwanese independence. The way the episode was handled suggested that the White House overruled Powell.

Whatever the explanation, though, the incident was the latest illustration of Washington's tendency to sow confusion regarding the volatile Taiwan issue. What may be seen in U.S. circles as caution and balance is likely seen in Taipei and Beijing as either duplicity or incompetence.

MORE TURMOIL AT THE END OF BUSH'S FIRST TERM

Washington tried to stay on its increasingly wobbly diplomatic tightrope as elections for Taiwan's national legislature approached in December 2004. As noted in chapter 4, Chen Shui-bian embraced a number of extremely assertive pro-independence measures during the final weeks of the campaign—particularly, proposals to remove "China" from the names of state-owned corporations and to include "Taiwan" in the official name of Taipei's representative offices in foreign countries. The U.S. reaction was quite critical. "These changes of terminology for government-controlled enterprises or economic and cultural offices abroad, in our view, would appear to unilaterally change Taiwan's status, and for that reason we're not supportive of them," stated State Department spokesman Adam Ereli.[48] That response was carefully calibrated, but it satisfied neither side. Beijing was clearly expecting a more definitive condemnation than a statement that the United States was "not supportive" of Taiwan's moves. The Chen government and its supporters, on the other hand, saw the comment as yet another case of attempted U.S. meddling in Taiwan's internal affairs.

Although they made no public statement on the legislative elections in Taiwan, U.S. officials were clearly relieved that Chen's Pan Green coalition failed in its bid to take control of the legislature. Washington saw the results as at least a mild rebuke by Taiwanese voters to the pro-independence faction and used the occasion to urge greater dialogue between Beijing and Taipei. The sense of relief in U.S. officialdom did not last long, however. Within days, Hu Jintao's government announced that it would propose an anti-secession law to the rubberstamp National People's Congress. Washington reacted with dismay. A senior State Department official stated that the proposed law posed "a difficult problem that is certainly a hazard to peace and stability in East Asia." The official added pointedly that "it's going to vitiate the positive effects" of the December 11 elections. He went on to say that he had hoped, "perhaps naively," that those elections would lead to "some breathing space while cooler heads on both sides of the Strait" could work on reducing tensions. Separately, State Department spokesman Richard Boucher expressed concern about "a hardening of positions."[49]

U.S. concern about the hardening of Beijing's position intensified a few days later when the PRC issued a new defense white paper warning that China's military would "crush" Taiwan if the latter created a "major incident" regarding independence. That inflammatory warning caused Secretary Powell to caution both Beijing and Taipei not to escalate tensions. Powell noted further that the United States had encouraged both sides to "find ways to reach out to one another."[50] Such a mind-numbing platitude suggested that either Washington did not fully comprehend the trends on Taiwan and the mainland, or that it did understand the alarming direction of policies in Beijing and Taipei but couldn't think of anything effective to do about them.

Washington's own actions added to the tensions—and to the confusion—on both sides of the Taiwan Strait. On successive days in late December 2004, the United States announced that it would station military officers at the American Institute in Taiwan—Washington's de facto embassy—for the first time, and that it was signing a 99-year lease for a new AIT site.[51] Those actions suggested that the United States expected Taiwan to be an independent political entity for a long time, and that relations between the two capitals would remain strong.

Immediately thereafter, however, Deputy Secretary of State Richard Armitage gave an interview on PBS television that created a rather different impression. Describing Taiwan as the biggest "land mine" in U.S.-PRC relations, the blunt-spoken Armitage adopted a very narrow view of the Taiwan Relations Act. "We are not obligated to go to defend [Taiwan]," Armitage stated, adding that it was up to the U.S. Congress to decide if America should go to war.[52] Given how often the executive branch has usurped the congressional war power over the past fifty-five years, such a statement was nothing less than astounding. To Taiwanese ears, it seemed likely that the second-ranking official in the State Department was looking for a pretext to absolve the United States from any responsibility to come to Taiwan's assistance in the event of an attack. If all that were not enough, Armitage said that he agreed with Beijing's one-China policy. Analysts noted that he, like Powell a few weeks earlier, had gone beyond Washington's usual policy of simply "acknowledging" the PRC's claim over Taiwan, and Armitage's comments drew a predictable blast from pro-Taiwan conservatives.[53]

The U.S. zig-zag policy took another zag again in the same month, however, in response to Beijing's decision to introduce the anti-secession law. As noted, Washington immediately criticized the proposal as destabilizing and unhelpful. That response was not nearly enough for some of the administration's conservative supporters, however. Not surprisingly, the ubiquitous John Tkacik called for much firmer action.

> If the U.S. administration is ruled by principle instead of craven expedience, it will respond to this Chinese ploy with the kind of forceful declaration usually reserved for Taiwan's leaders. So, President Bush should declare explicitly, in terms identical to his jibe at Taiwan's democratically elected president last December, that China's proposed anti-secession legislation 'indicates that China many be willing to make decisions unilaterally to change the status quo, which we oppose.'

Such a statement, Tkacik concluded sarcastically, "would be a nice bookend to President Bush's overreaction" to Chen Shui-bian's "rather benign effort" to hold referenda on security issues.[54]

Thomas Donnelly, an ultra-hawkish scholar at the American Enterprise Institute, was even more disgusted than Tkacik at the drift in U.S. policy on the Taiwan issue and toward China generally. Noting that Bush had campaigned in 2000 on the theme that China was a "strategic competitor," Donnelly charged that the administration had "reversed course 180 degrees." The evidence was especially clear regarding the U.S. attitude toward Taiwan. With some exaggeration he charged: "Arms sales to Taiwan, once a priority for the White House, have been all but cancelled, while the plucky democrats of Taipei have been reviled by President Bush and his lieutenants as independence-obsessed troublemakers." If one required an example of growing administration fecklessness, Donnelly argued, "witness the weak response by the State Department" to the anti-secession law. "Trading Taipei for Baghdad isn't much of a deal," he observed caustically.[55]

The discontent of the Bush administration's conservative base is not a trivial matter. It is likely to lead to renewed pressure on the White House to adjust its policy in a more pro-Taiwan direction. Another shift in the administration's policy, though, would be certain to upset Beijing, which has generally been pleased by U.S. actions on the Taiwan issue since December 2003. Once again, U.S. policymakers will find it impossible to satisfy all factions regarding this complex and emotional topic.

Whether in reaction to criticism from its political base or other reasons, Washington's policy seemed to show greater wariness, if not hostility, toward

China during the late winter and early spring of 2005. When the National People's Congress finally passed the anti-secession law in mid-March, the State Department's reaction was sharply critical. An even more significant sign of Washington's attitude toward Beijing involved the reaction to indications that the European Union was preparing to lift the arms embargo it had imposed on the PRC following the Tiananmen Square massacre. The Bush administration exerted utmost pressure on leading EU countries, especially Britain, to reconsider that course of action. During a trip to East Asia in March, Secretary of State Rice pointedly reminded the European allies that the United States, not Europe, had the responsibility and incurred the dangers of maintaining East Asia's stability.[56] The none-too-subtle implication is that lifting the arms embargo would lead to improvements in China's military capabilities, which would in turn pose a security threat to the region. Looming over the entire discussion was the prospect that China might use its greater military power to coerce Taiwan. As U.S. officials admittedly privately, that was the principal security threat that China might pose.

THE CHANGING POLITICAL AND ECONOMIC ENVIRONMENT IN EAST ASIA

Despite the vagueness of the Taiwan Relations Act and the at times frantic effort of the Bush administration to steer a middle course on the Taiwan issue, Bush probably spoke the undiplomatic truth in his April 2001 television interview. In all probability, the United States would try to come to Taiwan's aid militarily in the event of a PRC attack on the island. If it did so, however, the United States would not only find itself in a perilous military confrontation with China, it might have to wage the ensuing struggle virtually alone. The changing political and economic dynamics in East Asia make it likely that the nations in that region—even America's longtime allies such as Japan, South Korea, Australia, and the Philippines—would not jeopardize their own status with the PRC to back Washington. Signs of that reluctance have been evident for a decade.

Indeed, virtually all East Asian governments made a concerted effort to distance their policies from those of the United States when the Clinton administration dispatched two aircraft carrier battle groups to the western Pacific in response to Beijing's provocative missile tests in the Taiwan Strait in early 1996. South Korea and the Philippines both stressed that their mutual defense treaties with the United States did not cover contingencies in the Strait. Such countries as Malaysia, Indonesia, Thailand, and Australia contented themselves with the banal response of urging "restraint" on both sides, conspicuously declining to endorse Washington's moves. Indeed, they echoed Beijing's position that Taiwan was nothing more than a province of the PRC. Even Japan, the principal U.S. ally in the region, merely expressed "understanding" of Washington's decision to deploy the naval assets.[57]

The lack of allied support extends even beyond the Taiwan issue. The reaction in East Asian capitals to the April 2001 spy plane incident should have seemed a case of déjà vu to U.S. policymakers. Vocal support for the U.S. position was notably absent. Even Washington's treaty allies in the region—Japan, South Korea, Thailand, Australia, New Zealand, and the Philippines—declined to say that a U.S. apology to Beijing was unwarranted. Only Singapore's elder statesman, Lee Kuan Yew, unequivocally supported the U.S. position. Japan's tepid response epitomized the reaction of America's supposed friends and allies. Kauzuhiko Koshikawa, a spokesman for Prime Minister Yoshiro Mori, stated: "We strongly hope this case will be settled in an appropriate and acceptable manner."[58] Beijing could take as much comfort as Washington from such a comment.

U.S. officials tried to put the best face possible on a disturbing situation. In a letter to the *Washington Post*, Deputy Secretary of State Richard Armitage responded to criticism of the conduct of America's East Asian allies. "Asian friends and allies of the United States worked behind the scenes to be helpful to us—some of them right from the start, when it counted most. The top leaders of Japan, Korea, Australia and New Zealand all weighed in with the Chinese."[59]

Armitage is a master diplomat, and his phrasing was designed to conceal as much as enlighten. His description of alleged allied work "behind the scenes" in no way rebutted the point made by critics that the East Asian governments were unwilling to support the United States publicly, fearing that they would antagonize Beijing. Moreover, the United States does not need allies to conduct quiet diplomatic initiatives; neutral nations, or even allies of the opposing country, can play that role. One expects firm, public support of the U.S. position from loyal allies, not hedging behavior and cautious mediation efforts. Such support was not forthcoming from the East Asian allies in the spy plane incident any more than it had been in the 1996 crisis in the Taiwan Strait. The sole example that Armitage used to illustrate how the allies had been "helpful" to the United States confirmed just how weak his case was. "The Philippines offered us the use of its facilities as a transit point for the repatriation of our aircrew (we opted for Guam.)"[60] One could be excused for being underwhelmed at the boldness of such assistance.

The responses of the East Asian nations in both episodes underscore an important point. China's neighbors have no incentive to antagonize that rising power by backing the United States in disputes that do not seem vital to—or even relevant to—their interests. A Japanese scholar's explanation for his country's unwillingness to endorse publicly the U.S. naval deployment in 1996 was most revealing.

He did not cite the danger that a military collision between the United States and China might lead to Chinese attacks on Japanese territory because of the U.S. bases there, even though that was and remains a very real danger. Instead, he emphasized concerns that an endorsement of U.S. policy might jeopardize Japanese investments in China.[61] We can expect discreet neutrality from the East Asian countries in most, if not all, future squabbles between the United States and the PRC—especially on the Taiwan issue.

That point became apparent again in August 2004 when the governments of Australia and Singapore gave high-profile warnings to Taiwan to avoid actions that might provoke Beijing and create a military crisis in the Taiwan Strait. Both governments stressed that they would not come to Taiwan's aid if the island's increasingly assertive efforts to consolidate its de facto independence from China led to armed conflict. Lee Hsien Loong, Singapore's new prime minister, was blunt. "If Taiwan goes for independence, Singapore will not recognise it. In fact, no Asian country will recognise it. China will fight. Win or lose, Taiwan will be devastated," he warned. "Unfortunately, I only met very few [Taiwanese] leaders who understood this." Lest anyone miss the point, Lee stated emphatically: "A move by Taiwan towards independence is neither in Singapore's interest nor the region's interest."[62] Beijing expressed great satisfaction in response to the position Lee had adopted, but couldn't resist the reminder that "this stand is in line with Singapore's interests."[63]

PRC leaders had reason to be equally pleased with Australia's position. At a press conference during a visit to Beijing, Foreign Minister Alexander Downer emphasized that Australia's defense obligations under its treaty with the United States could be invoked only in the event of a direct attack on the United States or Australia. "So some other activity elsewhere in the world . . . doesn't invoke it."[64] Given the locale of his press conference, it did not require much imagination on the part of observers to discern what other contingency Downer meant.

The comments by Australia and Singapore reflect the growing concern throughout East Asia that tensions over the Taiwan issue are beginning to reach disturbing levels. It is clear that both countries were sending Taiwan a blunt message. What is less clear, but very important, is that they were also sending a crucial message to the United States: Do not count on your friends and allies in the region to help you if you try to defend Taiwan. Given the statements and actions of the East Asian governments over the past decade, such a message should not have come as a surprise to Washington.

Beijing has fostered the inclination toward neutrality through astute diplomacy that has lessened China's abrasive image among its neighbors, while quietly underscoring its economic importance to the economies of those countries.[65] As former ambassador J. Stapleton Roy pointed out in November 2004, "China is pursuing very skillful diplomacy to soften views" that other countries have toward its policies. Conversely, the United States "is seen as operating the opposite way, degrading its soft power." Roy singled out the Bush administration's doctrine of preemption, which he concluded created "unease" among many East Asian countries.[66]

The economic aspect of Beijing's strategy is especially important. Given current trends, China will surpass Japan as the world's second largest economy by 2020. Japan already imports more from China than it does from the United States, and China has become the largest trading partner of South Korea, the world's twelfth largest economy. Current trends indicate that China is likely to top America's trade with all of southeast Asia within a few years. James T. Laney, former U.S. ambassador to South Korea, and Jason T. Shapen, a foreign policy official during the 1990s, emphasize why such statistics are important.

> Because while Mao once claimed that power grows out of the barrel of a gun, today's leaders in China know that it also grows from trade. Tokyo and Seoul know this too. Aware that China is now vital to their economic well-being, they are no longer as willing as they once were to position themselves opposite Beijing, even if this means going against Washington. Put another way, while the Bush administration still thinks of the United States as the sole superpower in a unipolar world, Tokyo and Seoul do not share this view. To them, the United States and China are both powers to be reckoned with in a bipolar Asia.[67]

And what is true for Japan and South Korea is even more the case for less powerful countries in East Asia. A major reason for Australia's healthy economy is Chinese investment in liquid natural gas projects and other enterprises. Indonesians candidly describe their country's new economic relationship with Beijing as "feeding the dragon."[68] The situation is similar with regard to Australia. As *New York Times* correspondent Jane Perlez observed:

> These days, Australian engineers—like executives, merchants and manufacturers elsewhere in the region—cannot seem to work fast enough to satisfy the hunger of their biggest new customer: China. Not long ago, Australia and China regarded each other with suspicion. But through newfound diplomatic finesse and the seemingly irresistible lure of its long economic expansion, Beijing has skillfully turned around relations with Australia, America's staunchest ally in the region. The turnabout is just one sign of the broad new influence Beijing has accumulated across the Asian Pacific with American friends and foes alike.[69]

Perlez notes further that "more and more, Beijing is leveraging its economic clout to support its political preferences." In particular, the PRC "is dispersing aid and, in ways not seen before, pressing countries to fall in line on its top foreign policy priority: its claim over Taiwan."[70]

A major step in Beijing's diplomatic campaign came in late November 2004 when the PRC concluded an accord with the ten-member Association of Southeast Asian Nations (ASEAN) aimed at creating the world's largest free trade area by 2010. It would encompass a huge market of nearly two billion people. The measure removed tariffs on various goods immediately and created a mechanism to resolve trade disputes between China and ASEAN members. It also sought to end all tariffs by 2010.

China's motives were both economic and strategic. The Chinese economy's enormous appetite for oil and raw materials was clearly one factor, but PRC officials also apparently saw the pact as useful in securing vital sea lanes. Concern about China's sea lanes through southeast Asia is a high policy priority for Beijing. China has developed extremely close military ties with Burma and is in the process of building naval bases and electronic listening posts in that country. Beijing has also signed a military accord with Cambodia.[71] Such measures significantly enhance China's ability to protect the sea lanes in that region, or to deny those lanes to East Asian countries (e.g., Japan) if those countries supported the United States in a confrontation over Taiwan—a point that is probably not lost on those capitals.

Beyond such narrow military goals, foreign analysts saw the trade accord with ASEAN as another manifestation of how an increasingly bold China is forging new diplomatic and economic alliances that sought to challenge America's primacy in East Asia.[72] That potential was not lost on Taiwanese scholars. "China is using its huge market as a bait to lure ASEAN countries away from the U.S. and Japan and build closer relations," concluded Chao Chien-min, a China watcher and political science professor at Taiwan's National Chengchi University. "I think what Beijing has in mind is to forge good economic and trade relations now and then increase exchanges in other areas, particularly in the military and security arena."[73]

China's nuanced diplomacy was evident in the response to the tsunami crisis in late December 2004 and early January 2005. As *Los Angeles Times* correspondent Don Lee noted from the hard-hit city of Banda Aceh, Indonesia:

> China's presence in the global effort to aid tsunami victims is hard to miss here. The country's large, red tents are pitched in the middle of the town's air force base, the center of relief operations. Its team, which consists of 16 emergency doctors, is larger than that of any foreign country on the base and has made frequent runs to remote villages, treating about 1,000 victims a day. China's mone-

tary pledge has topped $63 million, its largest peacetime overseas humanitarian donation.[74]

The $63 million figure was actually quite modest, especially compared to the $335 million that the United States pledged and the $500 million that Japan provided, but Beijing cleverly allocated its assistance in ways that generated the most public attention in recipient countries. Moreover, that aid was concentrated in Indonesia and Thailand, within the sphere of influence the PRC hopes to cultivate in East Asia. Chinese generosity was far less pronounced in more distant countries such as India and Sri Lanka. The Chinese government also was careful not to dispatch units of the People's Liberation Army to southeast Asia to help in the relief effort, even though the U.S. military and the militaries of other countries were involved. With regard to Indonesia in particular, Beijing realized that the government and population still resented China's past attempts to interfere in their country's internal affairs (especially during the 1960s) and was cautious about doing anything that might revive those old sensitivities.

Beijing's diplomatic efforts to court countries in the region and further isolate Taiwan have provoked increasingly shrill protests from Taipei. Gary Song-Huan Lin, director general of East Asian and Pacific Affairs in Taiwan's Foreign Affairs Ministry, blasted Australian Foreign Minister Downer's comments on Australia's defense commitments. In an interview with the *Australian*, Lin warned that Australia's "one-sided" support of China was wrong and could make a war in the Taiwan Strait more, rather than less, likely. Downer, Lin charged, was like British prime minister Neville Chamberlain who, by appeasing Adolf Hitler, missed the chance to avoid World War II. "If Australia puts its weight behind the People's Republic of China, and the PRC feel they are assured that they will not face any opposition when they invade Taiwan, in that case they may really start a war."[75] The stridence of Lin's protest suggests how effective has been Beijing's strategy to cultivate its influence in East Asia and isolate Taiwan.

There is a crucial weakness in Washington's East Asia security strategy—especially as it pertains to the Taiwan issue. Because that policy developed during the Cold War, Washington could operate with confidence that its security clients would not have extensive economic ties with America's strategic adversaries. In other words, there would be no tension between the economic interests of those allies and their security relationships with the United States. The situation is now more ambiguous. For example, a chilly relationship (to say nothing of an armed confrontation) between the United States and the PRC would put the other East Asian nations in an extremely difficult position. They now have extensive investments in China and maintain lucrative trade relations with that country. As James

J. Przystup, a research fellow at the National Defense University in Washington states bluntly: "Today, China is East Asia's great power."[76] And no nation in the region wants to offend that great power, especially not over the issue of Taiwan. It is yet another reason why a hard-line U.S. policy in support of Taiwan, as suggested by some of President Bush's political supporters, is not sustainable.

Washington is making a concerted effort to counteract those regional trends and is trying to pressure its closest allies into providing assistance to the United States in the event of a conflict in the Taiwan Strait. One could discern that objective as far back as the 1997 revisions to the defense guidelines of the U.S.–Japan alliance. Washington sought and received a commitment from Japan that it would provide logistical assistance to U.S. forces if a breach to the peace of the region occurred. Previously, Japanese leaders had interpreted Article 9 of their country's constitution as permitting Japan's Self Defense Forces to assist U.S. military units only in the case of a direct attack on Japanese territory. The new guidelines expanded the role to include limited logistical support to deal with breaches of the peace "in areas surrounding Japan" that were relevant to Japan's defense.[77]

Although the operative phrase regarding the regional coverage was deliberately vague, most experts in Japan and the United States assumed that it referred to a possible crisis on the Korean Peninsula. But PRC officials worried that the language also might cover contingencies in the Taiwan Strait. Tokyo's steadfast refusal to clarify the coverage of the new defense guidelines did little to assuage Beijing's apprehension.

The Bush administration has sought to expand America's alliances with both Japan and South Korea to cover wider security problems in the region. Although administration officials have remained vague about what their concept of "broader alliances" would mean in practice, Korean and Japanese diplomats have the distinct impression that Washington's goal is to enlist their countries as security partners in the event of a conflict in the Taiwan Strait.[78] At the very least, that would mean letting the United States use its military bases in Japan and South Korea for operations against PRC forces. It also might mean that American officials would expect the military establishments of those two allies to lend assistance to U.S. units that were defending Taiwan.

South Korea seems firmly opposed to broadening its alliance with the United States to cover a Taiwan crisis. Japan is somewhat more ambivalent. In a joint security statement issued in February by the U.S.-Japan Security Consultative Committee (consisting of Secretary of State Condoleezza Rice, Secretary of Defense Donald Rumsfeld, and their Japanese counterparts), the two countries declared that among their "common strategic objectives" was the "peaceful resolution of issues concerning the Taiwan Strait through dialogue."[79] Although that statement was a long way from constituting a Japanese pledge to join the United States in defending Taiwan, it was the first time that Tokyo had made the Taiwan issue an explicit Japanese security interest. That step alone was enough to send Beijing into a fury, with PRC officials describing Japan's action as an "abominable act."[80]

Tensions between Beijing and Tokyo rose further in April 2005, when the PRC government expressed its opposition to Japan's becoming a permanent member of the UN Security Council. Perhaps more telling, large and violent anti-Japan demonstrations broke out in several Chinese cities—a reaction that took Japanese leaders aback.[81] Conflicting trends now appear to be under way. Economic factors continue to draw China and Japan closer together, but political tensions and Japan's own security interests may lead Tokyo ultimately to join Washington in a de facto containment policy toward the PRC. Whether such a containment policy would extend to Tokyo's support for a hard-line policy regarding the Taiwan issue is less certain.

Ultimately, officials in both Japan and South Korea may have to decide whether they will accede to Washington's wishes regarding Taiwan to maintain their alliances, which they believe benefit them in so many other respects. Time will tell how firmly they are prepared to resist growing U.S. pressure on this issue. U.S. leaders may be making a serious mistake, however, if they assume that even close allies will automatically line up with Washington against Beijing. At best, their role in a crisis is uncertain.

A POLICY IN DISARRAY

U.S. strategy regarding the Taiwan issue exhibits a troubling array of defects. At times it borders on incoherence. An example of the fuzzy thinking in U.S. policy circles can be gauged by the murky comments of a senior administration official on the eve of President Bush's December 2003 rebuke to Taiwan for trying to make unilateral changes in the status quo. "What you're seeing here is the dropping of the ambiguity for both sides because we cannot sort of imply to the Taiwan side that we're sort of agnostic towards moves toward Taiwan independence," the official said. "But at the same time, we've got to make it clear to the Chinese that this is not a green light for you to contemplate the use of force or coercion against Taiwan."[82] Assistant Secretary of State James Kelly's explanation of Washington's one-China policy was in the same vein. Testifying before the House Committee on International Relations, Kelly stated that he had "made the point of one China, and I really did not define it. I am not sure that I very easily could define it. I can tell you what it is not. It is not the one-China principle that Beijing suggests, and it may not be the definition that some would have in Taiwan, but it does convey a meaning of solidarity of a kind among the people on both sides of the Strait that has been our policy for a very long time."[83]

One could excuse officials in both Taiwan and the PRC if they were less than clear about the substance of U.S. policy following those explanations. But that U.S. policymakers must resort to such murky comments illustrates the underlying dilemma in U.S. policy regarding the Taiwan issue. Analyst Trevor Corson summarizes one aspect of Washington's growing predicament.

> For decades the United States has balanced its Taiwan policy on a contradiction: support for Taiwan and its nascent democracy on the one hand, suppression of the island's national ambitions in order to please Beijing on the other. So far Washington has managed to deliver the right combination of deterrence and reassurance to both parties. But Taiwan's drive to secure legal independence puts the United States in an increasingly untenable position.[84]

Unfortunately, the bulk of the U.S. foreign policy community still endorses Washington's "tightrope" policy and believes that it is sustainable. The Carnegie Endowment's Michael D. Swaine, for example, argues that the United States must maintain a strong deterrence posture but also provide reassurance to the PRC. "In particular, Washington must reassure the Chinese that their worst fear—independence for Taiwan—will not be realized without their consent."[85] Since there is almost no chance that any Chinese government will ever give its consent to Taiwanese independence, such a policy actually means that the United States must guarantee that Taiwan will not become independent. Yet the United States simultaneously must provide a security guarantee to Taiwan that is sufficiently robust to discourage a PRC challenge now and in the foreseeable future. What Swaine and others who advocate such a position fail to appreciate is how difficult it will be for Washington to achieve those objectives as both Taiwan and the PRC become more assertive.

An especially significant wild card is the attitude of the Taiwanese population. As political analyst Andrew Peterson observes, U.S. policy "has always aimed at making independence unattractive to Taiwan's leaders, but it has neglected the fact that an indefinite extension of the status quo is not particularly attractive to Taiwan's people. Domestic pressure for change is increasing, and an unanticipated pro-independence shift by Taiwan's leadership may not be the only path to independence."[86] Indeed, there is no evidence that Washington has even considered what it should do if popular sentiment in Taiwan for independence becomes irresistible.

Peterson persuasively argues that a Taiwanese bid for independence will not likely come as an abrupt declaration but as "the culmination of a series of steps taken by pro-independence activists." U.S. policy is not at all clear about what Washington would do in response to such a process. "What referenda topics are off limits? What constitutes a unilateral change in the status quo? What if a unilateral change is mandated by the vast majority of Taiwan's voters?" He concludes that "Taiwan and China may embark on courses that make U.S. requests for peaceful reunification impossible or at least unattainable without the active involvement of the United States on one side or the other."[87] Instead of confronting those issues, U.S. policy is currently in a state of denial about the growing danger.

The United States may be satisfied with the status quo, but the evidence is mounting that both Taipei and Beijing are increasingly dissatisfied. Taiwan lobbies hard for staunch U.S. support, even as it pursues initiatives that point clearly toward the ultimate goal of independence and antagonize Beijing. Conversely, the PRC is growing more insistent that Washington rein in its Taiwanese client. "Chen Shui-bian is bold and aggressive due to backing from the United States," contended Zhou Qing, a veteran Taiwan watcher for the PRC and a person who has connections to the highest decision-making echelons. "The United States is the key. We need to work on the United States."[88]

It has reached the point that Washington's admonitions to Beijing and Taipei to be cautious merely confuse, frustrate, and annoy the two capitals—and indeed the populations—on both sides of the Taiwan Strait. In addition, the regional economic and political environment is shifting rapidly, and not to America's advantage. Those changes may well encourage Beijing to become bolder in challenging the U.S. commitment to defend Taiwan.

Washington had better restructure its Taiwan policy before it produces a strategic train wreck. Above all, the United States needs to greatly reduce the danger of an armed confrontation with the PRC. There is a way out of the growing dilemma, but U.S. policymakers must spurn faulty alternatives and embrace the right kinds of changes.

CHAPTER 7

THE DYNAMIC MILITARY BALANCE

At present, the Chinese military would have little likelihood of success in an attempt to retake Taiwan by force. Deficiencies in the People's Liberation Army, Taiwan's advanced weapons systems, and uncertainty about the U.S. response to such an attack have thus far (since 1958) deterred any serious attempt by the People's Republic of China to use force against Taiwan.

However, the PRC's greatest military priority is to bolster its ability to make a credible threat of force against Taiwan. Beijing is focusing its defense spending in two areas: weapons systems that could be used to coerce Taiwan, including strategies for mining the Taiwan Strait or establishing a naval blockade of the Strait, and platforms that could present a credible deterrent to U.S. intervention. The key goal of thwarting U.S. intervention is to acquire the ability to sink an intervening U.S. aircraft carrier or the other vessels accompanying the carrier to denude the main ship of protection. The PRC may have massed as many as seven hundred short-range ballistic missiles (SRBMs) in the Nanjing military region, just across the Strait from Taiwan, in an effort to bring pressure to bear on the Taiwanese regime.[1] Beijing continues to deploy dozens of additional missiles each year.

The Defense Department's *Annual Report on the Military Power of the People's Republic of China*, issued in 2004, asserts that "the cross-Strait balance of power is steadily shifting in China's favor."[2] The report indicates that "China's force modernization, weaponry, pilot training, and command and control are beginning to erode Taiwan's qualitative edge.

> Over the next several years, given current trends, China most likely will be able to
> cause significant damage to all of Taiwan's airfields and quickly degrade Taiwan's

ground-based air defenses and associated command and control through a combination of SRBMs, land-attack cruise missiles, special operations forces, and other assets.[3]

If that is true, the PRC should seek to forestall any confrontation with Taiwan until the balance tips further in its favor. However, given the trends on Taiwan illustrated in chapter 4, it is uncertain whether such a confrontation can be put off much longer.

The Chinese are aware that a conflict may arise before their conventional forces have caught up to those of Taiwan, and may be experimenting with various contingency plans. An ancient concept from Chinese military history recently resurfaced in PLA strategic literature: *shashoujian*, or "the assassin's mace." While U.S. analysts remain unclear as to what exactly the "assassin's mace" refers, its usage in military journals indicates that it is some form of attack or attacks designed to allow a weaker power to defeat a stronger foe.[4]

The concept of the assassin's mace is part of a long history in Chinese strategic culture that emphasizes asymmetric warfare and the notion of a weaker force being able to defeat a stronger power. As Sun Tzu wrote in *The Art of War:* "All warfare is based on deception. Attack [an enemy] where he is unprepared, appear where you are not expected. These military devices, leading to victory, must not be divulged beforehand."[5]

Chinese strategic thinking continues to heavily emphasize surprise, asymmetric warfare, and attacking a stronger opponent in unsuspected ways that could reduce its numerical or other strengths.[6]

In this tradition, the Chinese have been pondering a quick, devastating strike against Taiwan that would create a fait accompli for the United States. Under such a scenario, the Taiwanese regime would be deposed and the PRC would be in control of the island well before adequate U.S. assistance could arrive. Upon arriving in theater, the United States would be forced to decide whether it wanted to attack a Chinese-held Taiwan and then attempt to give it back to a reformulated Taiwanese government or simply accept the PRC's conquest. In one simulation run recently by the Taiwanese, Chinese forces took the island in just six days.[7]

Even if such a scenario is unduly dire, the costs of a cross-Strait confrontation would be extremely high for all parties involved. With so much of the PRC's legitimacy staked to the credibility of its claims to Taiwan, it is unlikely that the Chinese would surrender easily, if at all, in a conflict over Taiwan. Their determination and persistence would mean that both the Taiwanese and the United States—should it decide to involve itself—would incur significant casualties.

There is also the considerable danger that a limited military confrontation could spiral out of control with disastrous consequences for both China and the United States.

This chapter will explore in greater depth the military balance as it currently exists and attempt to draw inferences from historical trends and the best estimates available as to where the military balance may shift. It will also assess various strategies that the PRC is likely to employ and the tools the Taiwanese may use to counter them, and evaluate the implications of a potential U.S. military response.

HOW STRONG IS CHINA'S MILITARY?

China's military, by all accounts, would be roundly defeated in a conventional war with the United States at the present time. Perhaps more important, however, several analyses have concluded that the PRC would be unable to win a conflict with Taiwan even if the United States did not intervene. For example, Michael O'Hanlon of the Brookings Institution wrote in 2000 that "China could not take Taiwan, even if U.S. combat forces did not intervene in a conflict . . . for at least a decade, if not much longer."[8] In 2003 analyst Ivan Eland noted Taiwan's qualitative military advantages and concluded that "China will probably remain deterred from attacking Taiwan, regardless of whether or not the United States guarantees Taiwanese security."[9]

Michael Swaine and James Mulvenon of the RAND Corporation assessed in 2001 what may happen if China were to attempt an "all-out air, missile, and naval strike against Taiwan followed immediately by attempted landings on at least some offshore islands, and possibly on the main island; or a direct and massive assault on Taiwan that passes the offshore islands entirely." They concluded that "Mainland China will likely remain unable to undertake such a massive attack over the medium term, and perhaps over the long term as well."[10] It is even less likely that a less comprehensive PRC military campaign could defeat Taiwan. Even the 2004 DoD report concedes, after presenting a long list of worst-case scenarios, that the "[a]symmetric capabilities that Taiwan possesses or is acquiring could deter a Chinese attack by making it unacceptably costly."[11]

Other assessments, though, are somewhat less sanguine. The Council on Foreign Relations report states that although "the PLA currently has the ability to undertake intensive, short-duration air, missile, and naval attacks on Taiwan, as well as more prolonged air and naval attacks . . . [t]he efficacy of either scenario would be highly dependent on Taiwan's political and military response, and especially on any actions taken by the United States and Japan."[12] The latter point is especially crucial. Robert S. Ross of Boston College went so far as to proclaim that "deterring China's use of force has never depended on Taiwan's capabilities; Taiwan alone cannot deter the mainland."[13] Writing in the late 1990s, Richard Bernstein and Ross H. Munro worried that, absent a U.S. security guarantee to Taiwan, "there would be very little standing in the way of Chinese domination of all of East Asia."[14]

The great disparity in assessments is likely due to several factors. First, the PLA is notoriously secretive, and, while professing its openness, releases white papers on its defense policy that actually reveal very little about its defense spending.[15] Beijing may have several reasons for concealing its true defense expenditures. It may be a manifestation of the lingering Communist tendencies toward secrecy within the PRC government. It may be that, after having lied for so long about its defense spending, it does not want to lose face by coming clean now. More alarmingly, it may be in order to keep the United States and China's regional competitors unclear on the scope of China's military modernization.[16] Compounding China's deceptiveness, there is an intellectual deficit when it comes to assessing the China-Taiwan military balance aside from America's capabilities.

As Eland points out, much of the foundational analysis of the PLA produced in the United States comes from the Defense Department, "a federal bureaucracy that has an inherent conflict of interest in developing assessments of foreign military threats. Because the department that is creating the threat assessments is the same one that is lobbying Congress for money for weapons, personnel, fuel, and training to combat threats, its threat projections tend to be inflated."[17] The work done by the DoD ends up laying the foundation for much of the work done by other government agencies and groups such as the CFR.

Moreover, perceptions of the national interest no doubt color most assessments of threats and appropriate U.S. policies. Since the prevailing view within the U.S. government has maintained for over half a century that an at least ambiguous security guarantee to Taiwan is a vital U.S. interest, a conclusion that Taiwan could defend itself would call into question a fundamental, long-standing institutional assumption. Perversely, as Michael O'Hanlon notes, overly pessimistic reports continually issued by the U.S. Department of Defense could help to convince the PRC that it had a decent chance of taking Taiwan.[18]

STRENGTHS AND WEAKNESSES OF THE PRC MILITARY

There are several ways in which the PRC could potentially attack Taiwan. As mentioned above, several hundred SRBMs are hosted in the Nanjing military region across from Taiwan, and the PRC is thought to be adding dozens more missiles to this battery each year.[19] The PRC could use these missiles either to target Taiwan's air bases and command, control, computer, communication, intelligence, surveillance, and reconnaissance (C4ISR) stations, or it could attempt to target Taiwan's military and civilian leadership. China could also attempt to target certain nodes of Taiwan's economic infrastructure, such as key communications sites and port facilities. The goal of such an assault would be to induce financial and economic panic, thereby causing severe damage to Taiwan's economy, at least in the short term. However, the economic impact of striking Taiwan's defense sites would likely be nearly as high, and would have the added benefit of prospectively taking out a portion of the means Taiwan could use to defend itself.

Swaine and Mulvenon note, however, that "[e]ven a large number of ballistic missile and air attacks alone, barring a rather quick collapse of Taiwan's will to resist, would take a considerable period of time to destroy strategic targets and seriously weaken Taiwan's morale."[20] The 2002 report of the U.S.-China Economic and Security Review Commission noted that "[a] barrage even of hundreds of Chinese ballistic and cruise missiles fired against Taiwan, however, would actually do limited (or at least not permanently devastating) damage, unless China resorted to chemical, biological or nuclear warheads or the missile strike is coordinated with other concurrent military operations such as air and maritime engagements."[21] O'Hanlon goes further, explaining that attacks on Taiwan's ample air defenses may not be incredibly effective:

> China's ballistic missiles are inaccurate. . . . They might achieve an occasional hit on a runway, but the missiles' accuracy—typically no better than three hundred meters—would be too poor to make that happen more than every tenth shot or so. And runways can absorb a number of hits before being incapacitated; as many as one hundred properly distributed craters could be needed to shut down operations at a single runway. China presently lacks advanced submunitions that could reduce the number of missiles required per base. To shut down a runway even temporarily using conventional munitions, therefore, literally hundreds of ballistic missiles might be required—virtually the entire PRC inventory.[22]

Although the PRC has made meaningful strides in increasing the accuracy of its SRBMs[23] (and has certainly increased the number massed across the Strait from the two hundred O'Hanlon was referring to in 2000), there is no reason to believe that the PRC could use missile attacks alone to defeat Taiwan. The PRC could attempt to bolster the missile attacks by using an aerial assault in addition to the missile barrage, but the PLA Air Force's fighters, with limited capabilities

for precision bombing, would need to fly low, and would face resistance from Taiwanese anti-aircraft defenses.[24] Moreover, Taiwan's air force would also respond,
and in an air war over the Taiwan Strait, the PLAAF could well be defeated by
the Taiwanese air force.

Taiwan has a modern air force that includes roughly three hundred and fifty
fourth-generation fighter planes.[25] By contrast, the PLAAF is quantitatively impressive, with nearly one thousand fighter aircraft. However, of that one thousand, the only fourth-generation fighters are the roughly seventy-eight Sukhoi
27s and seventy-six Sukhoi 30s purchased from Russia.[26] Thus, Taiwan has more
than twice as many fourth-generation fighters as the PLAAF.

Although Taiwan maintains air superiority at present, China is making attempts to shore up its fighter inventory by adding more fourth-generation fighters. The Russian news service RIA Novosti reported in December 2004 that
Sukhoi, the maker of the PLA's Su–27s and Su–30s, expected a new contract in
2005 for twenty-four more of the advanced Su–30 MK2s.[27] Sukhoi has licensed
the production of Su–27s to Shenyang Aircraft Corporation in China,[28] and has
nearly one hundred more to deliver under the terms of its contract. These measures will likely serve over time to erode Taiwan's advantage in the number of
fourth-generation fighters it can field.

There are other difficulties a PRC air assault would encounter. In an air war
over the Taiwan Strait, only roughly three hundred planes could physically fit
into the airspace.[29] Taiwan would likely limit its air force's response to the airspace over the Strait itself.[30] Thus, the PLA would be forced either to deploy all
or nearly all of its fourth-generation fighters to the conflict or else field 1950s-era
fighters against highly advanced F–16s, Mirage 2000s, and Indigenous Defense
Fighters.[31] At present, either strategy would be extremely risky and highly likely
to result in the serious losses for the PLAAF.

Given that the missiles massed in Nanjing, even if coupled with an attempt at
aerial bombing, would likely fail to be decisive in a conflict with Taiwan, one
could conclude that their presence serves in large part as a psychological deterrent to attempt to prevent Chen Shui-bian's government from going too far in its
campaign to assert a distinctive Taiwanese identity. But Taiwan's responses to
China's provocations during Taiwan's 1996 and 2000 elections seem to indicate
that bellicose rhetoric, let alone actions, have tended to have a counterproductive
effect on Taiwan's behavior. In the event China launched missiles at Taiwan, it
would have to hope that the damage done by the missiles would destroy Taiwan's
political will, which, while possible, seems unlikely given the historical record.
One unknown variable is how much pressure a spooked Taiwanese business community would put on the government to make concessions to halt the conflict be-

fore it would do irreparable damage to the island's economy. It is possible that such pressure could be a potent factor.

An even more ambitious option for the PRC would be to attempt an amphibious assault of Taiwan. This form of attack would involve ferrying PRC ground troops across the Taiwan Strait, attempting to establish a beachhead on Taiwan, and then using the beachhead to pour ground troops onto the island, starting a ground war there. This strategy is almost universally thought to be flawed, and is extremely unlikely to succeed.

First, for the PRC to launch an amphibious assault, it would need to prepare for the roughly one-hundred-mile voyage across the notoriously rough waters of the Taiwan Strait. Such a buildup would be easy to observe from satellite imagery, and the Taiwanese would have the ability to prepare before the PRC amphibious forces arrived. Not only would the Taiwanese know that an attack is coming, but it would take several hours for the PRC transports to cross the Strait.[32] Taiwan could prepare for the fight while the PRC ships were in transit (and possibly taking fire from Taiwan's air force). Taiwan could also deploy naval forces to meet and harass any amphibious force from China.[33] In January 2005, Taiwan announced that it had successfully tested its Hsiung Feng III, a highly advanced supersonic anti-ship missile that would cause serious problems for the technologically inferior Chinese amphibious forces.[34] If China moved its more advanced destroyers into the Strait, however, it is growing increasingly possible that it could overpower even Taiwan's more advanced technology with brute force.

Even if a PRC force could make it across the Strait safely, the DoD report notes that "[t]he PLA's amphibious lift assets are insufficient to project force much beyond China's shores. . . . [T]he PLA is assessed to lack lift assets for a conventional amphibious assault on Taiwan."[35] Some estimates claim that the PRC would only be able to sealift one division of troops (ten thousand men) to Taiwan.[36] The International Institute for Strategic Studies noted in 2001 that "it would take approximately 800–1,000 large landing craft nearly two weeks to transport the required 30 infantry divisions to Taiwan. At present, the Chinese Navy could move one, or perhaps two divisions."[37] As of 2004, those capabilities had improved substantially, although China still possesses fewer than three hundred fifty vessels capable of acting as landing craft, more than half of which are in reserve.[38] The 2004 DoD report notes that although "a number of newly designed landing ships have been under construction . . . the numbers currently believed to be under construction most likely are insufficient to support a sizable amphibious operation in the next 5 years."[39]

Any PLA amphibious force would be forced to choose from an extremely limited number of landing sites that are appropriate for amphibious assault.

O'Hanlon estimates that less than 20 percent of Taiwan's coastline would be suited to amphibious assault, due to the presence of mud flats on Taiwan's western shores and large cliffs on its eastern shores.[40] The Taiwanese, of course, know their coastline better than anyone, and they no doubt have assessed and planned for where amphibious assaults may come.

Taiwan, knowing in advance that an amphibious assault was coming from a force of ten to twenty thousand PLA soldiers, and having some knowledge of where the forces would be attempting to land, could draw from its two-hundred-thousand-strong active duty forces (let alone its more than one million reserves) to prepare to meet them. Taiwan could also launch an assault on the amphibious force from the air, exploiting Taiwan's air superiority and the vulnerability of China's amphibious forces to air attacks. Given all of these factors, an amphibious assault would be highly likely to fail, and is one of the least likely forms of Chinese attack.[41]

A more threatening (and consequently more likely) form of attack by the PRC would be a blockade of the Taiwan Strait. A blockade would be meant to strangle the Taiwanese economy, causing Taiwan to capitulate to the PRC's political demands, possibly even without a fight. David Shambaugh, an expert on the PLA military, characterized three different types of blockade the PRC may attempt:

1. A "low" blockade. In such a blockade, the PLA Navy would declare that it was blockading Taiwan and board and/or turn back any ships attempting to arrive at Taiwan, possibly exempting certain types of shipments.
2. A "medium" blockade. In a medium blockade, the PLAN would declare a blockade and possibly exempt certain craft, but openly state that ships attempting to break the blockade would be fired upon.
3. A "high" blockade. A high blockade would mean a total ban on ships arriving at or leaving Taiwan and an open threat of violence against any ships attempting to break the blockade.[42]

Any of the forms of blockade outlined by Shambaugh would present significant problems and serious questions for Taiwan, the People's Republic of China, and the United States. First, a blockade is considered an act of war under international law. This fact would certainly be cited by the Taiwanese regime in calling for U.S., if not international, condemnation of the blockade.

Taiwan's inevitable invocation of international law could become a severe point of contention, because the Chinese would assert sovereignty over Taiwan and assert that the measure was merely part of an internal conflict. In other words, China would be blockading itself and not violating international law. Given the fact that most countries do not recognize Taiwan, they would likely accept Beijing's position. The United States, and the international community generally, would have to determine which side they agreed with: Taiwan as part of China, or Taiwan as a sovereign country. Taiwan would likely also call for military assistance in breaking a blockade. Unlike in the case of a potential amphibious assault or missile strike, Taiwan may need substantial help to survive a naval blockade.[43]

Though it is possible that Taiwan's navy could forcibly break a PRC blockade on its own, it is by no means certain, and is becoming less likely. It is also possible that Taiwan could survive a blockade without responding with a direct military confrontation, but that is not certain either. The threat of a blockade is the most plausible of all conventional Chinese military options, since it is unclear if Taiwan could weather a blockade without a military confrontation or prevail in a subsequent military confrontation. There is a significant chance that a blockade could force Taiwan to capitulate or risk escalating matters to the military level with all the perils that step would entail. Consequently, the issue deserves closer examination.

Taiwan is almost entirely dependent on imports, particularly in strategically important commodities such as petroleum. It does not have a significant strategic petroleum reserve from which it could draw in the event of a crisis. It would be forced to plead for international assistance, attempt to break the blockade by itself, attempt to wait out the blockade with the resources it had, or even to attempt airdrops of supplies.[44] Questions remain as to whether the Organization of Petroleum Exporting Countries would stop oil exports to China in response to a blockade of Taiwan. If they did not, or if non-OPEC oil-producing countries continued to sell oil to China, the PRC would maintain a steady flow of oil during a conflict while Taiwan drained its small petroleum reserve and forced rationing on homes and businesses on Taiwan.

The economic impact of a blockade would be dire for Taiwan. Even during the 1995, 1996, and 2000 provocations by China, Taiwan's economy was seriously damaged. Between the Chinese missile tests in July 1995 and its military exercises in and across the Taiwan Strait in August of that year, the Taiwanese stock market crashed 20 percent.[45] During the 1996 crisis, Taiwan's foreign currency reserves sank by more than 8 percent and it took more than U.S. $7 billion to prop up its stock market. The 1996 missile firings halted merchant marine traffic for days and caused serious economic dislocations in Taiwan, even though they occurred during a crisis in which China was stating openly and publicly that it had no intention of mounting a campaign to retake Taiwan.[46] If China stated its intentions openly as having designs on Taiwan, the repercussions could be much deeper and last much longer.

There are two kinds of blockades that China could attempt: mining the harbors off Taiwanese ports or a submarine blockade. The PLAN possesses more than two hundred naval vessels that are or could be equipped to lay mines.[47] In addition to those surface vessels, the PLAN's submarine force, numbering roughly sixty-five, could be used to lay mines. Though this prospect appears intimidating, the PLAN may have difficulty getting the desired result using either strategy.[48]

If the PLAN were to try to use surface vessels to mine Taiwan's harbors it would be met by the Taiwanese air force, and possibly the Taiwanese navy in the Taiwan Strait, before it could reach its targets. Most of the Chinese minelaying surface vessels would be quite vulnerable to attacks from the air,[49] and Taiwan could deploy its new Hsiung Feng III anti-ship missile, which could aptly deal with Chinese amphibious vessels.

The situation would become much more dangerous if Taiwan's engagement of the PLAN minelayers caused the conflict to spiral into open naval warfare. Analysts Justin Bernier and Stuart Gold have pointed out in 2003 that, while the PLAN's minelaying surface vessels are not a grave threat, the PLAN could simply mount a traditional blockade with its destroyers and other naval assets. According to Bernier and Gold, "Taiwan is . . . unprepared today for a traditional blockade by the Chinese surface fleet, which is numerically and qualitatively superior. Its newest additions, two Russian-built Sovremenny-class destroyers fitted with the supersonic Sunburn ship-killing cruise missiles, present an edge over anything Taiwan has sent to sea this decade."[50] Avoiding escalation would be an important consideration for Taiwan in handling a surface blockade or minelaying attempt, but that might be extremely difficult to avoid.

The technique for implanting mines that would be even more dangerous to the Taiwanese is via submarine. The Strait itself is relatively shallow, and its underwater geography is uneven, both factors that increase the difficulty in detecting approaching submarines using sonar. It is unlikely that the Taiwanese could detect the submarines as they went about laying mines.

One recent analysis suggests that, although successfully mining the Strait would be a serious shock to Taiwan's economy and would likely sink several commercial vessels, it would not present a meaningful military threat, even in the short-term. Michael A. Glosny of the Massachusetts Institute of Technology ran three different scenarios in which PLAN submarines would mine the Taiwan Strait. Glosny concluded that:

> In all three simulations of the mine-laying analysis, the number of kills would be very small, even when a relatively favorable mine effectiveness ratio is used. In two

of the three simulations of the mine-clearing analysis, the Taiwanese would be able to clear q-routes [safe passages that had been de-mined] within a month, even under pessimistic conditions. Even with the risky strategy of laying mines with two-hundred-fifty-day delays, the total number of mines would still be very small by historical standards. With the inability to replenish minefields through aerial drops, and [with] a small number of submarines (even under optimistic conditions), the Chinese would not be able to lay enough mines to be militarily decisive.[51]

If Glosny is correct, the ability of Taiwan to endure a mine-based blockade would depend mostly on Taiwan's political will, and perhaps to some degree on economic support from abroad intended to shore up that political will. Although attempts to provide financial support to Taiwan could elicit harsh responses by China, it is unclear whether the PRC would have the wherewithal to mount additional military attacks on foreign countries agreeing to financial support for Taiwan.[52] On the other hand, China's ability to engage in political and economic retaliation—especially against its East Asian neighbors—is already considerable. That ability is certain to become even more formidable in the future. In terms of Taiwan's political will, given the responses to the PRC's attempts to coerce Taiwan in 1996 and 2000, it is unlikely that Taiwan would crumble immediately. Indeed, Taiwan's responses in 1996 and 2000 could be fairly considered the opposite policy outcomes than those the PRC sought. Yet it is also true that a blockade would exert pressure far greater than did the PRC moves in 1996 and 2000.

Glosny points out that Taiwan's response to those earlier provocations was rooted not in fear but rather in anger and defiance: "In a poll asking people in Taiwan how they felt in response to the PRC's military threats before the 1996 presidential election, 57 percent said not panicky at all and 28 percent said not very panicky."[53] If the Taiwanese were to feel that they were genuinely under attack, it seems unlikely that they would shift from a defiant position to one of capitulation. Moreover, given the trends highlighted in chapter 4, the Taiwanese people would likely feel themselves under attack from a foreign power and muster their defenses to protect what they see as their country. In the eyes of many Taiwanese, they would be facing their third foreign occupation in just over one hundred years.

In lieu of mining the Strait, the PRC may attempt a submarine blockade, in which PLAN submarines would take up positions in the Taiwan Strait and the East China Sea, threatening to torpedo any vessels violating a certain perimeter around Taiwan's ports. Using projections that "would produce higher kill ratios per patrol and exchange rates [the ratio between the number of merchant ships sunk versus submarines lost] than any other historical engagement," Glosny concludes in this case that "the PLAN's small fleet of submarines would inflict an amount of total damage that seems unlikely to be militarily decisive by historical standards."[54]

While Glosny's research is probably guilty of underestimating the nonmilitary costs that Taiwan would incur under a naval blockade,[55] it does suggest that the overall danger posed to Taiwan by a blockade may be overstated. If Taiwan were to bolster its ability to conduct antisubmarine warfare (ASW) and minesweeping, it could well defeat or live with, respectively, a submarine or mine blockade. Even absent advances in ASW and minesweeping, if political will were strong on Taiwan a blockade could possibly be endured.

One factor adding to the uncertain efficacy of a Chinese blockade is Taiwan's potential ability to re-route its shipping beyond the reach of the blockade. According to David Shambaugh, Taiwan for years has developed contingency plans to use the Palawan Passage in the South China Sea for its shipping.[56] Given the PLAN's current deficiencies, its ability to extend a blockade all the way into the South China Sea is dubious, and any attempt to do so would certainly elicit louder criticism from its neighbors and raise serious logistical problems, such as sorting out Taiwan-bound ships from other maritime traffic.

Lyle Goldstein and William Murray of the U.S. Naval War College disagree, however. In their view, "Taipei is unwilling or unable to devote the necessary resources to mount a credible defense against a sustained submarine [blockade] campaign."[57] Moreover, the authors go so far as to suggest that a U.S. attempt to break a PRC blockade of Taiwan could result in dozens of U.S. naval vessels sunk. Goldstein and Murray point out that the United States could encounter serious difficulties as a result of the PRC's:

- advances in undersea mapping, which increase the PRC's ability to sit submarines on the sea floor, making them nearly impossible to detect;
- refinements its submarines to make them quieter while running (and thus more difficult to defeat with sonar);
- possible strategy to use its antiquated Ming and Romeo submarines as decoys in order to draw attacks from U.S. submarines so that their identity is revealed and China's advanced Kilo submarines could then fire on U.S. submarines;
- advancements in its newest class of submarines to allow them to launch large, wake-homing torpedoes that are effective at sinking aircraft carriers.[58]

The prospect of the PRC being able to sink a U.S. aircraft carrier is incredibly troubling. Perhaps it is no coincidence, then, that the PRC again has focused its energies on attempting to develop a credible capability to sink an aircraft carrier. In the words of one PRC general:

[the PRC has] the ability to deal with an aircraft carrier that dares to get into our range of fire. Once we decide to use force against Taiwan, we definitely will consider an intervention by the United States. The United States likes vain glory; if one of its aircraft carriers should be attacked and destroyed, people in the United States would begin to complain and quarrel loudly, and the U.S. president would find the going harder and harder.[59]

If Goldstein and Murray are correct, a PRC blockade could pose a mortal threat to Taiwan. It could also create an extremely dangerous situation for U.S. forces if Washington decided to intervene to break the blockage. Indeed, all of the incentives are for the PRC to take action in the short term.

The murky view of China's ability and potential tactics is not the only area of uncertainty. The trends in the military balance have even come under scrutiny. Although the cross-Strait military balance is generally thought to be shifting in the PRC's favor, not all analysts even agree on that point. Justin Bernier and Stuart Gold argue precisely the opposite: that the balance is shifting away from the PRC, and that this fact may act as another influence toward rashness on the part of China. Bernier and Gold cite the taxing effects the global war on terrorism (GWOT) has placed on U.S. strategy and readiness, dramatically diminished Taiwanese defense budgets (from roughly one-third of government spending in 1991 to only 16.5% of government spending in 2002), deficiencies in Taiwan's navy, and a PRC defense acquisition policy that has been aimed directly at bolstering its ability to blockade Taiwan.[60] Bernier and Gold project that U.S. readiness will correct over the coming years, as will Taiwan's defense spending. In their view, Taiwan's greatest vulnerability is now. (One point in the authors' analysis has been corrected already: the "overwhelming advantage over the ROC air force" that the PLAAF enjoyed momentarily because of its acquisition of the AA–12 air-to-air missile has since been offset by Taiwan's acquisition of the AIM–120, a comparable weapon.[61])

The fact that nearly every widely held assumption about China's military capacity can reasonably be doubted is reflective of the degree of uncertainty about its capabilities. The bulk of the evidence, though, suggests that the PRC is beginning to acquire some viable military options with regard to Taiwan.

THE PRC'S CONTINGENCY PLANS: FAIT ACCOMPLI AND *SHASHOUJIAN*

Even the assessments that calculate China's military strength as inadequate believe that China's hand could be forced if the Taiwanese regime were to go too far in its quest for independence. The unclear and shifting rhetoric from the United States has caused confusion in China as to whether the United States would intervene in a conflict, or, more accurately, what type of scenario would elicit U.S. intervention. Accordingly, the PRC has developed a series of strategies designed to avoid U.S. intervention by appearing less warlike (such as a "low" blockade), as well as strategies for dealing with U.S. intervention if the line is crossed.

Given that low-level escalation such as a "low" blockade or provocations like those in 1995 and 1996 are likely to fail to achieve their political goals, it is worth investigating China's contingency plans for what to do if it goes too far and provokes the United States to intervene in a conflict in the Taiwan Strait.

It is common knowledge that PLA military strategists are diligent students of U.S. military doctrine, and that they have observed the last several U.S. military interventions, particularly those in the Balkans and in Iraq, with a mixture of awe and humility. However, the demonstrated might of the U.S. military has not deterred PLA planners from pursuing various strategies to achieve "victory" against the much stronger, more advanced, and swifter U.S. fighting force.

The lessons PLA strategists have gleaned from recent U.S. interventions have led to a shift and recalibration of PLA military doctrine. The vision that currently enjoys favor is commonly referred to as "local war under modern, high-tech conditions" (LWUMHTC).[62] Paul H. B. Godwin, a non-resident scholar at the Atlantic Council, explains that LWUMHTC, "recognizing the PLA's outdated arms and equipment . . . focuses on joint operations and logistics and directs the armed forces to prepare for 'information, electronic, mobile, and special warfare.'" The problem, according to Godwin, is that "[i]t will take over a decade for the PLA to master the skills required, and acquire the arms and equipment necessary, to conduct advanced technology warfare."[63]

The PLA's march toward a modern military doctrine was no doubt influenced by the dramatic changes that occurred in global military affairs during the 1990s. The change in military thinking and actions over the past two decades has been dubbed a revolution in military affairs, or RMA, by military analysts. The RMA is something of an amorphous concept, but a commonly accepted explanation has been offered by Andrew Krepinevich of the Center for Strategic and Budgetary Assessments, who states that an RMA "occurs when the application of new technologies into a significant number of military systems combines with innovative operational concepts and organizational adaptation in a way that fundamentally alters the character and conduct of conflict."[64]

Far from leveling the field of competition for the Chinese, the RMA adds another layer of deficiency to the PLA's capabilities. It has fallen two generations behind: It is behind the military capability possessed by the United States in 1980, and it has been leapfrogged by an RMA that has occurred since. Though PLA analysts have dutifully studied the RMA and sought—with some success—to incorporate it into PLA operations, Ahmed Hashim, a professor at the U.S. Naval War College, has pointed out that "[w]riting about and dissecting the RMA theoretically and conceptually and actually being able to exploit it are two totally different endeavors. Whether the PLA succeeds in the second is another matter altogether."[65]

If the PLA had intended to catch up to the United States' capabilities before the RMA, its task became doubly difficult afterward. Not only would the PLA have to catch up to the United States' conventional warfighting capabilities, but the developments that characterized the RMA, such as joint operations capability, vastly improved C4ISR capacity, and precision-guided munitions present another hurdle for the PLA to clear. For the PLA to catch up in both these arenas would take several decades at least. In the meantime, China has pursued asymmetric strategies that seek to maximize its strengths and minimize those of its prospective opponents.

The PLA finds itself in a position where it realizes that external events (on Taiwan) may force it to start a war that will likely draw in an opponent that it could definitely not defeat conventionally—perhaps not even unconventionally. This predicament defies much of the logic of Western military thinking. For China, however, the notion of engaging a stronger foe goes back to Mao Zedong and beyond.[66]

The first strategy the PRC developed to offset its conventional deficiencies was the concept of a fait accompli strike: striking at Taiwan so quickly and devastatingly that by the time U.S. troops could respond the Taiwanese regime would be deposed and the PRC would be in control of the island. The United States would then be forced to decide whether it wanted to attempt to unravel Chinese control of Taiwan and piece together a Taiwanese government to which it could hand back the island. One Chinese general, Zhang Wannian, reportedly claimed in 2000 that "during the period of [2001–2006], it is certain that war will break out in the Taiwan Strait" in the form of a "decapitation strike."[67]

The fait accompli approach has been joined by (or perhaps evolved into) the concept of *shashoujian*, or the assassin's mace. *Shashoujian* involves striking a deadly, unexpected blow with a weapon that the enemy is not prepared for.[68] Use of the term in Chinese military journals indicates that *shashoujian* may in fact refer to a particular weapons platform(s) or mode(s) of attack, as opposed to a loose conceptual tactic.[69] While U.S. analysts remain uncertain what, exactly, *shashoujian* refers to, various theories have advanced the notions that *shashoujian* is a weapon for:

- "blinding" an enemy so that his C4ISR capabilities are diminished;
- "decapitation," by which the opposing force's leadership is neutralized;

- "paralysis," damaging an opponent's ability to command and mobilize his fighting force; or even
- deterrence, when wielded in such a way that a potential opponent chooses not to fight.[70]

These conceptual interpretations could take operational form in many different ways. Electromagnetic pulse (EMP), electronic warfare (EW), information warfare (IW), and other forms of asymmetric warfare all have been suggested as potential *shashoujian* weapons. These forms of attack all seek to exploit vulnerabilities in the areas where the PRC is grossly outmatched, such as C4ISR. By severely limiting, for example, Taiwan's ability to conduct joint operations, the playing field would become at least partially leveled between the Chinese force and the Taiwanese force, taking away Taiwan's advantage.

An EMP, for example, could cripple Taiwan's entire communications network. An EMP results from a nuclear weapon being detonated in the atmosphere several miles above the target.[71] As the pulse from the detonation reaches Earth it causes communications and other networks to shut down. While not immediately harmful to humans, an EMP would be devastating to a high-tech society like Taiwan, particularly in a time of war. A scientist at the Lawrence Livermore National Laboratory described the effects of an EMP as "instantly regressing a country dependent on 21st century technology by more than 100 years."[72]

In addition to crashing Taiwan's networks, an EMP would seriously damage the communications and computers of any intervening U.S. force. The Executive Report of the Commission to Assess the Threat to the United States from Electromagnetic Pulse Attack noted that "[o]ur increasing dependence on advanced electronics systems results in the potential for an increased EMP vulnerability of our technologically advanced forces, and if unaddressed makes EMP employment by an adversary an attractive asymmetric option."[73]

Perhaps even more troubling for the United States would be the prospect of EW/IW attacks. In 2002, the *Los Angeles Times* reported that a classified CIA memo indicated that "the Chinese military is working to launch wide-scale cyber-attacks on American and Taiwanese computer networks, including Internet-linked military systems considered vulnerable to sabotage."[74] This could pose a serious problem for U.S. policymakers, because at the tactical level, EW/IW is in many ways the functional equivalent of terrorism: We have to be right all the time; they only have to be right once.

A potential EW/IW attack would fit perfectly the working definition of *shashoujian*: It would potentially be a "blinding" or "paralyzing" surprise attack that would take away a profound advantage of a stronger enemy. In addition, the ability to attribute a large-scale EW/IW attack to the PRC government is uncertain. The inability of governments on both sides to control the actions of all "combatants" in an EW/IW exchange could present an extremely dangerous scenario of decentralized escalation; that is, while acting purportedly on behalf of their countries, private hackers could become caught in an escalation where the opposite side cannot tell whether the attacks are state-sanctioned or not.

During the EP–3 crisis in 2001, thousands of EW attacks were launched by Chinese hackers, though not necessarily by the Chinese government. Private U.S. hackers responded by raining a deluge of cyber-attacks on Chinese websites (denoted by the suffix .cn.)[75] While the ability of Chinese hackers to penetrate U.S. defense systems is uncertain, crucial networks at home, such as the power grid, telecommunications networks, and others remain vulnerable.[76] Though the odds the Chinese would face in trying to penetrate U.S. cyberdefenses are great, they are not as great as the odds they would face on a battlefield. The Chinese would have every reason to prepare such a line of attack.

Certainly, the Chinese would not launch an EMP, an EW/IW attack, or any other asymmetrical attack against the United States or Taiwan lightly. But with the legitimacy and potentially the survival of the Chinese regime staked so closely to its claim to Taiwan, it is not impossible to envision a scenario where the Chinese feel their hand being forced. Depending on how "victory" is defined, which side may emerge victorious remains uncertain. What is certain, however, is that the potential costs to all parties involved would be very high, in human, economic, and geopolitical terms.

LOOKING AHEAD: PROSPECTS FOR THE PRC AND TAIWAN

Predicting what will happen on either side of the Taiwan Strait is difficult. There are any number of scenarios, most of which are undesirable, that one could envision. In the interest of prudent policymaking, however, U.S. analysts must look at what China *could* do to strengthen its ability to project power across the Strait, and what Taiwan *should* do to shore up its defenses against the most likely forms of Chinese attack.

The trends in defense spending as a percentage of economic output are moving in opposite directions for China and Taiwan. Taiwan's defense spending has shrunk to roughly 2.5 percent of its $280 billion gross national product.[77] China, on the other hand, has increased its defense spending to between 3.5 and 5 percent of its $1.43 trillion GDP.[78] Put another way, the best estimates consistently place China's defense spending between roughly $50 and $70 billion per year,[79] whereas Taiwan's defense spending comes in at roughly $6.6 billion.[80] Certainly the strategic advantages possessed by Taiwan can afford it a lesser need for defense spending, but the gross disparity in defense spending has Taiwan flirting with danger.

There are troubling indications that Taiwan does not take the Chinese military threat as seriously as it should. *The Economist* magazine, quoting James Mulvenon, put the problem thus: "[T]here is a 'fundamental perceptual difference' between Taiwanese officials and American ones about the nature of the Chinese threat. The Americans brief their Taiwan counterparts on Chinese military capabilities, he says, but are "flummoxed" by their unwillingness to accept that 'the threat is imminent.'"[81]

Domestic politics on Taiwan also seem to have surpassed its considerations for its own defense. Tseng Yung-chuan, the executive director of the opposition Kuomintang's Central Policy Committee, remarked in November 2004 that Taiwan's existing defense budget should be cut in half in order to fund social welfare projects.[82] Continued foot-dragging by Taiwan on the unfulfilled 2001 U.S. arms sales package to Taiwan has caused even staunch Taiwan supporters in Congress such as Rep. Tom Lantos (D-CA) to remark that Taiwan's position is "absurd at a time when clearly Taiwan's security is not as guaranteed as friends of Taiwan would like to see."[83]

The arms sales package, originally proposed in 2001, has remained bogged down in Taiwan's internal politics. Some of the package's opponents argue that domestic spending priorities in Taiwan should trump national security spending. Some argue that there is no way Taiwan can win an arms race in the long term and that there is no sense in trying. Taiwan's ruling Democratic Progressive Party finally approved a scaled-back version of the initial agreement in 2004, but ran into trouble because of continued opposition in the Legislative Yuan. DPP legislator Bikhim Hsiao lamented in December 2004, "How can we expect the Americans to support us if we are not willing to come to our own defense?"[84]

From a theoretical standpoint, Taiwan must be either wholly depending on U.S. military intervention in case of a PRC attack or else acting entirely irrationally. If the latter were true, it would unravel one of the principal shared assumptions about international politics. Theorists of nearly all ideological persuasions agree on this one fundamental point: States act rationally to pursue their interests. For Taiwan to simply ignore questions pertaining to its survival separate from China would defy millennia of historical precedent.

The former explanation seems more likely. The U.S. message to Taiwan has been muddled, but apparently Taiwan has heard what it wants to hear; especially the continued categorical pledges of a defense guarantee by the Taiwan Lobby in Congress. In 2004 one congressman, Tom Tancredo (R-CO), went so far as to propose a bill recommending that the administration confer diplomatic recognition on Taiwan as a sovereign country.[85]

For its part, however, it seems that China has been hearing what it wants to as well: worry on the part of U.S. policymakers about China's growing defense capability, and doubts as to whether the U.S. should defend Taiwan at all cost. Accordingly, China's thinking going forward seems to entertain two strategies: developing an ability to deter the U.S. by making the costs of intervention prohibitively high, or using a strategy of incremental escalation that would confuse and divide U.S. policymakers as to when and whether intervention should take place.

China's spending, while already enormous compared to Taiwan's, could easily increase dramatically. China's economy is large and growing rapidly. Its economic growth over the past nine years has averaged over 8 percent.[86] With its GDP growing from an already large $1.43 trillion,[87] even a marginal increase in the percentage of China's GDP devoted to defense spending could dramatically increase its advantage in defense spending and worsen the threat it could pose to U.S. forces deployed in defense of Taiwan. As an illustration, China's 2002 acquisition of two Sovremenny destroyers was estimated to cost $1.4 billion.[88] China recently bought twenty-four fighters, a combination of Su–27s and Su–30s, for $1 billion.[89] A 0.5 percent increase in China's proportion of non-PPP adjusted GDP devoted to defense spending could generate an extra $6 to 7 billion per year.[90] Thus, with continued economic growth, relatively small increases in defense spending can yield meaningful advances in China's military capability. At present, several areas of PRC defense spending are already causing alarm among U.S. military analysts.

China's acquisition of two Russian-built Sovremenny destroyers in 2000 that were subsequently equipped with Sunburn anti-ship missiles has raised concerns at the Pentagon. In the words of one former U.S. defense official, Sunburn anti-ship missiles are those that the U.S. Navy "fears most."[91] The Sunburn-equipped Sovremennys would pose a meaningful threat to a U.S. naval deployment to the region (including aircraft carriers), which may explain why China has been so determined to acquire and deploy them. China has reportedly ordered two more Sunburn-equipped Sovremennys to be delivered in 2006, and will end up with at least eight total, by 2010.[92]

In addition to the Sovremennys, China is developing two indigenous destroyers that may represent significant advances in China's domestic technological capacity for shipbuilding. In the words of one analyst: "All available evidence suggests that the performance and characteristics of the [two new Chinese destroyers] are at least comparable to, when not better than many of the most recent Western and Asian corresponding designs."[93]

In addition to its advances in destroyer acquisition and development, in May 2002 China signed a contract to acquire eight more Kilo class submarines via "expedited delivery," to add to the four it possesses already.[94] The Kilo submarine is a modern, technologically advanced weapon, and will be armed with wake-homing torpedoes, which could present a real danger to U.S. naval vessels, let alone Taiwanese ships. If Taiwan continues to stall in shoring up its ASW capabilities, a submarine blockade could well become an even more feasible option for the PRC. As William Murray of the U.S. Naval War College put it, "a relatively modest investment in submarines can give the U.S., Taiwan, and Japan more trouble than nearly any other military investment."[95]

The ubiquitous theme in assessing Chinese capabilities and strategy vis-à-vis the Taiwan issue is uncertainty. Unfortunately, a failure to recognize uncertainty about capabilities coupled with uncertainty about U.S., PRC, and Taiwanese intentions could result in a grave miscalculation that results in full-scale war in the Taiwan Strait. The "unknown unknowns" are too many to count. Will China succeed in developing its C4ISR capabilities so that it can integrate its advanced weapons systems? Will economic conditions in China continue, or could there be an economic downturn, limiting China's military capability? What will Hu Jintao's stewardship of the Taiwan issue look like? Will Chen Shui-bian's press toward independence continue? Will Taiwan's military spending, particularly on ASW and naval defense, increase to a realistic level? Would the United States intervene in a limited provocation by China, say, China's taking Kinmen (Quemoy) and Matsu? Would the United States back away from Chen if he began to press harder toward independence?

Unfortunately, not one of these questions has a clear answer. In assessing the trends in military spending and strategy, however, one thing seems clear: The Chinese are getting stronger and the Taiwanese are getting weaker. If the United States is willing to accept Taiwanese foot-dragging on acquiring weapons that can help it defend itself but simultaneously prepared to defend Taiwan at all cost, the policy of strategic ambiguity may end in a catastrophic exchange in the Taiwan Strait.

CHAPTER 8

AVOIDING CALAMITY

It is imperative that the United States formulate a new policy on the Taiwan issue, above all one with greater clarity and the right kind of clarity. The current ambiguity and inconsistency in Washington's policy invites miscalculation. One could easily envision a scenario in which Taiwan thought it had a secure defense commitment from the United States and pressed forward vigorously on its independence agenda. Meanwhile Beijing concluded that, since U.S. leaders had embraced a one-China policy and were increasingly impressed by the PRC's military capabilities, Washington would not come to Taiwan's rescue—especially if the authorities in Taipei engaged in provocative actions. Wars have started over less plausible miscalculations.

America's existing policy also invites attempts at manipulation by both Taipei and Beijing. That has become increasingly obvious in recent years, as each side tries to maneuver the United States to "tilt" toward its position. Indeed, both governments exert a great deal of time, money, and effort trying to influence key opinion leaders in the United States.

But most of the policy experts who criticize current U.S. policy offer alternatives that do not come to grips with the central problems in Washington's approach. One alternative suggested by several experts in the American foreign policy community is to accommodate Beijing and put pressure on the Taiwanese to abandon their quest for independence and become serious about negotiations for eventual reunification with the mainland. The other alternative, suggested primarily by staunch conservatives, would take the opposite course. It would involve vigorous and explicit backing for Taiwan—in some cases even going so far as to extend diplomatic recognition. Both alternatives not only fail to rectify the problems with current U.S. policy, they would make matters worse.

THE ACCOMMODATIONIST OPTION

Perhaps the most vocal and visible member of the accommodationist faction is former Assistant Secretary of Defense Joseph Nye. In a crucial March 1998 article in the *Washington Post*, Nye argued that it was imperative for the United States to move away from the "calculatingly ambiguous" language of the 1972 Shanghai Communiqué and the 1979 Taiwan Relations Act. "If we leave these ambiguities in place," Nye warned, "we may court disaster." He then proposed a policy bargain.

The first part would involve a U.S. statement "that if Taiwan were to declare independence, we would not recognize or defend it. Moreover, we would work hard to discourage other countries from recognizing Taiwan independence." At the same time, Washington would have to stress "that we would not accept the use of force [by Beijing] since nothing would change as a result of any abortive declaration of independence by Taiwan."

The second part would involve a PRC concession. If Taiwan decisively rejected the idea of declaring independence, Beijing would agree "not to oppose the idea of more international living space for Taiwan." Such living space would include more opportunities for Taiwan to expand its participation in international groups beyond its current involvement in the Olympics and the Asia Pacific Economic Forum. (Since Nye wrote his article, Taiwan also has been able to join the World Trade Organization.) The Taiwanese would have other venues in which they "could express themselves—as long as they acknowledge that Taiwan was part of one China." As a supposed sweetener, Nye speculated that Beijing could also indicate that its one country, two systems formula for Hong Kong "could be broadened to 'one country, three systems,' so as to make clear that Taiwan would continue to enjoy its own political, economic, and social systems."[1]

Nye's approach clearly made headway during the final years of the Clinton administration. Indeed, the same kind of thinking was evident in Clinton's "three nos" statement in Shanghai in June 1998. John Kerry, the 2004 presidential nominee of the Democratic Party, also appeared to be receptive to accommodationist logic. Perhaps more surprising, by the end of its first term, Secretary of State Colin Powell and some other officials in the Bush administration seemed rather close to that position.

Clearly, the most important change in U.S. policy that the accommodationist alternative would produce involves Taiwan's future political status. The position that earlier presidents adopted did not prejudge that status; U.S. officials merely acknowledged Beijing's position that there was only one China and that Taiwan would eventually have to agree to reunification. The accommodationist approach changes that attitude with vengeance; it places Washington squarely in Beijing's camp on the reunification issue. And that thinking has apparently had an impact on U.S. policy. Bush's statement in December 2003, and even more so Powell's media comments in October 2004, indicate that the United States is now firmly opposed to Taiwanese independence.

The question that Nye and other advocates of the accommodationist approach never address is: If the United States goes to such lengths to accommodate Beijing on the issue of Taiwan's political status, why should PRC leaders then believe that the United States would go to war to defend the island even under a relatively narrow set of circumstances? The policy that Nye proposed seven years ago and other experts have embraced since then virtually invites the kind of miscalculation that often leads to a major war.

Kenneth Lieberthal, a professor at the University of Michigan and a former special assistant to the president for national security affairs, has published an article in *Foreign Affairs* advocating a slightly milder version of the accommodationist approach.[2] In that piece he accurately describes America's dilemma, noting that "the United States now finds itself with a conditional commitment to protect a government in Taiwan that pushes the envelope on independence well beyond what Washington wants, while fending off constant requests from Beijing to do more to rein in Taiwan's actions."[3] His solution for that dilemma—and for the growing PRC-Taiwan tensions—is to press Beijing and Taipei to negotiate a twenty- to thirty-year "agreed framework" for stability. The framework would be designed to "eliminate the things that each side fears the most: for Taiwan, the threat that Beijing will attack; and for Beijing, the threat that Taiwan will cross the independence red line."[4] The essence of the agreement would be a pledge from Taiwan not to seek independence for the duration of the agreement in return for a pledge from the PRC renouncing the use of force during that same period.

The Lieberthal plan has some potential to dampen tensions. But the proposed concessions are hardly symmetrical. Taiwan would be conceding for an extended period the principal issue in its dispute with the mainland. Beijing, on the other hand, would be conceding relatively little; if Taiwan does not move toward independence, China has no incentive to resort to military force in the first place. From the perspective of Taiwan's independence advocates, the framework agreement would simply be surrender on the installment plan.

The accommodationist approach, either in its strong or mild form, is not likely to solve the underlying problem. Chinese leaders increasingly want the Taiwanese to make an explicit commitment to eventual reunification, not merely refrain from pushing the envelope regarding independence. Any effort to placate the PRC short of pressuring Taiwan to give up, now and forever, any hope of independence is not likely to satisfy Beijing.

THE ULTRA-HAWKISH ALTERNATIVE

At the opposite end of the policy spectrum from the accommodationists are the ultra-hawks. Each administration since the opening to China in the early 1970s has had to confront an array of hawks who press for a more confrontational line toward Beijing. That factor has become especially pronounced during the administration of George W. Bush. Thomas Donnelly, a scholar at the American Enterprise Institute and a member of the influential Project for a New American Century, claimed in November 2004 that one of the "biggest challenges for the Bush administration" was to integrate its China policy "into the Bush doctrine." Since the essence of the Bush doctrine is the vigorous promotion of democracy around the world, including through forcible regime change as in Iraq, that was an extraordinarily bold statement. Later in his remarks, Donnelly lamented "the return of the sort of panda-hugger crowd" in the Bush administration, as exemplified by the comments of Colin Powell.[5]

Daniel Blumenthal of AEI and Randy Scheunemann of PNAC have written that "it is most definitely not the position of the U.S. that Taiwan is part of China" and that the United States needs to "reaffirm our commitment to Taiwan's defense."[6] On another occasion, Blumenthal proclaimed that Washington's "traditional engagement policy with China" has become "a dangerous anachronism."[7] Other hawks have been equally forceful. Richard Fisher, now with the International Assessment and Strategy Center, argued in 2004 that the United States should sell offensive as well as defensive weapons to Taiwan. In Fisher's view, the United States should supply "either a limited number of ballistic missiles or cruise missiles, or [the] technology to make them." The goal of such a change in policy would be enable Taiwan "to build an effective 'offensive' capability that can pre-empt an imminent Chinese offensive strike."[8]

Alongside scholars and opinion-shapers who call for a more confrontational policy toward China are members of Congress who breezily advocate U.S. support for steps leading to Taiwan's independence. At a February 2004 lecture at the Heritage Foundation, Representatives Steve Chabot (R-OH) and Robert Andrews (R-NJ) both glibly expressed support for an independent Taiwan. Chabot stated: "Do I want to abandon the one-China policy? I would answer that so long as one China is not understood to mean that Taiwan is part of China, then I have no problem with it. But if carelessness or inattention to nuance or force of habit leads America's political leaders to the mistaken conclusion that Taiwan is part of China, then 'one China' must be done away with." He stressed that the United States should have no "philosophical problem" with Taiwan's independence. "If that is what the people of Taiwan want, they have every right to have it. After all, the sovereignty over Taiwan doesn't rest in Beijing or Taipei, but with Taiwan's people."[9]

Andrews' views were similar, making U.S. policy dependent on the wishes of the Taiwanese people and their democratically elected government regarding the independence issue. If reunification were rejected by Taiwan's democratic leadership, Andrews stated, "then we should recognize Taiwan as a free and independent state."[10]

Some strongly pro-Taiwan individuals have gained positions of influence in the Bush administration. Before joining AEI, Blumenthal was senior director for China, Taiwan, and Mongolia in the secretary of defense's office of international security affairs. Aaron L. Friedberg, a scholar from Princeton University, became a national security adviser to Vice President Dick Cheney. Before joining the administration, Friedberg had published a controversial essay, "Will We Abandon Taiwan?" in *Commentary* magazine. In that essay, he advocated a revision of U.S. policy on the Taiwan issue.

> The primary objective of our policy must be to repair the frayed fabric of deterrence—deterrence, that is, of mainland China. Under the terms of such a policy, the United States would make it clear not only that it strongly favors a mutually acceptable resolution to the Taiwan issue, if and when one can be found, but that it will *not* accept, under any circumstances, an outcome imposed by force.[11]

A careful reading of that paragraph reveals some important implications. By insisting on a "mutually acceptable" resolution, Friedberg would give Taiwan veto power. That is precisely the position of the Taiwanese government, and a view that is anathema in Beijing. Friedberg's position regarding America's response to the PRC's use of force—that the United States would not accept an outcome imposed by force "under any circumstances"—eliminates even the slightest ambiguity in Washington's policy. His prescription amounts to an unqualified U.S. security guarantee to Taiwan. Pro-independence Taiwanese could implement their agenda secure in the knowledge that the United States would defend the island come what may.

The ultra-hawks adopt an irresponsible position. Of course, no reasonable American would be happy about the possibility of a democratic Taiwan being forcibly absorbed by an authoritarian China. But preserving Taiwan's de facto independence—much less giving tacit encouragement to campaign for de jure independence—is not worth risking war with a nuclear-armed great power. America should never incur that level of risk except in the defense of its own vital security interests.

And the risk of war is not far-fetched. The status of Taiwan is a hot button issue for most mainland Chinese. Even those Chinese who are not especially fond of the Communist regime in Beijing tend to believe that the island is rightfully part of China. From their perspective, Japan stole that province from their country in 1895 and the United States prevented reunification following the defeat of Chiang Kai-shek's Nationalist forces in 1949. They want the territory back and their patience is beginning to wear thin. At the same time, Taiwan is developing an ever stronger sense of a separate identity. A growing number of Taiwanese have no interest in reunification with China, now or in the future.

The ingredients exist for a nasty confrontation between Beijing and Taipei at some point. The two sides have mutually incompatible agendas, and it is not easy to see how such profound differences can be bridged. The United States needs to be careful lest it get caught in the middle of such a conflict. True, the PRC is not in a strong position at the moment to militarily challenge the U.S. commitment to defend Taiwan. Indeed, as noted in chapter 7, it is likely to be many years before China's military can match the overall capabilities of the U.S. military. But there are two important caveats. First, China does not need to match the U.S. military globally or even regionally; it only needs to raise the cost of a confrontation in the Taiwan Strait to such a painful level that U.S. officials would face an agonizing decision whether to honor the commitment. And China may be fairly close to having that capability. Second, when emotional issues of national pride are at stake, nations sometimes resort to military action even when they have little hope of victory. Taiwan may be such an issue for China.

DUBIOUS ASSUMPTIONS ABOUT DETERRENCE

Washington's security commitment to Taiwan is based on an excessive confidence in the reliability of extended deterrence—confidence based almost entirely on this country's Cold War experience deterring the Soviet Union. The conventional wisdom about extended deterrence is that aggressors will always be deterred from molesting a U.S. ally or client whenever Washington provides an unambiguous security commitment. Advocates of a more pro-Taiwan policy seem to embrace that assumption with little reflection. According to Blumenthal and Scheunemann: "Avoiding military conflict over Taiwan has always required a strong deterrent posture from Washington so the People's Republic of China understands the cost of any precipitous action."[12]

But the assumption that the deterrence of Soviet aggression during the Cold War can be replicated with regard to China over Taiwan is dubious. A strategy of extended deterrence is hardly infallible. Indeed, the historical record is littered with the wreckage of deterrence failures. Many Europeans in the early years of the twentieth century assumed that the Continent's elaborate system of alliances would make war unthinkable. The tragic events of 1914 demonstrated how wrong they were. A generation later, the explicit British and French security guarantees to Poland did not deter Germany from launching an invasion of that country.

In addition to the balance of military forces, three factors are especially important in determining whether extended deterrence is likely to succeed: (1) the importance of the stakes to the protector; (2) the importance of the stakes to the challenging power; and (3) the extent of the challenging power's inclination to gamble. All three factors worked to Washington's advantage to an unusual degree in its confrontation with the Soviet Union.

America's major Cold War security guarantees—those in which the United States was prepared to put the safety of its own country at risk—were confined to western Europe and northeast Asia. Both regions were considered crucial to America's own security and economic well-being, and U.S. policymakers were determined to prevent those power centers from coming under the control of the rival military superpower. It was therefore credible to leaders in the Kremlin that the United States would be willing to incur significant risks—even the possibility of a nuclear war—to thwart a Soviet conquest.

Conversely, while those regions would have been a significant strategic and economic prize for the Soviet Union, neither area was essential to Moscow. Nor did Soviet leaders or the Soviet population have an emotional attachment to either region. There was, therefore, a definite limit to the risks the Kremlin was willing to run to gain dominion. Although Soviet leaders could never be sure that the United States would really go to war on behalf of its allies, challenging the commitment would have been an extraordinarily reckless gamble.

Fortunately for the United States, the Soviet leadership tended to be relatively risk averse. Most of Moscow's challenges occurred on the periphery, primarily in the Third World. Although Soviet leaders occasionally tested the U.S.-led alliance network (especially over West Berlin), they did not put their prestige on the line to such an extent that a tactical retreat became impossible. Indeed, as believers in Leninist doctrine, the Soviets were patient—pocketing geopolitical gains whenever they could be obtained at relatively low risk but backing off when the risk appeared excessive—supremely confident that their system would prevail in the long run.

There are crucial differences in all three deterrence factors when it comes to the prospect of a showdown over Taiwan. Taiwan may have some importance to the United States, since it is a significant trading partner and a sister democracy. Nevertheless, its relevance to American economic and security interests hardly compares to the central importance U.S. policymakers thought that western Europe and northeast Asia had during the Cold War.

The problem is that Chinese officials probably understand that point as well. Soviet leaders may have considered it credible that the United States would risk a major war to keep western Europe and northeast Asia out of Moscow's orbit. But it is far less likely that the Chinese believe that Washington will incur the same risk merely to defend Taiwan—a "country" the United States does not even officially recognize. Wang Zaixi, vice minister of the Taiwan Affairs Office, clearly expressed that assumption. If the Taiwan "'separatists' believe that they will get protection from the United States in the event of war, they are being "extremely naive," Wang stated. "The Americans will protect their own national interests, but they are expected to neither protect Taiwan independence nor shed blood for Taiwan independence."[13]

While Taiwan's importance to the United States is much less, the island's importance to China is much greater than western Europe or northeast Asia was to the Soviet Union. To Beijing, Taiwan is not merely a political and economic prize; the status of the island is caught up in issues of national pride and prestige. Taiwan is a reminder of China's long period of humiliation at the hands of outside powers. When such potent emotions are engaged, even normally dispassionate political leaders do not always act prudently or even rationally. The bottom line is that, as political scientist Robert Ross contends, Taiwan "is a vital interest" of the PRC but "does not entail a vital interest of the United States."[14] Given the difference in the stakes, for the United States to attempt to deter the PRC is profoundly dangerous.

Nor is it as certain that the Chinese leaders will be as risk averse as the old Soviet hierarchy. When Admiral Dennis Blair, then commander of U.S. forces in the Pacific, warned high-ranking PRC military officers in the spring of 2001 that the United States would come to Taiwan's aid in the event of an unprovoked attack, their reaction was not reassuring. The military officers reportedly reacted with disbelief verging on scorn.[15] That attitude is reinforced by a pervasive impression within the PRC military hierarchy, based on an interpretation of the rapid U.S. withdrawal from Somalia and the way the U.S. military waged the Gulf and Kosovo conflicts, that the American people are so averse to casualties that they would simply be unwilling to fight a serious war over Taiwan.[16] That belief is not likely altered by the bitter divisions in American public opinion over the relatively modest casualties suffered in the Iraq war and occupation.

It matters little whether Chinese skepticism about U.S. intentions is right or wrong. If PRC leaders believe the U.S. commitment is a bluff, they will be inclined to call that bluff. Applying the supposed lessons of the Cold War to deter China from settling the Taiwan issue on its own terms could, therefore, lead to either a humiliating U.S. retreat or a disastrous armed conflict.

Those Americans who believe that the United States can deter the PRC from coercing Taiwan for the indefinite future base their confidence on the superiority of American military forces. But as we have seen in chapter 7, China is searching for ways to offset that advantage—a classic attempt to adopt a strategy of asymmetric warfare. Even if that strategy does not succeed on a global basis, it may prove effective in the limited theater of the Taiwan Strait, and that may be sufficient for Beijing's purposes. If China can raise the potential cost of a U.S. military intervention on Taiwan's behalf high enough, any American president would face a dire decision if the United States sought to honor its security commitment to the island.

Moreover, even if the PRC cannot fully overcome America's military superiority in the Taiwan Strait, that does not guarantee that China would not challenge the U.S. commitment if it concluded that its vital interests were threatened. The credibility of a promise to defend an ally or client does not depend merely on the balance of forces, although that factor is certainly important. An equally crucial consideration is the relative importance of the issue to the guarantor power and to the challenging power—what might be termed the "balance of fervor." On that scale, there is no question that the PRC would have the advantage. As Carnegie Endowment for Peace scholar Michael D. Swaine observes, the Chinese leadership "would almost certainly fight to avoid the loss of Taiwan if it concluded that no other alternative existed, even if its chances of prevailing in such a conflict were low." Exactly how much blood and treasure Beijing would be willing to spend is uncertain, Swaine admits, "but it might be considerably more than the United States would be prepared to shoulder."[17]

Aside from the problems of deterrence in the event of a crisis in the Taiwan Strait, there is the ever-present danger of uncontrolled escalation if deterrence failed. Swaine notes that Taiwan's proximity to China makes it difficult for the United States to interdict Chinese attacks without striking the mainland itself. Yet, if the U.S. forces did that, it would be very difficult for the PRC to back down, even if it was losing the military engagement. The danger of escalation is especially acute because both sides have a history of emphasizing the need to display resolve in a crisis, and to display that resolve through rapid and decisive military action.[18] Those are the perfect ingredients for a war that could spiral out of control. Since both sides possess nuclear weapons and the ability to deliver strikes on the other's homeland, that prospect is especially dangerous.

Finally, even if the United States "won" a military confrontation with China over Taiwan, it would be a Phyrric victory. In a worst-case scenario, the victory would come only after bitter fighting with possible nuclear implications and the prospect of many thousands dead on both sides. Even if the belligerents managed to avoid that nightmare scenario and China backed off after relatively minor skirmishes, the consequences would be horrific. The important U.S.-PRC political and economic relationship so laboriously constructed over the past three and one-half decades would be in a shambles. Indeed, it is not an exaggeration to say that America's relations with China would be poisoned for at least the next generation.

Moreover, America's victory would always be tenuous. U.S. leaders could never be certain that China would not make another military attempt at some point to validate its claim to Taiwan. How many decades would the United States be willing to stand guard in the Taiwan Strait—especially if China, after the initial setback from its defeat in war, became ever stronger, economically and militarily? How many wars would the United States be willing to fight to maintain an independent Taiwan?

The current strategy is a loser, certainly in the long term if not the short term. It is imperative for the United States adopt a different strategy—one that preserves the crucial relationship with the PRC but still gives Taiwan a chance at a separate existence, if that is what the Taiwanese people want to pursue.

TOWARD A BALANCED AND PRUDENT TAIWAN POLICY

A clear distinction should be made between selling arms to Taiwan and giving the island a U.S. security guarantee. That distinction points the way to a new, more sustainable, and more prudent U.S. policy on the Taiwan issue. That new strategy should incorporate a continued willingness to sell arms to Taipei with a withdrawal of any security commitment—even an implicit one.

Selling weapons to Taiwan is a reasonable course of action. A militarily capable Taiwan makes it less likely that Beijing will contemplate using coercion to pursue its goal of national reunification, since the cost of doing so would be excessively high. That is the essence of a "porcupine" strategy for Taiwan.[19] It also would increase the likelihood that, as the economic ties between Taiwan and the mainland continue to grow, both sides will seek a peaceful resolution to their differences. Moreover, the issue of credibility that is always a troubling factor in a case of extended deterrence would be less prominent. Beijing has a legitimate reason to wonder whether U.S. leaders would risk their own country to defend Taiwan. There would be little doubt that the Taiwanese would fight to prevent their own subjugation by armed force.

Washington should couple its policy of arms sales to Taiwan with a firm statement that the United States will not become involved in any armed struggle between Taiwan and the PRC. It would be appropriate for U.S. officials to convey that message privately to Taipei, at least a short period before making a public statement. That would give the Taiwanese some time to adjust their own policies to reflect the impending loss of the U.S. security umbrella.

Critics of a public pledge of nonintervention typically argue that it would embolden the PRC to use force against Taiwan. One cannot rule out that possibility, but it is not an inevitable outcome. Beijing would still have to take into account Taiwan's military capabilities, which could be formidable if Taipei took full advantage of U.S. arms sales and further developed its own nascent defense industry. Even without U.S. military intervention, China could not be certain that it would be able to prevail in a war against a well-armed Taiwan. Moreover, the PRC could no longer count on the United States to strong arm Taiwan into cautious behavior in exchange for the defense commitment. Without U.S. involvement, Beijing might have to open a real dialogue with Taipei instead of incessantly badgering Washington to make the Taiwanese "behave."

Finally, Beijing would have to realize that, given the political realities in the United States, horrendous diplomatic repercussions and economic sanctions would certainly occur in response to an attack on Taiwan. A pledge that the United States would not intervene militarily would not preclude such measures. PRC leaders would still have to ask themselves if they wish to pay the political and economic price of trying to forcibly regain a province inhabited by a population that clearly does not want to live under Beijing's authority.

With the withdrawal of the U.S. security umbrella, the Taiwanese could make their own decisions about whether to opt for independence, seek to preserve the ambiguous status quo, or attempt to negotiate the best terms possible for eventual reunification with the mainland. Whatever the course they decided to pursue, it would be done at their own risk, not America's. The Taiwanese would have to make hard and realistic decisions about their future instead of engaging in largely cost-free political posturing, as they sometimes do at present.

Analyst Trevor Corson notes that such a dramatic change in U.S. policy "would require delicate diplomacy" because it would "infuriate" both Taipei and Beijing.[20] That is a bit of an overstatement. Both capitals would have mixed emotions about the strategy. Taiwan would be relieved that arms sales would continue and perhaps even intensify, assuming the Taiwanese people and their elected representatives would be willing to absorb the financial cost. Many Taiwanese also might be relieved that they would no longer be subjected to U.S. lectures and pressure about their policy decisions. On the other hand, the loss of even the vague security commitment in the Taiwan Relations Act would be unsettling.

Beijing, of course, would be gratified that the United States had withdrawn the security pledge, but PRC officials would be extremely unhappy about the prospect of U.S. arms sales for an indefinite duration. The PRC wants the best of both worlds: the withdrawal of the security guarantee and an end to arms sales. U.S. officials need to inform their PRC counterparts that such a combination is a political nonstarter in the United States. It will be difficult enough to overcome the opposition of Taiwan's American supporters to terminating the defense commitment. There is absolutely no chance of eliminating both the security pledge and arms sales. Indeed, the only possible way of selling the idea of terminating the former is to emphasize the continuation of the latter.

A U.S. policy of continued arms sales but no security guarantee is based on the recognition that Taiwan is a limited or "peripheral," not a vital, American interest.[21] Advocates of a security commitment to Taiwan typically fail to make that distinction. Indeed, some of them exaggerate Taiwan's importance to absurd levels. Tom Donnelly argues that the island is "the functional equivalent of the Fulda Gap [the gateway for a Warsaw Pact invasion of western Europe during the Cold War.]"[22] He ignores the important difference that China, unlike the USSR, does not have global messianic, expansionist ambitions. Ross Munro, a senior scholar at the Center for Security Studies and co-author of *The Coming Conflict with China*, is even more apocalyptic than Donnelly. According to Munro, "The United States is finished as a world power if it does not come to the aid of Taiwan in an unprovoked attack by China."[23] Ross Terrill offers a slightly less shrill, but still alarmist, view that "the entire balance of power in East Asia would change if Taiwan went out of existence as a separate entity. Japan's confidence in its security relationship would be reduced; the Philippines, Vietnam, and others would reconsider their view of China."[24]

Much of what Terrill laments is already taking place because of China's growing economic, political and military influence, even though the United States retains an implicit commitment to defend Taiwan. And, contrary to Donnelly and Munro, one suspects that the United States—a nation with a $12 trillion economy, thousands of strategic nuclear warheads, and a culture that permeates the world scene—would still be a major player in the international system, even if Taiwan succumbed to a PRC takeover.

Certainly, the American people would not like to see prosperous, democratic Taiwan forcibly incorporated into the dictatorial PRC. And if the United States can help prevent that result with minimal risk to itself, then it would be beneficial to do so. But a security guarantee entails enormous, not minimal, risks. China already has some two dozen ICBMs capable of reaching American cities. In the years to come, that number could well grow to several hundred. Even an armed skirmish originally confined to the Taiwan Strait might spiral out of control regardless of the intentions of U.S. or PRC policymakers. Such a level of risk should never be incurred except in defense of a vital American security interest. Preserving Taiwan's de facto independence does not meet that test.

The Bush administration has adopted the worst possible combination of policies regarding Taiwan. On the one hand, the administration is pressuring a sister democracy to abstain from exercising some of its important democratic prerogatives. On the other hand, in the weeks following President Bush's chastisement of the Chen government in December 2003, Washington renewed its pledge to protect Taiwan's security.[25] The same pattern occurred after Secretary of State Colin Powell's surprisingly pro-Beijing comments in October 2004. In taking these actions, the administration has compromised its moral position while still exposing the United States to the needless risk of eventual military conflict.

Although it is imprudent for the United States to pledge to defend Taiwan, it is equally inappropriate for Washington to tell Taiwan what its policies ought to be.

Instead of either risking going to war to defend Taiwan or kowtowing to Beijing regarding Taiwan's political status, the Bush administration should adopt an entirely different approach. The president should state that the United States takes no position on the question of Taiwan's independence. It is not our place to support or oppose that outcome. At the same time, we should not retain any obligation to defend an independent (de facto or de jure) Taiwan.

A policy of arms sales but no security guarantee is an approach that would respect Taiwan's dignity as a democratic society while limiting America's risk exposure.[26] Washington's current strategy does exactly the opposite. It pressures Taiwan not to exercise its prerogatives as a vibrant democracy while it keeps America's risk exposure at a dangerously high level if a conflict should erupt. That is the essence of a risky and bankrupt policy. America can and should do better.

NOTES

INTRODUCTION

1. Susan V. Lawrence, "U.S. Presses China on Arms, Quietly," *Wall Street Journal*, October 30, 2003, p. A14; and David E. Sanger, "U.S. Punishes 8 Chinese Firms for Aiding Iran," *New York Times*, January 17, 2005, p. A1.
2. U.S. House of Representatives, *Report of the Select Committee on U.S. National Security and Military/Commercial Concerns with the People's Republic of China*, 3 vols., 105th Cong., 2nd sess., 1999.
3. *Report to Congress of the U.S.-China Security Review Commission—The National Security Implications of the Economic Relationship between the United States and China*, July 2002, http://www.uscc.gov. See also Evelyn Iritani, "China Trade Poses Security Threat to U.S., Asia Panel Says," *Los Angeles Times*, July 12, 2003, p. A25.
4. William R. Hawkins, "Are We Serious about China?" *Washington Times*, November 6, 2003, p. A21.
5. Ibid.
6. Qiao Liang and Wang Xiangsui, *Unrestricted Warfare* (Beijing: PLA Literature and Arts Publishing House, 1999).
7. Michael Pillsbury, *China Debates the Future Security Environment* (Washington, D.C.: National Defense University Press, 2000), p. 71.
8. Ibid., p. 77.
9. Yiwei Wang, "China's Defensive Realism," *Asia Times*, December 22, 2004, www.atimes.com.
10. James Pomfret, "A Protest Beijing Can Endorse," *Washington Post*, May 10, 1999, p. A18.
11. Paul Eckert, "China Chat Room Seethes after U.S. Plane Collision," *Reuters*, April 1, 2001; and Lynne O'Donnell, "Surfers Talk Up Extreme Responses," *The Australian*, April 3, 2001, p. 9.
12. Author's conversations with PRC diplomats, Washington, D.C., November and December 2004.
13. For a discussion of the growth of a distinct Taiwanese identity, see Philip P. Pan, "New National Identity Emerges in Taiwan," *Washington Post*, January 2, 2004, p. A13.
14. Keith Bradsher, "Still Wary, Taiwan Split over Change on the Mainland," *New York Times*, November 16, 2002, p. A6; and William Foreman, "Taiwanese on Mainland Support China," *Washington Times*, February 7, 2004, p. A7.
15. Nikolas K. Gvosdev and Travis Tanner, "Wagging the Dog," *National Interest*, no. 77 (Fall 2004): 5–10.

16. Quoted in "Dancing with the Enemy: A Survey of Taiwan," *Economist*, January 15, 2005, p. 12.

CHAPTER 2

1. The history of Taiwan pre-1895 is taken from Johnathan I. Charney and J. R. V. Prescott, "Resolving Cross-Strait Relations between China and Taiwan," *American Journal of International Law* 94, no. 3 (July 2000): 453–477.
2. Republic of China, *Taiwan Yearbook 2003* (Taipei: Government Information Office, 2003), pp. 39–40.
3. Much of this section draws on S. C. M. Paine's excellent history, *The Sino-Japanese War of 1894–1895* (Cambridge, U.K.: Cambridge University Press, 2003).
4. Paine, *Sino-Japanese*, p. 87.
5. Stewart Lone, *Japan's First Modern War: Army and Society in the Conflict with China, 1894–1895* (New York: St. Martin's Press, 1994), p. 26.
6. Ibid., p. 16.
7. Paine, *Sino-Japanese*, p. 115.
8. Ibid., p. 117.
9. British journalist W. T. Stead, cited in Marius B. Jansen, *Japan and China: From War to Peace, 1894–1972* (Chicago, Ill.: Rand McNally College Publishing Company, 1975), p. 22. For more examples of Western skepticism of Japan's capabilities, see Paine, pp. 125–127; 138–139, Lone, p. 29.
10. Paine, *Sino-Japanese*, pp. 133–134.
11. Taken from Zenone Volpicelli (published under the pseudonym "Vladimir"), *The China-Japan War Compiled from Japanese, Chinese, and Foreign Sources* (Kansas City, Mo.: Franklin Hudson Publishing Company, 1905), Appendix D, p. 245.
12. "Japanese Next Station," *New York Times*, February 20, 1895, p. 5. Cited in Paine, p. 152 n. 230.
13. Paine, *Sino-Japanese*, pp. 165–243.
14. The Chinese approach was bizarre. During its attempts to broker peace, it escalated its rhetoric, shifting from referring to the Japanese as "dwarfs" to referring to them as "dwarf bandits." It also sent low-level diplomats and even negotiators without vested authority to conduct the peace negotiations (Paine, pp. 254–257).
15. Edward I-te Chen, "Japan's Decision to Annex Taiwan: A Study of Ito-Mutsu Diplomacy, 1894–1895," *Journal of Asian Studies* 37, no. 1 (November 1977): 61–72.
16. Frank W. Ikle, "The Triple Intervention: Japan's Lesson in the Diplomacy of Imperialism," *Monumenta Nipponica* 22, no. 1/2 (1967): 122–130.
17. Chen, "Japan's Decision," p. 70.
18. Quoted in Ikle, "The Triple Intervention," pp. 127–128.
19. For a complete analysis of the dynamics of the Triple Intervention, see Ikle, pp. 122–130.
20. For a thorough history of the republican experience in Taiwan, see Harry J. Lamley, "The 1895 Taiwan Republic: A Significant Episode in Modern Chinese History," *Journal of Asian Studies* 27, no. 4 (August 1968): 739–762.
21. A. J. Grajdanzev, "Formosa (Taiwan) under Japanese Rule," *Pacific Affairs* 15, no. 3 (September 1942): 311–324.
22. Shimpei Goto, "The Administration of Formosa (Taiwan)," in Shigenobu Okuma, *Fifty Years of New Japan* (London, 1909), vol. 2, p. 530. Cited in Hyman Kublin,

"The Evolution of Japanese Colonialism," *Comparative Studies in Society and History* 2, no. 1 (October 1959): 67–84.

23. Edward I-te Chen, "Japanese Colonialism in Korea and Formosa: A Comparison of the Systems of Political Control," *Harvard Journal of Asiatic Studies* 30 (1970): 126–158.
24. Kublin, p. 68.
25. Ibid., p. 83.
26. By one account, in 1942 the Japanese government owned approximately two-thirds of the land in Taiwan, with Japanese corporations and businesses owning much of the remaining third. See Grajdanzev, "Formosa," p. 318.
27. Joseph W. Ballantine, *Formosa: A Problem for United States Foreign Policy* (Washington, D.C.: The Brookings Institution, 1952), p. 35.
28. Ibid., p. 39.
29. Ibid., pp. 41–44.
30. See, for example, Spencer's two-volume *Principles of Biology* (Honolulu: University Press of the Pacific, 2002 [1864–67]) and Robert L. Carneiro, ed., *The Evolution of Society: Selections from Herbert Spencer's Principles of Sociology* (Chicago: University of Chicago Press, 1967).
31. For a thorough analysis of the 100 Days Reform, see Young-Tsu Wong, "Revisionism Reconsidered: Kang Youwei and the Reform Movement of 1898," *Journal of Asian Studies* 51, no. 3 (August 1992): 513–544.
32. For example, General Douglas MacArthur believed that legal clarification was necessary. See Jon W. Huebner, "The Abortive Liberation of Taiwan," *China Quarterly*, no. 110 (June 1987): 262. Additionally, the position that Taiwan's legal status was undetermined became official U.S. policy by 1950. See, for instance, President Truman's letter to Warren Austin dated August 27, 1950, available from the Truman Presidential Library at http://www.trumanlibrary.org/whistlestop/study_collections/korea/large/sec3/mac_6_1.htm.
33. Ballantine, *Formosa*, p. 54.
34. Tse-han Lai, Ramon H. Myers, and Wei Wou, *A Tragic Beginning: The Taiwan Uprising of February 28, 1947* (Stanford, Calif.: Stanford University Press, 1991), pp. 44–49.
35. General Albert Wedemeyer, cited in ibid., pp. 65–66.
36. Douglas H. Mendel, Jr., "Japanese Policy and Views toward Formosa," *Journal of Asian Studies* 28, no. 3 (May 1969): 513–534.
37. Some reports indicate Chen may actually have developed "a lucrative clandestine trade" with the Japanese as governor of Fukien province, and in some quarters his allegiance was suspect. See, for example, F. A. Lumley, *The Republic of China under Chiang Kai-shek* (London: Barrie and Jenkins Ltd., 1976), p. 55.
38. Ballantine, *Formosa*, pp. 62–63.
39. Lai, Meyers, and Wou, "A Tragic Beginning," pp. 180–182.
40. Ibid., pp. 192–193.
41. Fred W. Riggs, "Chinese Administration in Formosa," *Far Eastern Survey* 20, no. 21 (December 12, 1951): 209–215.
42. Jansen, *Japan and China*, p. 442.
43. See Frank S. T. Hsiao and Lawrence R. Sullivan, "The Chinese Communist Party and the Status of Taiwan, 1928–1943," *Pacific Affairs* 52, no. 3 (Autumn 1979): 446–467. The particular statement about Taiwan appears on pp. 453–454,

and appeared originally in Edgar Snow's *Red Star over China* (New York: Random House, 1948), pp. 88–89.

44. Hsiao and Sullivan, "The Chinese Communist Party," p. 446.

45. To some degree, the 1947 uprising rattled the KMT and its leadership started thinking about reforms even as early as 1947. It also marked the beginning of a coherent Taiwan independence movement. See Lai, Myers, and Wou, *A Tragic Beginning*, pp. 188–193.

46. For a thorough investigation of the KMT's restructuring, see Bruce J. Dickson, "The Lessons of Defeat: The Reorganization of the Kuomintang on Taiwan, 1950–52," *China Quarterly*, no. 133 (March 1993): 56–84.

47. For more on the Wedemeyer Report, see *United States Relations with China with Special Reference to the Period 1944–1949*, Department of State Publication 3575, Far Eastern Series 30 (Washington, D.C.: U.S. Government Printing Office, 1949), pp. 260–261.

48. Huebner, "The Abortive Liberation of Taiwan," p. 260.

49. See, for example, *Foreign Relations of the United States: 1950* (volume VI), p. 543.

50. Quote taken from President Truman's letter to Warren Austin dated August 27, 1950, available from the Truman Presidential Library at http://www.trumanlibrary.org/whistlestop/study_collections/korea/large/sec3/ mac_6_1.htm.

51. Nancy Bernkopf Tucker, *Taiwan, Hong Kong, and the United States, 1945–1992* (New York: Twayne Publishers, 1994), p. 31.

52. Denny Roy, *Taiwan: A Political History* (Ithaca, N.Y.: Cornell University Press, 2003), pp. 109–113.

53. Walter Sullivan, "Main Formosa Battle Expected this Summer," *New York Times*, April 30, 1950, p. E5.

54. Huebner, "The Abortive Liberation of Taiwan," p. 271.

55. *Selected Works of Zhou Enlai*, vol. 2, p. 52. Cited in Hao Yufan and Zhai Zhihai, "China's Decision to Enter the Korean War: History Revisited," *China Quarterly*, no. 121 (March 1990): 94–115.

56. Hao and Zhai, "China's Decision," p. 109.

57. See, for example, Leonard A. Kusnitz, *Public Opinion and Foreign Policy: America's China Policy, 1949–1979* (Westport, Conn.: Greenwood Press, 1984), p. 49. Kusnitz reports that public support for Taiwan grew steadily during late 1950, and that by mid-1951 "[t]he public was quite willing to help the 'free Chinese,' probably reflecting its increasingly hostile attitude toward Peking."

58. Ibid., p. 273.

59. Kenneth S. Chern, "Politics of American China Policy, 1945: Roots of the Cold War in Asia," *Political Science Quarterly* 91, no. 4 (Winter 1976–77): 631–647.

60. See interview with Francis R. Valeo, "From China to Washington," pp. 31–34. Available online at http://www.senate.gov/artandhistory/history/resources/pdf/valeo_interview__01.pdf.

61. Gayle B. Montgomery and James W. Johnson, *One Step from the White House: The Rise and Fall of Senator William F. Knowland* (Berkeley, Calif.: University of California Press, 1998), pp. 91–92.

62. Bennett C. Rushkoff, "Eisenhower, Dulles and the Quemoy-Matsu Crisis, 1954–1955," *Political Science Quarterly* 96, no. 3 (Autumn 1981): 465–480. See also Gordon C. Chang, "To the Nuclear Brink: Eisenhower, Dulles, and the Quemoy-Matsu Crisis," *International Security* 12, no. 4 (Spring 1988): 96–123 and Gordon H. Chang, *Friends and Enemies: The United States, China, and the Soviet Union*,

1948–1972 (Stanford, Calif.: Stanford University Press, 1990), pp. 116–121. Rushkoff puts the figure at forty thousand troops on Quemoy, but Chang claims there were more than fifty thousand.

63. For an analysis that claims Eisenhower and Dulles were pragmatic and risk-averse, see Nancy Bernkopf Tucker, "John Foster Dulles and the Taiwan Roots of the 'Two Chinas' Policy," in Richard H. Immerman, ed., *John Foster Dulles and the Diplomacy of the Cold War* (Princeton, N.J.: Princeton University Press, 1990), pp. 235–262.

64. Dwight D. Eisenhower, *The White House Years: Mandate for Change, 1953–1956* (Garden City, N.Y.: Doubleday and Co., Inc., 1963), p. 464.

65. Chang, "To the Nuclear Brink," p. 100.

66. The text of the Mutual Defense Treaty is available online at www.taiwandocuments.org/mutual01.htm.

67. Document in author's possession.

68. Cited in Rushkoff, "Eisenhower and the Quemoy-Matsu Crisis," p. 473.

69. Chang, "To the Nuclear Brink," pp. 101–104.

70. Rushkoff claims that an unsigned document in the Dulles Papers, likely written by Dulles or a close associate, drew parallels between the prospect of giving up the offshore islands to the PRC and ceding Czechoslovakia to Hitler. Rushkoff indicates Dulles believed that the Chinese Communists would continue to advance until the United States rose to meet them, by military conflict, if necessary. Rushkoff, "Eisenhower, Dulles, and the Quemoy-Matsu Crisis," pp. 474–475.

71. Chang, "To the Nuclear Brink," p. 106. Chang also alleges the prospect of nuclear confrontation did not altogether discomfort Eisenhower, who had "for some time . . . wanted to change public attitudes about the atomic bomb and reduce the widespread squeamishness about its use." By 1954 the United States had fully functional nuclear weapons on Okinawa, and by 1958 (the time of the second Strait crisis) they were stationed on Taiwan itself. See Robert S. Norris, William M. Arkin, and William Burr, "Where They Were," *Bulletin of Atomic Scientists* (November/December 1999): 26–35. Available online at http://www.bullatomsci.org/issues/1999/nd99/nd99norris.pdf.

72. Ibid., p. 108.

73. Ibid., p. 112.

74. Chang, "To the Nuclear Brink," pp. 116, 121. Chang suggests that the PRC would definitely have considered a blockade (whether or not it was labeled such) as an act of war, let alone the mining of the Strait, as Dulles had recommended. Chang further wonders if the lack of clarity on the part of the United States could have led a less cautious PRC government to attack parts of the Seventh Fleet or Taiwan itself.

75. Quoted in Dwight D. Eisenhower, *White House Years: Mandate for Change, 1953–1956*, p. 482.

76. Some in the administration were pushing for a fuller, formal resolution of the Taiwan matter. State Department political advisor Robert Murphy reportedly recommended that if the PRC would formally pledge not to attack the Penghus or Taiwan, the United States should formally eschew any plan to attack the mainland and should "use its influence to assure that Taiwan and the Penghus are not used as a base for attack against . . . the mainland." Cited in Leonard H. D. Gordon, "United States Opposition to Use of Force in the Taiwan Strait, 1954–1962," *Journal of American History* 72, no. 3 (December 1985): 637–660. Quote is on p. 640 n. 6.

77. Gordon, "United States Opposition," p. 641.

78. Tang Tsou, "The Quemoy Imbroglio: Chiang Kai-shek and the United States," *The Western Political Quarterly* 12, no. 4 (December 1959): 1075–1091.

79. Though this strategy was highly suspect from a military perspective, by 1958 the Eisenhower administration either believed Chiang's argument or was going along with it without actually believing it. See, for example, Roy, *Taiwan*, p. 122. Additionally, Assistant Secretary of State Walter Robinson told the *New York Times* in October 1958 that "[i]t is not really anyone above the intelligence of a military moron who would for one moment think that these islands would be selected as bases from which to attack the mainland." Quoted in Tsou, "The Quemoy Imbroglio," p. 1078. For another argument that the islands' military significance was minimal, see Gordon, "United States Opposition," p. 645, n. 21.

80. Tucker, *Taiwan, Hong Kong, and the United States*, p. 42.

81. Quoted in Gordon, "United States Opposition," pp. 644–645.

82. "Radio and Television Report to the American People Regarding the Situation in the Formosa Straits," September 11, 1958, *Public Papers of the Presidents*. Available online at http://www.presidency.ucsb.edu/site/docs/pppus.php?admin=034&year=1958&id=261.

83. *New York Times*, September 20, 1958, p. A3. Cited in Tsou, "The Quemoy Imbroglio," p. 1084.

84. Tsou, "The Quemoy Imbroglio," p. 1085.

85. Gordon, "United States Opposition," pp. 651–652.

86. Reuters, "Peiping Offer of Week's Quemoy Truce," *New York Times*, October 6, 1958, p. A3.

87. Melvin Gurtov, "The Taiwan Strait Crisis Revisited: Politics and Foreign Policy in Chinese Motives," *Modern China* 2, no. 1 (January 1976): 91. The PRC would continue to sporadically shell Quemoy into the early 1960s. See John Wilson Lewis, "Quemoy and American China Policy," *Asian Survey* 2, no. 1 (March 1962): 13.

88. Roy, *Taiwan*, p. 123.

89. John Gittings, "Co-Operation and Conflict in Sino-Soviet Relations," *International Affairs* 40, no. 1 (January 1964): 60–75. For more on U.S. attempts to foment a Sino-Soviet split during the period, see Chang, *Friends and Enemies*, chapter six.

90. Tucker, *Taiwan, Hong Kong, and the United States*, p. 45. See also Gordon, "United States Opposition," pp. 656–658.

91. Tucker, *Taiwan, Hong Kong, and the United States*, p. 94.

92. "China, the United Nations and United States Policy: An Analysis of the Issues and Principal Alternatives with Recommendations for U.S. Policy: A Report of a National Policy Panel Established by the United Nations Association of the United States of America," *International Organization* 20, no. 4 (Autumn 1966): 705.

93. For a discussion of the two-Chinas concept and the U.S. effort to implement it in the United Nations, see Henry Kissinger, *White House Years* (Boston: Little, Brown and Company, 1979), pp. 770–774 and 784–787.

94. William Burr and Jeffrey T. Richelson, "Whether to 'Strangle the Baby in the Cradle': The United States and the Chinese Nuclear Program, 1960–1964," *International Security* 25, no. 3 (Winter 2000–2001): 54–99.

95. Tucker, *Taiwan, Hong Kong, and the United States*, p. 96.

96. Official records of these meetings have been declassified and can be viewed online at http://www.gwu.edu/~nsarchiv/NSAEBB/NSAEBB106/index.htm.

97. Quoted in Kissinger, *White House Years*, pp. 759–760.

98. Ibid., p. 1062.

99. Richard Nixon, *RN: The Memoirs of Richard Nixon* (New York: Grosset & Dunlap, 1978), p. 570.

100. William Burr, *The Kissinger Transcripts: The Top Secret Talks with Beijing and Moscow* (New York: The New Press, 1998), p. 66.

101. The text of the Shanghai Communiqué can be found online at http://www.taiwan-documents.org/communique01.htm.

102. Quoted in Robert B. Semple, Jr., "2 Senate Leaders Will Go to China: Invited by Chou," *New York Times*, March 1, 1972, p. A1.

103. Quoted in John W. Finney, "Nixon Wins Broad Approval of Congress on China Talks but Some Criticism Arises," *New York Times*, February 29, 1972, p. A17.

104. Quoted in Carroll Kilpatrick, "President Stresses Peace as His Aim," *Washington Post*, February 18, 1972, p. A1.

105. James C. Thomson, Jr. points out that some of the groundwork for a shift in China policy was laid during the 1960s. See "On the Making of U.S. China Policy, 1961–9: A Study in Bureaucratic Politics," *China Quarterly*, no. 50 (April-June 1972): 220–243.

106. Kusnitz, *Public Opinion and Foreign Policy*, pp. 132–134.

107. Gottfried-Karl Kindermann, "Washington between Beijing and Taipei: The Restructured Triangle, 1978–80," *Asian Survey* 20, no. 5 (May 1980): 461.

108. Ibid., pp. 135–138.

109. Victor H. Li and John W. Lewis, "Resolving the China Dilemma: Advancing Normalization, Preserving Security," *International Security* 2, no. 1 (Summer 1977): 11.

110. Martin L. Lasater, *The Taiwan Issue in Sino-American Strategic Relations* (Boulder, Colo.: Westview Press, 1984), p. 156.

111. Quoted in Gerald McBeath, "Taiwan in 1976: Chiang in the Saddle," A Survey of Asia in 1976, Part I, *Asian Survey* 17, no. 1 (January 1977): 25.

112. Steven I. Levine, "China Policy during Carter's Year One," *Asian Survey* 18, no. 5 (May 1978): 438.

113. Ibid., p. 440.

CHAPTER 3

1. In accordance with the shift of recognition in 1979, references hereinafter to "Taiwan" will indicate the de facto state on the island, previously referred to as the Republic of China.

2. David Tawei Lee, *The Making of the Taiwan Relations Act: Twenty Years in Retrospect* (New York: Oxford University Press, 2000), pp. 16–17.

3. Portions of the speech were reprinted in Ronald Reagan, "Decency for Taiwan," *New York Times*, January 28, 1979, p. E17.

4. Barry Goldwater, "Has the President Broken the Law?" *New York Times*, Letter to the Editor, February 8, 1979, p. A18.

5. Richard M. Pious, "The Taiwan Relations Act: The Constitutional and Legal Context," in Louis W. Koenig, James C. Hsiung, and King-yuh Chang, eds., *Congress, the Presidency, and the Taiwan Relations Act* (New York: Praeger, 1985), pp. 141–165.

6. These provisions can be found in Sections 2(b)(6), 3, 4, and 6 of the TRA, respectively.

7. See, for example, Peter Brookes, "Remain Resolute on Taiwan," *Defense News*, April 20–26, 1998, p. 31.

8. Lee, *The Making of the Taiwan Relations Act*, pp. 130–131.

9. Bush argues forcefully that the TRA does not represent an unconditional pledge on behalf of the United States to defend Taiwan. See, for example, "Helping the ROC to Defend Itself," in Ramon H. Myers, ed., *A Unique Relationship: The United States and the Republic of China under the Taiwan Relations Act* (Stanford, Calif.: Hoover Institution Press, 1989), pp. 79–118. See also Cecil V. Crabb, Jr., "An Assertive Congress and the TRA: Policy Influences and Implications," in Koenig, Hsiung, and Chang, eds., *Congress, the Presidency and the Taiwan Relations Act,* p. 93.

10. Quoted in Ted Galen Carpenter, "Let Taiwan Defend Itself," Cato Institute Policy Analysis, no. 313, August 24, 1998, p. 11.

11. For more on the erosion of the constraints on presidential war-making power, see the author's "Global Interventionism and a New Imperial Presidency," Cato Institute Policy Analysis, no. 71, May 16, 1986.

12. Quoted in Ralph Clough, "The People's Republic of China and the Taiwan Relations Act," in Myers, ed., *A Unique Relationship.*

13. Ibid.

14. Quoted in Robert S. Hirschfield, "The Reagan Administration and U.S. Relations with Taiwan and China," in Koenig, Hsiung, and Chang, eds., *Congress, the Presidency, and the Taiwan Relations Act,* pp. 111–139.

15. Cited in Hong N. Kim and Jack L. Hammersmith, "U.S.-China Relations in the Post-Normalization Era, 1979–1982," *Pacific Affairs* 59, no. 1 (Spring 1986): 69–91.

16. Ibid., p. 74.

17. Ibid., pp. 76–77.

18. Robert A. Manning, "Reagan's Chance Hit," *Foreign Policy,* no. 54 (Spring 1984): 90.

19. Lt. Col. William J. Frey, "The F–20: Saga of an FX," *Air University Review* (May-June 1986). Available online at http://www.airpower.maxwell.af.mil/airchronicles/aureview/1986/may-jun/frey.html.

20. Hirschfield, "The Reagan Administration and U.S. Relations with Taiwan and China," p. 126.

21. The full text of the third communiqué can be found online at http://www.taiwan-documents.org/communique03.htm.

22. *Human Events* 43, no. 9 (February 26, 1983): 19. Quoted in Hirschfield, "The Reagan Administration and U.S. Relations with Taiwan and China," p. 126.

23. Tucker, *Taiwan, Hong Kong, and the United States,* p. 139.

24. Dennis Van Vranken Hickey, *United States-Taiwan Security Ties: From Cold War to Beyond Containment* (Westport, Conn.: Praeger, 1994), p. 45.

25. Kim and Hammersmith, "U.S.-China Relations," pp. 86–87.

26. Zhang Jia-Lin, "The New Romanticism in the Reagan Administration's Asian Policy: Illusion and Reality," *Asian Survey* 24, no. 10 (October 1984): 999.

27. Robert S. Ross suggests that U.S.-PRC relations improved not because the states' interests were converging, but rather because President Reagan took a hard line against the Soviets and demonstrated to the Chinese their "reduced importance in American security policy." See Ross's "China Learns to Compromise: Change in U.S.-China Relations, 1982–1984," *China Quarterly,* no. 128 (December 1991): 742–773.

28. Richard Conroy, "China's Technology Import Policy," *Australian Journal of Chinese Affairs,* no. 15 (January 1986): 27.

29. Kim and Hammersmith, "U.S.-China Relations," p. 82.

30. Ibid., p. 83. See also Associated Press, "China Cautious on U.S. Offer," *The Globe and Mail,* September 26, 1983, p. 13.

31. Ibid., p. 84.
32. See Jane Mayer, "Searching for Substance: Reagan, in China, Focuses on TV," *Wall Street Journal*, April 27, 1984.
33. Kim and Hammersmith, "U.S. China Relations," p. 86.
34. Editorial, "Panda Bear Diplomacy," *Wall Street Journal*, April 16, 1984.
35. For a full analysis of the U.S.–China nuclear cooperation that emerged after Reagan's visit, see Qingshan Tan, "U.S.-China Nuclear Cooperation Agreement: China's Nonproliferation Policy," *Asian Survey* 29, no. 9 (September 1989): 870–882.
36. Joseph Fromm and Walter A. Taylor, "What Reagan Got—and Gave," *U.S. News & World Report*, May 7, 1984, p. 22.
37. Underpinning this new policy stance were what came to be known as the "Nine Principles." A brief outline of the substance of the nine principles can be found online at http://www1.chinataiwan.org/web/webportal/W5096185/A5113227.html.
38. Parris Chang, "Beijing's Policy toward Taiwan: An Elite Conflict Model," in Tun-jen Chang, Chi Huang, Samuel S. G. Hu, eds., *Inherited Rivalry: Conflict across the Taiwan Straits*, (Boulder, Colo.: Lynne Rienner Publishers, 1995), p. 68.
39. Quoted in Roy, *Taiwan*, p. 148.
40. Maria Hsia Chang, "Political Succession in the Republic of China on Taiwan," *Asian Survey* 24, no. 4 (April 1984): 424.
41. Tun-Jen Cheng, "Democratizing the Quasi-Leninist Regime in Taiwan," *World Politics* 41, no. 4 (July 1989): 471–499.
42. Edwin A. Winckler, "Institutionalization and Participation on Taiwan: From Hard to Soft Authoritarianism?" *China Quarterly*, no. 99 (September 1984): 481–499.
43. Ibid., pp. 482–483.
44. Christopher Howe, "The Taiwan Economy: The Transition to Maturity and the Political Economy of Its Changing International Status," *China Quarterly*, no. 148 (December 1996): 1172.
45. Ibid., p. 1171. See also Roy A. Werner, "Taiwan's Trade Flows: The Underpinning of Political Legitimacy?" *Asian Survey* 25, no. 11 (November 1985): 1110.
46. Werner, "Taiwan's Trade Flows," p. 1098.
47. Howe, "The Taiwan Economy: The Transition to Maturity and the Political Economy of Its Changing International Status."
48. Though recognition in the United Nations was officially a part of the DPP's platform, its public statements and rhetoric on the reunification issue represented a serious step back from the positions taken by its members as part of the APP.
49. Antonio Chiang, the editor who made this statement, also gave a glimpse of the mindset that would increasingly take root in Taiwan over the ensuing years. He noted that "[t]he majority of people here don't know about China and haven't been there. We want to trade and communicate (with China), as long as this doesn't touch politics." See Jim Mann, "Taiwan's Nationalists Face Dramatic Political Changes," *Los Angeles Times*, December 3, 1986, p. A1.
50. Roy, *Taiwan*, p. 173.
51. Cheng, "Democratizing the Quasi-Leninist Regime," pp. 489–490.
52. Ibid., p. 494.
53. Quoted in Nicholas D. Kristof, "Taiwan's Risky Refrain: 'Self Determination,'" *New York Times*, December 14, 1986, p. A14.
54. Roy, *Taiwan*, p. 185.
55. Ibid., pp. 187–188.

56. Ibid., pp. 192–195.
57. Linda Chao and Ramon H. Myers, "The First Chinese Democracy: Political Development and the Republic of China on Taiwan, 1986–1994," *Asian Survey* 34, no. 3 (March 1994): 226–227. See also Roy, *Taiwan*, pp. 194–195.
58. Quoted in Kent Chen, "Lord Hits Out at U.S. Sale of F–16 Fighters," *South China Morning Post*, December 15, 1992, p. 10.
59. Quoted in Mary Curtis, "China Says U.S. Jet Sale to Taiwan Perils Ties," *Boston Globe*, September 4, 1992, p. A2.
60. Robert Benjamin, "China Expresses Outrage over Jets' Sale to Taiwan," *Baltimore Sun*, September 4, 1992, p. 3A. Some estimates claimed that only three thousand jobs would be saved by the deal. See Amy Borrus, Joyce Barnathan, and Stewart Toy, "An Arms Sale That Suits Everyone but Beijing: Taiwan Wants F–16s, Texans Want Jobs, and Bush Wants Their Votes," *BusinessWeek*, September 14, 1992, p. 30.
61. Charles Aldinger, "Bush Using Incumbent's Advantage Well, Analysts Say," *Reuters*, September 2, 1992.
62. Xu Shiquan, "The 1992 Consensus: A Review and Assessment of Consultations between the Association for Relations across the Taiwan Strait and the Straits Exchange Foundation," *American Foreign Policy Interests* 23, no. 3 (June 2001): 126–127.
63. Statement of Taiwan's National Unification Council, August 1, 1992, reprinted in ibid., p. 125.
64. Chen Qimao, "The Taiwan Strait Crisis: Its Crux and Solutions," *Asian Survey* 36, no. 11 (November 1996): 1057.
65. Cited in ibid., p. 1058.
66. Martin L. Lasater, *The Taiwan Conundrum in U.S.-China Policy* (Boulder, Colo.: Westview Press, 2000), pp. 193–194 and 205–210. See also James McGregor, "Taiwan's Foreign Policy: From Cold War to Cold Cash," *Wall Street Journal*, August 16, 1989.
67. Chen Qimao, "New Approaches in China's Foreign Policy: The Post–Cold War Era," *Asian Survey* 33, no. 3 (March 1993): 237–251.
68. Richard K. Betts, "Wealth, Power, and Instability: East Asia and the United States after the Cold War," *International Security* 18, no. 3 (Winter 1993–1994): 47–54.
69. Quoted in Donald M. Rothberg, "Administration Criticized for Refusing Visa to Taiwan President," *Associated Press*, February 9, 1995.
70. H.Con.Res. 53 passed by a margin of 396 to 0, and S.Con.Res. 9 passed 91 to 1. See Roy, *Taiwan*, p. 197.
71. From wire reports, "China Threatens Reprisals if Taiwan Foe Visits U.S.," *Baltimore Sun*, May 26, 1995, p. A3.
72. Quoted in *Agence France-Presse*, "Ex-Diplomat Blames U.S. for Imbroglio with China," June 1, 1995.
73. Quoted in "China Threatens Reprisals."
74. Tim Healy and Laurence Eyton, "Perils of Money Diplomacy," *Asiaweek*, December 20, 1996, p. 23.
75. Alan D. Romberg, "The Role of the United States in Seeking a Peaceful Solution," in Steve Tsang, ed., *Peace and Security across the Taiwan Strait* (New York: Palgrave Macmillan, 2004), p. 121.
76. Chen Qimao, "The Taiwan Strait Crisis," p. 1058. Former DPP party member Annette Lu would later collect $160,000 from Taiwanese citizens and attempt to simply donate it to the UN, but that too was refused. See Cheng, "Taiwan in 1996," p. 48.

77. This analysis is taken from Suishang Zhao, "Changing Leadership Perceptions: The Adoption of a Coercive Strategy," in Suisheng Zhao, ed., *Across the Taiwan Strait: Mainland China, Taiwan, and the 1995–1996 Crisis* (New York: Routledge, 1999), p. 100.

78. Hung-mao Tien, "Taiwan in 1995: Electoral Politics and Cross-Strait Relations," *A Survey of Asia in 1995, Part I, Asian Survey* 36, no. 1 (January 1996): 36.

79. For an analysis on the broader origins of the 1995–96 Taiwan Straits crisis that is very critical of Beijing's policies, see Edward Friedman, "The Prospects of a Larger War: Chinese Nationalism and the Taiwan Strait Crisis," in Suisheng Zhao, *Across the Taiwan Strait: Mainland China, Taiwan, and the 1995–1996 Crisis*, pp. 243–275.

80. Quoted in *Agence France-Presse*, "Chinese Diplomat Dismisses Taiwan Concerns over Missile Exercise," July 19, 1995.

81. Jane Macartney, "China Fires another Salvo at Taiwan's President," *Reuters*, July 25, 1995.

82. Quoted in James Mann, "Between China and the U.S., Taiwan, Even More than Human Rights, Is the Most Dangerous Issue," *Washington Post*, January 10, 1999, p. C1.

83. Qimao, "The Taiwan Strait Crisis," p. 1055.

84. Dana Priest and Judith Havemann, "Second Group of U.S. Ships Sent to Taiwan; Christopher Calls Exercises by China 'Risky,' 'Reckless,'" *Washington Post*, March 11, 1996, p. A1.

85. Alice Hung, "Lee Hails Approach of *Nimitz* on Eve of Taiwan Poll," *Reuters*, March 22, 1996.

86. While unintentional, the Chinese were aware that a hard-line approach could bolster Lee's support in Taiwan. A recently declassified State Department cable authored by U.S. Ambassador to the PRC James Sasser noted that the PRC was "fully aware that the missile exercises could have a counterproductive affect [sic] and [that they could] actually bolster support for Lee, but had 'taken that into consideration.' [redacted] said that for China, there was too much at stake not to take a stand." See "Nationalism Strong Factor in China's Taiwan Stanch [sic]," Confidential Cable 008278, March 15, 1996. National Security Archive #CH01947.

87. Quoted in James Kynge, "Taiwan Blasts China, Says No Surrender to Pressure," *Reuters*, July 26, 1995.

88. With over 76 percent of the electorate turning out, Lee won 54 percent of the vote in a four-way race, with the closest opponent getting less than 22 percent. See Tun-jen Cheng, "Taiwan in 1996: From Euphoria to Melodrama," *A Survey of Asia in 1996, Part 1, Asian Survey* 37, no. 1 (January 1997): 43–44.

89. Quoted in Jim Wolf, "Helms to Invite Taiwan Leader to U.S.," *Reuters*, March 27, 1996.

90. Quoted in Dara Akiko Tom, "Chinese Leader Leaves United States on an Upbeat Note," *Associated Press*, November 3, 1997.

91. Quoted in *Agence France-Presse*, "Taiwan Carefully Examines Sino-U.S. Joint Statement," November 3, 1997.

92. Quoted in Guy Gugliotta and Thomas B. Edsall, "Laurels and Lingering Doubts; President's Critics, Backers Await Concrete Change," *Washington Post*, July 4, 1998, p. A1.

93. Quoted in ibid.

94. Ted Galen Carpenter, "Roiling Asia: U.S. Coziness with China Upsets the Neighbors," *Foreign Affairs* 77, no. 6 (November/December 1998): 2–6.

95. Tom Carter, "China Takes a Beating on Hill on Tibet, Army's U.S. Activities," *Washington Times*, November 7, 1997, p. A17.
96. Statement of the William J. Casey Institute of the Center for Security Policy, cited in Robert S. Ross, "Why Our Hardliners Are Wrong," *National Interest*, no. 49 (Fall 1997): 42–51.
97. Richard D. Fisher, "How America's Friends Are Building China's Military Power," *Heritage Foundation Backgrounder*, November 5, 1997.
98. The bill in question was S.693 in the Senate and H.R. 1838 in the House. It should also be noted that the Taiwanese government had continued its relationship with Cassidy and Associates, the Washington consulting group that aided in the Lee visit in 1995, in order to help it win support in Congress.
99. Quoted in Stan Crock and Joyce Barnathan, "Will China-Bashers in Congress Shower Taiwan with Arms?" *BusinessWeek*, June 7, 1999, p. 55.
100. John Pomfret and Michael Laris, "China Suspends some U.S. Ties; Protesters Trap Ambassador in Embassy," *Washington Post*, May 10, 1999, p. A1.
101. Sheng Lijun, "Chen Shui-bian and Cross-Strait Relations," *Contemporary Southeast Asia* 23, no. 1 (April 2001): 122–148.
102. Quoted in Stephen Fidler, "A Relationship Reduced to Rubble," *Financial Times*, May 15, 1999, p. 11.
103. Sheng, "Chen Shui-bian."
104. Philip Liu, "Chen Shui-bian's Victory: What Does It Mean?" *Taiwan Economic News*, March 26, 2000.
105. Editorial in *PLA Daily*, quoted in Sheng, "Chen Shui-bian."
106. *China Defense Daily*, March 24, 2000, p. 2. Cited in ibid.
107. BBC Monitoring Service, "Mainland on Leader's Speech: One China a Reality, not 'Future' Issue," May 22, 2000. The notion that the Taiwan issue could not be forestalled indefinitely officially emerged in a White Paper released in 2000 by the PRC. See People's Republic of China, The Taiwan Affairs Office and the Information Office of the State Council, "White Paper—The One China Principle and the Taiwan Issue," February 21, 2000.

CHAPTER 4

1. Michael D. Swaine, "Trouble in Taiwan," *Foreign Affairs* 83, no. 2 (March-April 2004): 45.
2. Ross Terrill, *The New Chinese Empire: And What It Means for the United States* (New York: Basic Books, 2003), p. 212.
3. For an analysis of growth of the independence movement in Taiwan, see Steven Phillips, "Building a Taiwanese Republic: The Independence Movement, 1945-Present," in Nancy Bernkopf Tucker, ed., *Dangerous Strait: The U.S.-Taiwan-China Crisis* (New York: Columbia University Press, 2005), pp. 44–69.
4. Reuters, "Poll: Hong Kong Handover Swells Taiwan Independence Mood," *Inside China Today*, July 4, 1997.
5. "Independence Gains Support in Taiwan," *Inside China Today*, January 30, 1997.
6. Taiwan Thinktank, "Taiwanese Nationals 'Perception About the Anti-Secession Law," December 31, 2004, http://www.taiwanthinktank.org/indexl.php.
7. Poll results in National Chengchi University (Taipei), "Changes in the Taiwanese/Chinese Identity of Taiwanese as Tracked in Surveys by the Election Study Center, NCCU (1992–2004), http://www2.nccu.edu.tw/~s00/eng/data/Political%20Attitude02.htm.

8. Tun-jen Cheng, "Taiwan in 1996: From Euphoria to Melodrama," *Asian Survey*, January 1997, pp. 44–45.
9. Ibid.
10. Emile C. J. Sheng, "Cross-Strait Relations and Public Opinion on Taiwan," *Issues & Studies* 38, no. 1 (March 2002): 17–46.
11. Ibid., pp. 27–28.
12. Ibid., p. 37.
13. Ibid., p. 39.
14. Ibid.
15. Quoted in Ted Galen Carpenter, "Beijing Smothers Hong Kong, Drives Taiwan Away," *FoxNews.com*, June 2, 2004, http://www.foxnews.com/printer_friendly_story/0/3566,121607,00.html.
16. For discussions of the economic relationship, see Karen M. Sutter, "Business Dynamism across the Taiwan Strait: Implications for Cross-Strait Relations," *Asian Survey* 42, no. 3 (May-June 2002): 523–540; Chien-min Chao, "Will Economic Integration between Mainland China and Taiwan Lead to a Congenial Political Culture?" *Asian Survey* 43, no. 2 (March-April 2003): 280–304; T. J. Cheng, "China-Taiwan Economic Linkage: Between Insulation and Superconductivity," in Tucker, ed, *Dangerous Strait*, pp. 93–130; and Gary H. Jefferson, "Like Lips and Teeth: Economic Scenarios of Cross-Strait Relations," in Gerrit W. Gong, ed., *Taiwan Strait Dilemmas: China-Taiwan-U.S. Policies in the New Century* (Washington, D.C.: CSIS Press, 2000), pp. 97–116.
17. Sutter, "Business Dynamism across the Taiwan Strait: Implications for Cross-Strait Relations," p. 534.
18. Sheng Lijun, *China and Taiwan: Cross-Strait Relations under Chen Shui-bian* (London: Zed Books, 2002), p. 75. See also, Suisheng Zhao, "Economic Interdependence and Political Divergence: A Background Analysis of the Taiwan Strait Crisis," in Suisheng Zhao, ed., *Across the Taiwan Strait: Mainland China, Taiwan, and the 1995–1996 Crisis* (New York: Routledge, 1999), pp. 21–40.
19. Sheng Lijun, *China and Taiwan*, pp. 75–76.
20. Trevor Corson, "Strait-Jacket," *Atlantic Monthly* (December 2004), http://www.theatlantic.com/doc/print/200412/corson.
21. "Dancing with the Enemy: A Survey of Taiwan," *The Economist*, January 15, 2005, p. 7.
22. Quoted in Sheng Lijun, *China and Taiwan*, p. 83.
23. Sutter, "Business Dynamism across the Taiwan Strait: Implications for Cross-Strait Relations," p. 534.
24. For a discussion of some of the economic and security dilemmas regarding economic ties in one industry, see Chyan Yang and Shiu-Wan Hung, "Taiwan's Dilemma across the Strait: Lifting the Ban on Semiconductor Investment in China," *Asian Survey* 43, no. 4 (July-August 2003): 681–696.
25. For a view that the economic linkages are probably sufficient to prevent the outbreak of war between the mainland and Taiwan, see "Dancing with the Enemy: A Survey of Taiwan."
26. Chao, "Will Economic Integration between Mainland China and Taiwan Lead to a Congenial Political Culture?" p. 283.
27. Quoted in Corson, "Strait-Jacket."
28. Andrew Peterson, "Dangerous Games across the Taiwan Strait," *Washington Quarterly* 27, no. 2 (Spring 2004): 23.
29. Republic of China Tenth-Term President, Chen Shui-bian Delivers Inauguration Address, May 20, 2000, p. 6, http://www.taipei.org/chen/chen0520.htm.

30. See ibid., p. 4.
31. Sheng Lijun, *China and Taiwan*, p. 53.
32. Ibid.
33. "Taiwan President: Reunification Is Not Taiwan's Only Choice," *Associated Press*, August 18, 2000; Mark Landler, "Risking China's Ire, Taiwan Leader Questions Unification," *New York Times*, September 2, 2000, p. A1.
34. Quoted in Sheng Lijun, *China and Taiwan*, p. 58.
35. Ibid.
36. Lin Mei-chun, "President Backs Siew's 'Common Market' Concept," *Taipei Times*, March 27, 2001, p. 1.
37. Quoted in "Taiwan's Ruling DPP Moves to Play Down Pro-Independence Flavour," *Agence France-Presse*, October 21, 2001.
38. Quoted in "DPP Passes 'Conflicting Interpretations," *China Post*, October 22, 2001, p. 1.
39. Quoted in Xing Zhigang, "Refusal of Principle May Spark Tension," *China Daily*, November 1, 2001, p. 1.
40. For a discussion of some of Chen's early attitudes and policies, see Sheng Lijun, *China and Taiwan*, pp. 51–59.
41. Chien-min Chao, "Will Economic Integration between Mainland China and Taiwan Lead to a Congenial Political Culture?" p. 289.
42. Ibid., p. 291.
43. "Text—Taiwan President Details Proposed Referendum," *Reuters*, January 16, 2004.
44. Alice Hung, "Taiwan Referendum Fails to Gain 50 Percent Vote," *Reuters*, March 20, 2004.
45. President Chen's Inaugural Address, "Paving the Way for a Sustainable Taiwan," http://www.president.gov.tw/php-bin/prez/showenews.php4, p. 8.
46. Ibid.
47. Ibid., p. 7.
48. Ibid., pp. 6–7.
49. Quoted in Tiffany Wu, "Taiwan to Appoint New China Policy Maker," *Reuters*, May 6, 2004.
50. Quoted in Nailene Chou Wiest and Jacky Hsu, "Beijing Blasts Threat of Retaliation: Taiwanese Premier's Remarks on Balance of Terror 'a Serious Provocation," *South China Morning Post*, September 30, 2004, p. 4.
51. Quoted in I-wei J. Chang, "Taiwan Dances on a Tightrope," *Washington Times*, July 30, 2004, p. A19. Emphasis added.
52. Quoted in Kathrin Hille, "Taiwan's Chen Hardens Stance toward China," *Financial Times*, October 1, 2004, http://news.ft.com/cms/s/10d710e6–12ed–11d9-b869–00000e2511c8.html.
53. Chang, "Taiwan Dances on a Tightrope."
54. Quoted in Tiffany Wu, "EXCLUSIVE—Taiwan Must Stand Up to China Bullying—Ex-President," *Reuters*, November 19, 2004.
55. Quoted in Huang Tai-lin, "Chen Pledges to Change Names," *Taipei Times*, December 6, 2004, p. 1. Emphasis added.
56. Alice Hung, "History Textbooks to Promote Separate Identity," *Washington Times*, December 10, 2004, p. A19.
57. Quoted in Philip P. Pan, "A New National Identity Emerges in Taiwan," *Washington Post*, January 2, 2004, p. A13.

58. Quoted in Hung, "History Textbooks to Promote Separate Identity."
59. Joseph Kahn, "Taiwan Voters Weighing How Far to Push China," *New York Times*, March 18, 2004, p. A1.
60. Quoted in Hung, "History Textbooks to Promote Separate Identity."
61. "President Chen Shui-bian's November 10, 2004 Statement on National Security," *Taiwan Update*, November 29, 2004, p. 2.
62. Ibid.
63. Quoted in "U.S. Praises President Chen's Peace Plan," *Taiwan Update*, November 29, 2004, p. 1.
64. Quoted in Huang Tai-lin, "Chen Pledges to Change Names."
65. Quoted in Edward Cody, "Taiwan Vote May Boost Independence," *Washington Post*, December 11, 2004, p. A16.
66. Benjamin Kang Lim and John Ruwitch, "China Warns Taiwan against Provoking Conflict," *Reuters*, November 15, 2004.
67. Quoted in Edward Cody, "Taiwan Vote May Boost Independence."
68. Quoted in William Foreman, "Taiwan Says China Is Threat to Region," *Associated Press*, August 15, 2004.
69. Keith Bradsher, "Small Pro-Independence Party Gaining in Taiwan," *New York Times*, December 9, 2004, p. A14.
70. Joseph Kahn, "China's Saber Rattling: Paying Off?" *New York Times*, December 13, 2004, p. A8.
71. "Chen and China," editorial, *Financial Times*, December 13, 2004, p. 16.
72. "Table—Vote Count for Taiwan's Legislative Election," *Reuters*, December 11, 2004.
73. Quoted in Kahn, "Taiwan Voters Weighing How Far to Push China."
74. Ibid.
75. "Dancing with the Enemy: A Survey of Taiwan," p. 5.
76. For an analysis of the breakdown of the vote in the legislative elections, see "Taiwan Holds Legislative Elections," *Taiwan Update*, December 23, 2004, pp. 1–3, 9.
77. Quoted in Alice Hung and Tiffany Wu, "Chen Loses Taiwan Poll, China Strains Seen Easing," *Reuters*, December 12, 2004.
78. Taiwan Thinktank, "Taiwanese Nationals' Perception about the Anti-Secession Law," www.taiwanthinktank.org/print_preview.php?id=552.
79. Quoted in "Taiwan's Chen Accuses China of Threatening Peace," *Reuters*, January 1, 2005.
80. Quoted in ibid.
81. Quoted in Kathrin Hille, "China-Taiwan Charter Flight Talks to Resume," *Financial Times*, January 3, 2005, p. 3.
82. Quoted in ibid.
83. For a discussion of Lee's "two states" theory, see Sheng Lijun, *China and Taiwan*, pp. 11–18.
84. Min Lee, "China, Taiwan Ok First Direct Flights," *Associated Press*, January 15, 2005.
85. Katherin Hille and Mure Dickie, "Taiwan Seeks New Era of Links with China," *Financial Times*, January 16, 2005, p. 1.
86. Quoted in Tan Ee Lyn, "Taiwan, China Clinch Deal on Landmark Direct Flights," *Reuters*, January 15, 2005.
87. Quoted in Lee, "China, Taiwan Ok First Direct Flights."
88. "Taiwan May Call Referendum to Counter China Law," *Reuters*, January 21, 2005.

89. Quoted in Benjamin Kang Lim, "China Offers Talks with Taiwan on Eve of Flights," *Reuters*, January 28, 2005.

90. Kathrin Hille, "Chen and Opposition Leader Agree to Relax Restrictions on Ties with China," *Financial Times*, February 25, 2005, p. 6.

91. Alice Hung, "Taiwan's Chen, Opposition Head Inch Closer on China," *Reuters*, February 24, 2005.

92. Keith Bradshar, "China's Hard Line Stirs Throng in Taiwan," *New York Times*, March 27, 2005, p. A10; Tim Culpan, "Thousands Protest in Taiwan," *Washington Post*, March 27, 2005, p. A19; and Alice Hung, "Taiwanese Protest Anti-Secession Law," *Reuters*, March 26, 2005.

93. Eugene Hoshiko, "Taiwanese Opposition Leader in China on Historic Visit," *Associated Press*, March 28, 2005; Benjamin Kang Lim, "China Dangles Economic Sweeteners for Taiwan," *Reuters*, March 30, 2005; and Philip P. Pan, "China Reaches Out to Opposition Party," *Washington Post*, April 1, 2005, p. A18.

94. Tiffany Wu, "Ruling Party Accuses KMT of Selling Out Taiwan," *Reuters*, March 30, 2005.

95. Kathrin Hille, "Taiwan Investigates Politicians for Treason over Links with China," *Financial Times*, April 7, 2005, p. 4.

96. Sheng, "Cross-Strait Relations and Public Opinion on Taiwan," p. 20.

97. Quoted in Nikolas K. Gvosdev and Travis Tanner, "Wagging the Dog," *National Interest*, no. 77 (Fall 2004): 5–10.

98. Corson, "Strait-Jacket."

CHAPTER 5

1. Quoted in William Matthews, "U.S. Delegation: Be Wary of Chinese Intentions," *Defense News*, January 24, 2005, p. 7.

2. "China Political Document Summaries," www.csis.org/isp/taiwan/china/political.pdf.

3. See Richard McGregor, "Beijing to Display More Potent Army," *Financial Times*, July 20, 2004, p. 6.

4. Quoted in Juliana Liu, "China Invokes Ex-Leader to Send Tough Taiwan Message," *Reuters*, August 21, 2004.

5. Sheng Lijun, *China and Taiwan: Cross-Strait Relations under Chen Shui-bian* (London: Zed Books, 2002), p. 44.

6. People's Republic of China, The Taiwan Affairs Office and the Information Office of the State Council, "White Paper—The One-China Principle and the Taiwan Issue," February 21, 2000, p. 6.

7. Sheng Lijun, *China and Taiwan*, p. 49.

8. Ibid., p. 70.

9. Quoted in ibid., p. 71.

10. Quoted in Philip P. Pan, "China Rebukes Taiwan's Leader on New Plans for Referendum," *Washington Post*, January 20, 2004, p. A13.

11. Quoted in Alice Hung, "China Likely to Spurn Taiwan Peace Overture—Analysts," *Reuters*, October 12, 2004.

12. Quoted in Elaine Kurtenbach, "Taiwan Leader's Peace Overture Rebuffed," *Associated Press*, October 11, 2004.

13. Quoted in Benjamin Kang Lim, "China Spurns Taiwan President's Peace Overture," *Reuters*, October 13, 2004.

14. Quoted in Mark Magnier, "China Lashes Out at Taiwan's Call for Renewed Dialogue," *Los Angeles Times*, October 14, 2004, p. A3.
15. Quoted in Benjamin Kang Lim and John Ruwitch, "China Warns Taiwan against Provoking Conflict," *Reuters*, November 15, 2004.
16. Embassy of the People's Republic of China in the United States of America, "Opening Remarks By Sun Weide," July 13, 2004. Transcript in author's possession.
17. Quoted in "China Slams U.S. Plan to Post Military Officers in Taiwan," *Agence France-Presse*, December 21, 2004.
18. Quoted in Mark Magnier, "Ties with China Dominate as Taiwan Heads to Polls," *Los Angeles Times*, December 11, 2004, p. A5.
19. Shelly Rigger, "Making Sense of Taiwan's Legislative Election," Foreign Policy Research Institute E-Note, January 4, 2005, pp. 3–4, www.fpri.org.
20. Quoted in "China, Taiwan Spat Expected to Persist—Chinese Media," *Reuters*, December 13, 2004.
21. Quoted in Joseph Kahn, "China's Saber Rattling: Paying Off?" *New York Times*, December 13, 2004, p. A8.
22. Quoted in "China Sends Fresh Warning to Chen," CNN.com, December 15, 2004, http:edition.cnn.com/2004/world/asiapcf/12/14/Taiwan.china.react/.
23. Katherin Hille, "China Criticized over Denial of Hong Kong Visa to Taipei Mayor," *Financial Times*, January 6, 2005, p. 3.
24. K. C. Ng and Philip P. Pan, "Critics See China behind Hong Kong's Snub of Taipei Mayor," *Washington Post*, January 11, 2005, p. A11.
25. Hille, "China Criticized over Denial of Hong Kong Visa to Taipei Mayor."
26. Joe McDonald, "China Plans to Enact Secession Law," *Associated Press*, December 17, 2004; and Lindsay Beck, "China to Introduce Law Opposing Taiwan Secession," *Reuters*, December 17, 2004.
27. Quoted in Stephanie Hoo, "China Mulls Linking Taiwan to Mainland," *Associated Press*, May 12, 2004.
28. Mark Magnier, "China Achieves More by Doing Less in Elections," *Los Angeles Times*, December 17, 2004, p. A5.
29. Joseph Kahn, "China's Army May Respond if Taiwan Fully Secedes," *New York Times*, December 18, 2004, p. A7; and Ching-Ching Ni, "Move by Chinese Congress Alarms Taiwan," *Los Angeles Times*, December 19, 2004, p. A6.
30. Joseph Kahn, "China's Army May Respond if Taiwan Fully Secedes."
31. Quoted in "Chen Says Taiwan Must Not Lower Guard against China," *Reuters*, September 3, 2004.
32. John J. Tkacik, "The Invasion of Taiwan: A Chinese Law Would Make It Legal," *National Review Online*, January 10, 2005, http://www.nationalreview.com/script/printpage.asp?ref=/comment/tkacik2005010011715.asp.
33. Quoted in McDonald, "China Plans to Enact Secession Law."
34. Quoted in Richard Dobson, "Taiwan Says China Forming Legal Basis to Attack," *Reuters*, December 18, 2004.
35. Ibid.
36. Philip P. Pan, "China Planning to Enact Law against Secession," *Washington Post*, December 18, 2004, p. A24.
37. Ibid.
38. *China's National Defense in 2004*, Section I, "The Security Situation," p. 2, http://english.people.com.cn/whitepaper/defense2004/defense200491)html.

39. Ibid., Section 11, "National Defense Policy," p. 1.
40. "Expert: White Paper Taiwan Part Has Six Fresh Meanings," *China Daily Online*, December 30, 2004, http://english.peopledaily.com.cn/200412/30/print20041230_169169.html.
41. Ibid.
42. Quoted in Patrick Goodenough, "Taiwan Seeks Int'l Support for Referendum Plan," CNSNews.com, January 8, 2004, townhall.com/news/politics/200401/for20040108c.shtml.
43. Ibid.
44. "China to Send Envoys to Koo's Funeral in Taiwan," *Reuters*, January 30, 2005.
45. Quoted in Benjamin Kang Lim, "China Offers Talks with Taiwan on Eve of Flights," *Reuters*, January 28, 2005.
46. Quoted in "China Seeks Conditional Talks with Taiwan's Ruling Party," *Kyodo News Service*, January 28, 2005.
47. Ibid.
48. Sheng Lijun, *China and Taiwan*, p. 121.
49. Edward Cody, "Nationalists Return to Chinese Mainland; Trip Seen as Undermining Taiwan Leader," *Washington Post*, April 27, 2005, p. A13.
50. Patrick Goodenough, "Taiwanese Divided over Mainland Visit," CNSNews.com, April 27, 2005, cnsnews.com/viewforeignbureaus.asp?page=/foreignbureaus/archive/200504/for20050427c.html.
51. "Anti-Secession Law Adopted by the NPC (full text)," *China Daily*, March 14, 2005, http://www.chinadaily.com.cn/english/doc/2005–03/14/content_424643.htm.
52. Ibid.
53. Greg Jaffe and Marc Champion, "Europe Is Likely to Delay Lifting China Embargo," *Wall Street Journal*, March 22, 2005, p. A13.
54. Robert Marquand, "Beijing Growing Restless over Taiwan," *Christian Science Monitor*, July 21, 2004, htttp://csmonitor.com/2004/0721/p01s04-woap.htm.
55. Richard McGregor and Caroline Gluck, "China Issues New Warning to Taiwan," *Financial Times*, December 28, 2004, p. 1.
56. Marquand, "Beijing Growing Restless over Taiwan."
57. Robert Marquand, "Would China Invade Taiwan?" *Christian Science Monitor*, July 22, 2004, http://csmonitor.com/2004/0722/p06s03-woap.htm.
58. Ibid.
59. Ibid.
60. Chien-min Chao, "Will Economic Integration between Mainland China and Taiwan Lead to a Congenial Political Culture?" *Asian Survey* 43, no. 2 (March-April 2003): 300–301.
61. Quoted in Trevor Corson, "Strait Jacket," *Atlantic Monthly*, December 2004, http://www.theatlantic.com/doc/print/200412/corson.
62. For a discussion about how extensive and growing economic ties may induce policy caution by both Beijing and Washington, see Joseph P. Quinlan, "Ties That Bind," *Foreign Affairs* 81, no. 4 (July-August 2002): 116–126.
63. Michael D. Swaine, "Trouble in Taiwan," *Foreign Affairs* 83, no. 2 (March-April 2004): 41–42.
64. Ross Terrill, *The New Chinese Empire: And What It Means for the United States* (New York: Basic Books, 2003), p. 216.
65. Quoted in Daniel Bolger, Mure Dickie, and Katherin Hille, "China Rejects Taiwan Flight Concessions," *Financial Times*, October 14, 2004, p. 7.

CHAPTER 6

1. Dan Blumenthal and Randy Scheunemann, "Tense Strait," *National Review Online*, January 27, 2005, http://nationalreview.com/script/printpage.asp?ref=/comment/blumenthal200501270741.asp.
2. See ibid.
3. Written testimony of John F. Copper, February 6, 2004, http://www.uscc.gov/hearings/2004hearings/written_testimonies/04_02_06/cooper.htm.
4. For a detailed discussion of the Taiwan Relations Act, see *Legislative History of the Taiwan Relations Act: An Analytic Compilation with Documents on Subsequent Developments*, ed. Lester L. Wolff and David L. Simon (Jamaica, N.Y.: American Association for Chinese Studies, 1982). The text is on pp. 288–295 and the quoted passage is on p. 288.
5. Ibid., p. 289.
6. "Mutual Defense Treaty between the United States and the Republic of China (Taiwan), Washington, December 3, 1954," in *United States Treaty System*, ed. J. A. S. Grenville and Bernard Wasserstein (New York: Metheun, 1987), p. 123.
7. Ibid.
8. Ibid., pp. 123–124.
9. Robert Kagan and William Kristol, "A National Humiliation," *Weekly Standard*, April 16–23, 2001, pp. 11–16.
10. Fox News Network, *Fox Special Report with Brit Hume*, April 3, 2001, transcript no. 040303cb.254, pp. 2, 3.
11. "Top U.S. Lawmaker Calls Air Crew 'Hostages' in China," *Reuters*, April 7, 2001.
12. Ibid.
13. For a full listing of U.S. arms sales to Taiwan since 1990, see Shirley A. Kan, "Taiwan: Major U.S. Arms Sales since 1990," Congressional Research Service Report RL30957, April 18, 2003.
14. Quoted in Indira A. R. Lakshmanan, "Deal Gets Arms to Taiwan Sooner; Submarines May Prove Bigger than Aegis," *Boston Globe*, April 25, 2001, p. A9.
15. Quoted in David E. Sanger, "U.S. Would Defend Taiwan, Bush Says," *New York Times*, April 26, 2001, p. A1.
16. Quoted in Brian Mitchell, "As Bush Vows to Defend Taiwan, How Far Will the U.S. Really Go?" *Investor's Business Daily*, April 26, 2001, p. A22.
17. Quoted in Edwin Chen and Henry Chu, "Bush Remarks on Taiwan Cause a Furor over U.S. Policy," *Los Angeles Times*, April 26, 2001, p. A1.
18. Project for a New American Century, "Statement on the Defense of Taiwan," August 20, 1999, www.newamericancentury.org/taiwandefensestatement.htm.
19. Bruce Herschensohn, "Bush Shakes Free from the State Department on Taiwan," *Los Angeles Times*, April 27, 2001, p. A17.
20. Quoted in Chen and Chu, "Bush Remarks on Taiwan Cause a Furor over U.S. Policy."
21. "Committed to Taiwan," editorial, *Wall Street Journal*, April 26, 2001, p. A20.
22. CNN, "Inside Politics," April 25, 2001, transcript.
23. Quoted in Bill Sammon, "White House Sees 'No Change' in Taiwan Policy," *Washington Times*, April 26, 2001, p. A1.
24. Charles Hutzler, "China Lashes Out at Bush for His Pledge to Defend Taiwan," *Wall Street Journal*, April 27, 2001, p. A15.

25. Brian Hu, "U.S. Navy Official Made Secret Visit," *Taipei Times*, April 30, 2001. Also see William Foreman, "U.S. Commander Visited Taiwan," *Associated Press*, May 1, 2001.

26. Walter Pincus, "U.S. Considers Shift In Nuclear Targets," *Washington Post*, April 29, 2001, p. A23.

27. Sheng Lijun, *China and Taiwan: Cross-Strait Relations under Chen Shui-bian* (London: Zed Books, 2002), p. 97.

28. Ibid.

29. For a discussion of Chinese influence on North Korea, see Ted Galen Carpenter and Doug Bandow, *The Korean Conundrum: America's Troubled Relations with North and South Korea* (New York: Palgrave Macmillan, 2004), pp. 82–84. Although U.S. officials tend to overestimate Beijing's influence on Pyongyang, China is by far the most significant player in that regard.

30. Steven Lee Myers, "Taiwan Chief Drops Plan for Meeting in California," *New York Times*, August 13, 2000, p. A9.

31. See, for example, Willis Witter, "Leader's New York Speech a Prod; Beijing Frowns on High Profile," *Washington Times*, October 31, 2003, p. A19.

32. Robert Burns, "No. 2 Pentagon Official Scheduled to Meet with Senior Taiwanese Officials in Florida," *Associated Press*, March 8, 2002.

33. On the extent of U.S.–Taiwanese security cooperation, see Michael S. Chase, "U.S.-Taiwan Security Cooperation: Enhancing an Unofficial Relationship," in Nancy Bernkopf Tucker, ed. *Dangerous Strait: The U.S.-Taiwan-China Crisis* (New York: Columbia University Press, 2005), pp. 162–185.

34. That trend has continued and even intensified. See David E. Sanger and William J. Broad, "U.S. Asking China to Increase Pressure on North Korea to End Its Nuclear Program," *New York Times*, February 9, 2005, p. A6.

35. Hamish McDonald, "Beijing Threatens War over Taiwan," *Sydney Morning Herald*, November 20, 2003, http://www.smh.com.au/articles/20–03/11/19/1069027192249.html.

36. "Bush, Wen Meet at White House: Text of the Chinese and American Leaders' Comments," *WashingtonPost.com*, December 9, 2003, http://www.washingtonpost.com.

37. William Kristol, Robert Kagan, and Gary Schmitt, Project for a New American Century Memorandum, "U.S.-China-Taiwan Policy," December 9, 2003.

38. Quoted in Dana Milbank and Glenn Kessler, "President Warns Taiwan on Independence," *Washington Post*, December 10, 2003, p. A1.

39. "Mr. Bush's Kowtow," editorial, *Washington Post*, December 10, 2003, p. A30. The president's statement did attract a few defenders, though. See Michael D. Swaine, "Trouble in Taiwan," *Foreign Affairs* 38, no. 2 (March-April 2004): 39–49.

40. Willy Wo-Lap Lam, "China Claims a Big Win over Taiwan," *CNN.com*, December 14, 2003.

41. Bonnie S. Glaser, "Washington's Hands-On Approach to Managing Cross-Strait Tension," Center for Strategic and International Studies Pacific Forum, *PacNet*, May 13, 2004, p. 1.

42. Bradley Graham, "Pentagon Announces Plans to Sell Radars to Taiwan," *Washington Post*, April 1, 2004, p. A27.

43. "U.S. Welcomes New Terms of Taiwan Referendum," *Reuters*, January 16, 2004.

44. Scott Hillis, "China Says Taiwan Referendum Plan Is Provocative," *Reuters*, January 17, 2004.

45. Transcript, interview with Anthony Yuen of Phoenix TV, October 25, 2004, http://www.state.gov/secretary/rm/37361.htm.

46. Quoted in Joseph Kahn, "Warnings by Powell to Taiwan Provoke a Diplomatic Dispute," *New York Times*, October 28, 2004, p. A5.

47. John J. Tkacik, Jr. "Kung Pao Taiwan," *National Review Online*, October 29, 2004, http://nationalreview.com/script/printpag.asp?ref=/comment/tkacik200410290885.asp.

48. Quoted in Katherin Hille, "Taipei's Name Plan Brings U.S. Warning," *Financial Times*, December 7, 2004, p. 3.

49. Quoted in Carol Giacomo, "U.S. Sees Proposed China Law as Threat to Peace," *Reuters*, December 20, 2004.

50. Quoted in Bill Gertz, "U.S. Calls for Calm from Beijing, Taipei," *Washington Times*, December 28, 2004, p. A12.

51. "U.S. to Send Military Officers to Taiwan—Official," *Reuters*, December 21, 2004; and "U.S. Signs 99-Year Lease for Site of New De Facto Embassy in Taiwan," *Agence France-Presse*, December 22, 2004.

52. Quoted in Tiffany Wu, "Taiwan Plays Down China-U.S. 'Land Mine' Remark," *Reuters*, December 23, 2004.

53. See, for example, Blumenthal and Scheunemann, "Tense Strait."

54. John J. Tkacik, "The Invasion of Taiwan," *National Review Online*, January 10, 2005, http://www.nationalreview.com/script/printpage.asp?ref=comment/tkacik200501010715.asp.

55. Thomas Donnelly, "Who Forgot China?" American Enterprise Institute, January 3, 2005, http://www.aei.org/include/news_print.asp?newsID=21771.

56. Glenn Kessler, "Rice Warns Europe Not to Sell Advanced Weaponry to China," *Washington Post*, March 21, 2005, p. A12.

57. Willis Witter, "U.S. Gets No Help from East Asians in Backing Taiwan," *Washington Times*, March 14, 1997, p. A15; Steve Glain, "U.S. Probably Shouldn't Count on Help from Japan in Resolving Taiwan Flap," *Wall Street Journal*, March 11, 1996, p. A10; "Downer Urges Restraint in China-Taiwan Tension," Melbourne, Radio Australia, in *Foreign Broadcast Information Service Daily Report—East Asia*, March 13, 1996, electronic version, document Odo8cfk040v69n; "Alatas on Tense China-Taiwan Relations," Jakarta, Radio Republik Indonesia in *FBIS—East Asia*, 96–050, March 13, 1996, p. 50; "Further Comment on Assistance to U.S.," *Business World* (Manila) in *FBIS—East Asia*, March 13, 1996, electronic version, document Odoag3j03m9trn; Statement by Tan Sri Ahman Kamil Jaafar, Secretary General of the Foreign Ministry of Malaysia, March 1996, text provided by Malaysian Embassy, November 18, 1996.

58. Quoted in Ted Galen Carpenter, "With Friends Like These . . . ," *Washington Post*, April 18, 2001, p. A11.

59. Richard Armitage, "Help from Our Friends," letter to the editor, *Washington Post*, April 22, 2001, p. B6.

60. Ibid.

61. Witter, "U.S. Gets No Help from East Asians in Backing Taiwan."

62. Quoted in John Burton, "Singapore Warns Taipei on Independence," *Financial Times*, August 23, 2004, p. 4. Lee's effort to placate Beijing was all the more telling because he had just recently annoyed the PRC by visiting Taiwan.

63. Quoted in "China Hints Row with Singapore Over, Warns Japan," *Reuters*, August 26, 2004.

64. Quoted in Janaki Kremmer, "Official Clouds Support for U.S.," *Washington Times*, September 8, 2004, p. A11.
65. Philip P. Pan, "China's Improving Image Challenges U.S. in Asia," *Washington Post*, November 15, 2003, p. A1. For an incisive analysis of Beijing's supple diplomatic and economic strategy in East Asia, see David Shambaugh, "China Engages Asia: Reshaping the Regional Order," *International Security* 29, no. 3 (Winter 2004–2005): 64–99.
66. Quoted in James K. Glassman, "Examining America's Role in Asia," *Tech Central Station*, December 1, 2004.
67. Jason T. Shapen and James Laney, "China Trades Its Way to Power," *New York Times*, August 28, 2004, p. A23.
68. Quoted in Jane Perlez, "China Is Romping with the Neighbors (U.S. Is Distracted)," *New York Times*, December 3, 2003, p. A1.
69. Jane Perlez, "Across Asia, Beijing's Star Is in Ascendance," *New York Times*, August 28, 2004, p. A1.
70. Ibid.
71. Bill Gertz, "China Builds Up Strategic Sea Lanes," *Washington Times*, January 18, 2005, p. A1.
72. For an extreme interpretation of how the PRC is using its growing economic and political clout to enhance its strategic position in East Asia and, in the view of the author, pursue the goal of creating a de facto Chinese empire, see Ross Terrill, *The New Chinese Empire: And What It Means for the United States* (New York: Basic Books, 2003).
73. Quoted in Vijay Joshi, "China, Southeast Asia Sign Trade Accord," *Associated Press*, November 29, 2004.
74. Don Lee, "China Steps Up to Role of Rising Regional Leader," *Los Angeles Times*, January 6, 2005, p. A1.
75. Quoted in Catherine Armitage, "Taiwan Slams Downer over Region," *The Australian*, September 24, 2004, http://www.theaustralian.news.com.au/printpage/0,5942,10860469.00.html.
76. Quoted in Perlez, "China Is Romping with the Neighbors (U.S. Is Distracted)."
77. U.S.-Japan Security Consultative Committee, Completion of the Review of the Guidelines for U.S.-Japan Defense Cooperation, New York, NY, September 23, 1997, http://www.jda.go.jp/e/policy/f_work/sisin4_.htm, pp. 2–3.
78. Author's conversations with Japanese and South Korean diplomats, October and November, 2004, Washington, D.C. See also Jong-Heon Lee, "U.S. Intent Questioned: Seoul Seen as Base for Role in China-Taiwan Fight," *Washington Times*, December 3, 2004, p. A17.
79. U.S. Department of State, Joint Statement of the U.S.-Japan Security Consultative Committee, February 19, 2005, http://www.state.gov/r/pa/prs/ps/2005/42490.htm.
80. Quoted in David Pilling, "Issue of Taiwan Raises Stakes between Tokyo and Beijing," *Financial Times*, February 25, 2005, p. 6.
81. Norimitsu Onishi, "Tokyo Protests Anti-Japan Rallies in China," *New York Times*, April 11, 2005, p. A8.
82. Quoted in David E. Sanger, "U.S. Asks Taiwan to Avoid a Vote Provoking China," *New York Times*, December 9, 2003, p. A1.
83. Testimony of Assistant Secretary of State James Kelly, *The Taiwan Relations Act: The Next Twenty-Five Years*, Hearing Before the Committee on International Relations, House of Representatives, 108th Cong., 2d sess. April 21, 2004, Serial Number 108–107, p. 76.

84. Trevor Corson, "Strait-Jacket," *Atlantic Monthly*, December 2004, http://www.the-atlantic.com/doc/print/200412/corson.
85. Michael D. Swaine, "Trouble in Taiwan," *Foreign Affairs* 83, no. 2 (March-April 2004): 43.
86. Andrew Peterson, "Dangerous Games across the Taiwan Strait," *Washington Quarterly* 27, no. 2 (Spring 2004): 37–38.
87. Ibid., p. 37.
88. Quoted in Benjamin Kang Lim, "China Eyes U.S. to Rein In Taiwan, Avert Conflict," *Reuters*, December 8, 2004. See also Joseph Kahn, "Beijing Urges Bush to Act to Forestall Taiwan Vote," *New York Times*, February 6, 2004, p. A3.

CHAPTER 7

1. The Council on Foreign Relations' Independent Task Force Report, *Chinese Military Power* (New York: Council on Foreign Relations, 2003) put the figure at a mere three hundred fifty (p. 53). The Department of Defense estimates five hundred missiles. U.S. Department of Defense, "Annual Report on the Military Power of the People's Republic of China," 2004, p. 37. Chen Shui-bian claimed the correct figure was six hundred. *Reuters*, "Taiwan's Opposition Emboldened by Vote," December 16, 2004. In early 2005, a Taiwanese diplomat said that the number of missiles was approaching seven hundred. Author's conversation, February 2005.
2. U.S. Department of Defense, Annual Report on the Military Power of the People's Republic of China, p. 46, www.defenselink.mil/pubs/d20040528prc.pdf.
3. Ibid., p. 49.
4. Jason E. Bruzdzinski, "Demystifying Shashoujian: China's 'Assassin's Mace' Concept," in Andrew Scobell and Larry Wortzel, eds., *Civil-Military Change in China: Elites, Institutes, and Ideas After the 16th Party Congress* (Carlisle, Penn.: Strategic Studies Institute, 2004), pp. 309–364.
5. Sun Tzu, *The Art of War* Lionel Giles, trans. (Mineola, N.Y.: Dover Publications, 2002), pp. 42–43.
6. For a brief summary of contemporary examples of this phenomenon, see Mark Burles and Abram N. Shulsky, *Patterns in China's Use of Force: Evidence from History and Doctrinal Writings* (Washington, D.C.: RAND Corporation, 2000), pp. 5–20.
7. *Agence France-Presse*, "Taiwan Stages War Games as Report Shows China Could Win in Six Days," August 11, 2004. See also Kathrin Hille, "Taiwan Conquest 'Would Take Days,'" *Financial Times*, August 12, 2004, p. 6.
8. Michael O'Hanlon, "Why China Cannot Conquer Taiwan," *International Security* 25, no. 2 (September 22, 2000): 53.
9. Ivan Eland, "The China-Taiwan Military Balance: Implications for the United States," Cato Institute Foreign Policy Briefing no. 74, February 5, 2003, p. 8.
10. Michael Swaine and James Mulvenon, *Taiwan's Foreign and Defense Policies: Features and Determinants* (Santa Monica, Calif.: RAND Corporation, 2001), p. 124. Although Swaine and Mulvenon are not clear in defining "medium term" and "long term," the context of their work indicates that long term would mean until roughly 2020.
11. U.S. Department of Defense, "Annual Report on the Military Power of the People's Republic of China," p. 52.
12. CFR, "Chinese Military Power," p. 3.
13. Robert S. Ross, "Navigating the Taiwan Strait: Deterrence, Escalation Dominance, and U.S.-China Relations," *International Security* 27, no. 2 (Fall 2002): 82. Oddly,

Ross had argued previously that "Taiwan's assets alone could enable it to frustrate a mainland effort to occupy the island." It is unclear why China would be undeterred by the knowledge that Taiwan could frustrate an effort to occupy the island. See Ross, "The Stability of Deterrence in the Taiwan Strait," *The National Interest* (Fall 2001): 70.

14. Richard Bernstein and Ross H. Munro, *The Coming Conflict with China* (New York: Vintage Books, 1997), p. 165.

15. U.S. Department of Defense, "Annual Report on the Military Power of the People's Republic of China," p. 27.

16. See Ted Galen Carpenter, "China's Defense Budget Smoke and Mirrors," *United Press International*, March 15, 2004, www.nexis.com.

17. Ivan Eland, "Is Chinese Military Modernization a Threat to the United States?" Cato Institute Policy Analysis no. 465, January 23, 2003, p. 2.

18. O'Hanlon, "Why China Cannot Conquer Taiwan," p. 86.

19. The International Institute for Strategic Studies (*The Military Balance: 2004–2005* [London: Oxford University Press, 2004], p. 161) claims that the missile presence may be growing by as many as seventy-five missiles per year. Taiwan's vice president Annette Lu claimed that the PRC could have eight hundred missiles pointed at Taiwan by the end of 2005. See Tiffany Wu, "China Missile Build-Up Raises Stakes on Taiwan," *Reuters*, August 11, 2004.

20. Swaine and Mulvenon, *Taiwan's Foreign and Defense Policies*, p. 124.

21. U.S.-China Economic and Security Review Commission, *The National Security Implications of the Economic Relationship between the United States and China*, July 2002, chapter 8, p. 4.

22. O'Hanlon, "Why China Cannot Conquer Taiwan," pp. 57–58.

23. For example, Andrew Yang of Taiwan's Chinese Council of Advanced Policy Studies claims that as of 2004 their accuracy had been increased to between thirty to fifty meters. Tiffany Wu, "China Missile Build-Up Raises Stakes on Taiwan," *Reuters*, August 11, 2004.

24. As the PRC makes progress integrating the fourth-generation fighters into the PLAAF (particularly its Su–30s, which have a ground-attack capability), the Taiwanese will need to spend more money to bolster its air defense. Thus far Taiwan has relied on its preponderant air superiority, but the combination of PLAAF advances and Taiwan's failure to spend adequately on its military is causing the gap in capabilities to slowly close. This is an area in which Taiwan's vulnerability is increasing.

25. IISS, *The Military Balance*, p. 190.

26. Ibid., p. 172.

27. *RIA Novosti*, "China Contemplating New Contracts for Supply of Fighter Jets from Russia," December 20, 2004. Earlier reports had indicated that forty-eight planes would be sold to China. See Igor Zuyev, "Export of Russian 'Sukhoi' Fighters to Asia Expected to Grow," *Itar-Tass*, November 24, 2004.

28. Kenneth B. Sherman, "Flashpoint: Taiwan Straits," *Journal of Electronic Defense* 27, no. 11 (November 1, 2004): 51–59.

29. David Shambaugh, "A Matter of Time: Taiwan's Eroding Military Advantage," *The Washington Quarterly* 23, no. 2 (Spring 2000): 121. Taiwan possesses more than twice as many fourth-generation fighters as China. In the event of an aerial attack, Taiwan could use these planes to flood the airspace over the Strait.

30. Although its air force would likely seek to restrain the conflict to the direct vicinity of the Taiwan Strait, recent comments by Taiwanese Premier Yu Shyi-kun have

caused concern that Taiwan may attempt to retaliate by striking the mainland with missiles. In September 2004, Yu explained the logic: "You fire 100 missiles at me, I fire 50 at you. You hit Taipei and Kaohsiung, I at least hit Shanghai. This is what we call balance of terror." See Nailene Chou Wiest and Jacky Hsu, "Beijing Blasts Threat of Retaliation; Taiwanese Premier's Remarks on Balance of Terror 'A Serious Provocation,'" *South China Morning Post*, September 30, 2004, p. 4.

31. Even if the PRC were to put all of its advanced fighters at risk by deploying them to a battle over the Taiwan Strait, the Taiwanese pilots are better trained, the Taiwanese aircraft are better maintained, and their C4 capabilities are greater than the PRC's.

32. Denny Roy, "Tensions in the Taiwan Strait," *Survival* 42, no.1 (Spring 2000): 84.

33. If Taiwan were to purchase the proposed Kidd-class destroyers from the United States, it would bolster Taiwan's ability not only in an amphibious scenario, but would give it an increased ability to combat the PLAN's Kilo-class submarines in the Taiwan Strait. See "ROC Negotiating with U.S. on Four Destroyers—Jane's Defence," *The China Post*, December 4, 2000.

34. Kathrin Hille, "Taiwan Success with 'Counter-Strike' Missile," *Financial Times Asia Edition*, January 8, 2005, p. 4.

35. U.S. Department of Defense, "Annual Report on the Military Power of the People's Republic of China," p. 40.

36. Michael Richardson, "Don't Rule Out a Military Showdown over Taiwan," *South China Morning Post*, March 26, 2004, p. 15.

37. International Institute for Strategic Studies, "Taiwan's Military: Assessing Strengths and Weaknesses," *Strategic Comments* 6 (May 2001).

38. IISS, *The Military Balance*, p. 172.

39. Department of Defense, "Annual Report to Congress," p. 40.

40. O'Hanlon, "Why China Cannot Conquer Taiwan," p. 63.

41. Here again, though, there is dissent. Richard L. Russell argues that either "by readily deceiving outside observers about the scope of their sealift and airlift capabilities" or by using "massive barrages of surface-to-surface missiles armed with weapons of mass destruction" China could succeed in invading Taiwan. See Richard L. Russell, "What If . . . 'China Attacks Taiwan!'" *Parameters* 31, no. 3 (Autumn 2001): 76–91.

42. Shambaugh, "A Matter of Time," p. 130.

43. Lyle Goldstein and William Murray, "Undersea Dragons: China's Maturing Submarine Force," *International Security* 28, no. 4 (Fall 2004): 161–196. Goldstein and Murray suspect that after a blockade were imposed, "[w]hile the United States considered its options, Taiwan's navy might try to break the blockade on its own. Its chances of success, however, would be relatively low" (p. 181).

44. China's reaction to any states assisting Taiwan would likely be extremely harsh, and would probably deter states from participating.

45. Michael A. Glosny, "Strangulation from the Sea? A PRC Submarine Blockade of Taiwan," *International Security* 28, no. 4 (Spring 2004): 149.

46. Steven Mufson, "China-Taiwan Conflict 'in Remission, not Resolved,'" *Washington Post*, April 22, 1996, p. A17. IISS, *The Military Balance*, pp. 171–172. Peter Harmsen, "Sooner or Later, Taiwan Pays the Price of Cross-Strait Tensions," *Far Eastern Economic Review*, March 28, 1996, p. 58. John J. Tkacik, Jr., "Stating America's Case to China's Hu Jintao: A Primer on U.S.-China-Taiwan Policy," *Heritage Foundation Backgrounder* no. 1541, April 26, 2002, p. 8.

47. IISS, *The Military Balance*, pp. 171–172.

48. Though implanting mines by air is possible, most analysts rule this out because of Taiwan's air superiority.

49. Glosny, "Strangulation from the Sea?" pp. 140–141.

50. See Justin Bernier and Stuart Gold, "China's Closing Window of Opportunity," *Naval War College Review* 56, no. 3 (July 1, 2003). Of course, these ships would now be facing the Hsiung Feng III, but it is not clear how many of the new missiles Taiwan would have available. It should also be noted that a traditional blockade is a less subtle instrument than simply mining the Strait and the PLAN would be risking a harsh international reaction by actually massing ships and shooting at unarmed commercial vessels. Mining the Strait would allow them to present a fait accompli to the world community and appear less menacing.

51. Glosny, "Strangulation from the Sea," p. 145.

52. Again, however, China would almost certainly issue an unequivocal warning that economic assistance to Taiwan at that point would be viewed as a violation of its sovereignty. States violating China's claim would very likely face retaliation—especially economic retaliation. Given China's regional and increasing global economic clout (see chapter 6); it would be extremely dangerous economically to risk arousing China's anger.

53. Glosny, "Strangulation from the Sea," p. 150.

54. Ibid., pp. 138–139.

55. For example, Glosny claims that merchant shipping to Taiwan was not deterred during the 1996 crisis. In fact, air and sea traffic was diverted for nine days. (See *Associated Press*, "China Ends Live-Fire Drills: Other Exercises Continue," March 20, 1996.) Glosny also notes that insurance companies have historically made large profits from insuring merchant ships during wars and therefore would likely continue to insure ships bound for and coming from Taiwan, but he fails to attempt a calculation at what these costs may be and what they may mean to the Taiwanese economy. Taiwan's ability to endure sustained increases in costs for its imports and exports (which comprise nearly all its economy) would certainly bear on the outcome of a confrontation.

56. Shambaugh, "Taiwan's Eroding Military Advantage," p. 131. Though it would be difficult, Taiwan could also develop the ability to use its eastern ports for routing some of its traffic away from the Chinese blockade.

57. Goldstein and Murray, "Undersea Dragons," p. 183.

58. Ibid.

59. Maj. Gen. Huang Bin, original quote from Hong Kong's *Ta Kung Palo* daily newspaper on May 13, 2002. Reprinted in Richard D. Fisher, "To Take Taiwan, First Sink a Carrier," *Jamestown Foundation China Brief* 2, no. 14, July 8, 2002.

60. Bernier and Gold, "China's Closing Window of Opportunity."

61. See Audra Ang, "China: Use of Force May Be 'Unavoidable' if Taiwan Pursues Independence," *Associated Press*, November 19, 2003.

62. For an in-depth discussion of the significance and evolution of PLA doctrine over the recent past, see Paul H. B. Godwin, "Compensating for Deficiencies: Doctrinal Evolution in the Chinese People's Liberation Army: 1978–1999," in James C. Mulvenon and Andrew N. D. Yang, eds., *Seeking Truth from Facts: A Retrospective on Chinese Military Studies in the Post-Mao Era* (Santa Monica, Calif.: RAND Corporation, 2001): 87–118.

63. Ibid., p. 111.

64. Andrew F. Krepinevich, "Cavalry to Computer: The Pattern of Military Revolutions," *The National Interest* (Fall 1994): 30–42.

65. Ahmed S. Hashim, "The Revolution in Military Affairs Outside the West," *Journal of International Affairs* 51, no. 2 (Spring 1998): 440.

66. For example, Mao wrote of the war against Japan: "The enemy is strong and we are weak, and the danger of subjugation is there. But in other respects the enemy has shortcomings and we have advantages. The enemy's advantage can be reduced and his shortcomings aggravated by our efforts. On the other hand, our advantages can be enhanced and our shortcoming remedied by our efforts." See Mao Zedong, *The Selected Works of Mao Zedong*, vol. II (Peking: Foreign Languages Press, 1967), p. 134.

67. Quoted in Sherman, "Flashpoint."

68. Alastair Iain Johnston has warned against mystifying or "orientalizing" the term. He points out that it is also used in sports and even "love advice" columns in China. He likens the term to "silver bullet" in English parlance. See Johnston's "Toward Contextualizing the Concept of a Shashoujian (Assassin's Mace)," unpublished manuscript, August 2002. Available online at http://www.people.fas.harvard.edu/~johnston/shashoujian.pdf.

69. Bruzdzinski, "Demystifying *Shashoujian*," pp. 326–329.

70. Ibid., pp. 344–348.

71. For more information on the potential threat posed by EMP, see Jack Spencer, "The Electromagnetic Pulse Commission Warns of an Old Threat with a New Face," *Heritage Foundation Backgrounder* no. 1784, August 3, 2004.

72. Quoted in ibid.

73. *Report of the Commission to Assess the Threat to the United States from Electromagnetic Pulse (EMP) Attack*, Volume 1, Executive Report, p. 47. Available online at http://www.house.gov/hasc/openingstatementsandpressreleases/108thcongress/04–07–22emp.pdf.

74. Eric Lichtblau, "CIA Warns of Chinese Plans for Cyber-Attacks on U.S. Defense," *Los Angeles Times*, April 25, 2002, p. A1.

75. Vincent Wei-cheng Wang, "Winning the War without Fighting? Overcoming the Superior with the Inferior," paper presented to the 2002 Annual Meeting of the Conference Group on Taiwan Studies of the American Political Science Association, August 29-September 1, 2002, p. 30. Available online at http://www.la.utexas.edu/research/cgots/Papers/53.pdf.

76. Jon Swartz, "Cyberterror Impact, Defense under Scrutiny: But Al Qaeda not Seen as Primary Threat in E-Attack," *USA Today*, August 3, 2004, p. B2.

77. IISS, *The Military Balance*, p. 325. Here, Taiwan's GNP and China's GDP figures are not adjusted for purchasing power parity (PPP) so that they can be compared to their estimated defense spending.

78. IISS, *The Military Balance*, p. 322.

79. The CIA estimates China's defense spending at $60 billion annually, DoD places it between $50 and $70 billion, IISS estimates $56 billion, and the CFR report suspects it is somewhere between $44 and $67 billion.

80. The CIA World Factbook estimates Taiwan's defense spending to be as high as $8 billion.

81. "The Dragon Next Door: War with China May Not Be Likely, but if It Happened, It Would Be Devastating," *The Economist: A Survey of Taiwan*, January 15, 2005, pp. 6–7.

82. Luis Huang, "Arms Budget Should Be Slashed to Improve Social Welfare: KMT Chief," *Central News Agency*, November 14, 2004.

83. Jason Dean, "U.S. Lawmaker Criticizes Taiwan over Arms Budget," *Asian Wall Street Journal*, January 18, 2005, p. A6.

84. Quoted in Edward Cody, "Politics Puts Hold on Taiwan Arms Purchase: $18.2 Billion Deal for U.S. Weapons Stalled Despite American Warning of China Threat," *Washington Post*, October 10, 2004, p. A28.

85. U.S. Fed News, "Rep. Tancredo Introduces Resolution Pushing Official U.S. Recognition of Taiwan," June 3, 2004.

86. International Monetary Fund, "World Economic Outlook: The Global Demographic Transition," September 2004, p. 205, http://www.imf.org/external/pubs/ft/weo/2004/02/.

87. Again, this figure is not adjusted for PPP so as to allow for comparison to China's defense spending, which is not adjusted for PPP.

88. RIA Oreanda, "Deliveries," January 9, 2002, www.oreanda.ru.

89. IISS, *The Military Balance*, p. 161.

90. The CIA figure of $6.5 trillion, when reverted from PPP, indicates China's real GDP at $1.2 trillion. The IISS figures estimate $1.4 trillion. The estimates of $6 to $7 billion indicated above show the difference of a half-percent increase of GDPs at both $1.2 and $1.4 trillion.

91. "Dragon Next Door," *Economist*, p. 6.

92. "China Builds up Sovremenny Fleet as Russia's Fades," *Forecast International—Naval Systems Group*, August 12, 2004. See also IISS, *The Military Balance*, pp. 327–328.

93. Massimo Annati, "The Asian DDG Race," *Military Technology* 28, no. 11 (November 2004): 37.

94. Goldstein and Murray, "Undersea Dragons," pp. 162, 166.

95. Quoted in David Lague, "China Beefs Up Undersea Force—High-Tech Submarine Fleet Could Pose Threat to Neighbors, U.S.," *Asian Wall Street Journal*, November 29, 2004, p. A1. For a recent analysis of how much difficulty the United States might encounter in confronting China's increasingly modern military, see Robert D. Kaplan, "How We Would Fight China," *Atlantic Monthly*, June 2005, http://www.theatlantic.com/doc/print/200506/kaplan.

CHAPTER 8

1. Joseph S. Nye, Jr., "A Taiwan Deal," *Washington Post*, March 8, 1998.

2. Kenneth Lieberthal, "Preventing a War over Taiwan," *Foreign Affairs* 84, no. 2 (March-April 2005): 53–63.

3. Ibid., p. 55.

4. Ibid., p. 60.

5. Remarks by Thomas Donnelly at the American Enterprise Institute forum, "Foreign Policy in the Second Bush Administration," November 9, 2004. Transcript available online at http://www.aei.org/events/filter.all.eventID.952/transcript.asp.

6. Daniel Blumenthal and Randy Scheunemann, "Tense Straits: Washington Signals Timidity toward Chinese Bellicosity," *National Review Online*, January 27, 2005, http://www.nationalreview.com/comment/blumenthal200501270741.asp.

7. Daniel Blumenthal, "Unhelpful China," *Washington Post*, December 6, 2004, p. A21.

8. Richard Fisher Jr., "Deterring a Chinese Attack against Taiwan: 16 Steps," Center for Security Policy Decision Brief no. 04-D 14, April 2, 2004.

9. The Honorable Robert E. Andrews and the Honorable Steve Chabot, "Two Congressmen Look at 'One China,'" Heritage Lecture no. 821, February 6, 2004, http://www.heritage.org/Research/AsiaandthePacific/h1821.cfm.

10. Ibid.
11. Aaron L. Friedberg, "Will We Abandon Taiwan?" *Commentary*, May 2000, p. 31. Emphasis in original.
12. Blumenthal and Scheunemann, "Tense Straits."
13. Quoted in Hamish McDonald, "Beijing Threatens War over Taiwan," *Sidney Morning Herald*, November 20, 2003, http://www.smh.com.au/articles/2003/11/19/1069027192249.html.
14. Robert Ross, "The Geography of the Peace: East Asia in the Twenty-First Century," *International Security* 23, no. 4 (Spring 1999): 113.
15. "China Policy Check," *Washington Times*, March 20, 2001, p. A18.
16. For a discussion of these attitudes, see Thomas J. Christensen, "Posing Problems without Catching Up: China's Rise and Challenges for U.S. Security Policy," *International Security* 25, no. 4 (Spring 2001): 17–20.
17. Michael D. Swaine, "Trouble in Taiwan," *Foreign Affairs* 83, no. 2 (March-April 2004): 42.
18. Ibid., pp. 42–43.
19. For a discussion of arms sales and the logic of the porcupine strategy, see Ted Galen Carpenter, "Let Taiwan Defend Itself," Cato Institute Policy Analysis no. 313, August 28, 1998, pp. 15–17. The porcupine strategy even reduces the likelihood of military blackmail by the PRC, which may be an even more likely scenario than the actual use of military force.
20. Trevor Corson, "Strait-Jacket," *Atlantic Monthly*, December 2004, http://www.theatlantic.com/doc/print/200412/corson.
21. For a discussion of how to categorize vital, secondary, and peripheral interests, see Ted Galen Carpenter, *A Search for Enemies: America's Alliances after the Cold War* (Washington, D.C.: Cato Institute, 1992), pp. 170–179.
22. Quoted in Brian Mitchell, "As Bush Vows to Defend Taiwan, How Far Will the U.S. Really Go?" *Investor's Business Daily*, April 26, 2001, p. A22.
23. Quoted in Mitchell, "As Bush Vows to Defend Taiwan."
24. Ross Terrill, *The New Chinese Empire: And What It Means for the United States* (New York: Basic Books, 2003), p. 216.
25. Philip P. Pan, "Myers Stresses U.S. Stance on Taiwan," *Washington Post*, January 16, 2004, p. A14.
26. For a generally favorable discussion of this option, see Corson, "Strait-Jacket."

INDEX